ELEPHANT HAVE
RIGHT OF WAY

ELEPHANT HAVE RIGHT OF WAY

Betty and Jock Leslie-Melville

Introduction by Jack Paar

DOUBLEDAY & COMPANY, INC., GARDEN CITY, NEW YORK
1973

ISBN: 0-385-07943-5
Library of Congress Catalog Card Number 72–84927
Copyright © 1973 by Betty and Jock Leslie-Melville
All Rights Reserved
Printed in the United States of America

Photo Credits:

Photos 14 and 25: Marc and Evelyne Bernheim from Rapho
 Guillumette
Photos 4, 7, 12, 20, 23: Courtesy of Betty and Jock Leslie-Melville
All remaining photos were taken by Mrs. Leslie-Melville

To

RICK AND DANCY AND MCDONNELL

Acknowledgment

Without not the aid but full-time help of my husband, Jock, this book would be "incoherent, inarticulate, and ungrammatical" (his quotes). And he is right. As with lecturing, taking safaris, and making films, we also write together.

Since I want to be famous and he doesn't care, he let me write this book in the first person, but so I won't have to feel guilty about it the rest of my life, I confess right here it was a joint effort. (And I still hope many people will skip this part so I can get all the credit myself.)

Betty Leslie-Melville

Contents

Introduction

I have said many times on television that the happiest moments in my life have been spent in Africa and most of those moments were shared with Betty and Jock Leslie-Melville, the two attractive, charming and amusing people who wrote this book. Indeed, I can claim some credit for this book in that my wife Miriam and I over the years have encouraged them to write it.

We have traveled over East and Central Africa with Betty and Jock many times and some of those hilarious and exciting moments are included.

Let me tell you about them. Betty, a former fashion model from Baltimore, who looks like a movie star, first went to Africa fourteen years ago and later fell in love with this handsome former Britisher, now a Kenyan, who was raised in Africa, though educated at Eton and Sandhurst in England. The mother of three children, Betty has a figure like a gazelle and in a safari jacket and pants makes the men in Nairobi pant. It's a good thing that elephant can't whistle! And it's quite true that many male hippopottomussess have wanted to leave their wives. (Incidentally, how does one spell the plural? Usually, I just type "hippo" and then keep hitting the "ssssssssssssss.")

Jock, who never wore shoes until he was eight, speaks Swahili
with great ease but more than that, hooks up with Africans in a
way that is remarkable. He is very sophisticated and damned
amusing. Several times over the years he has out-talked me—his
only bad manners. (It was actually only three times in five years
but I remember things like that.) Whenever I thought he was out-
talking me, I would suggest we go snorkling. I felt that with those
tubes in his mouth, I would have a chance to get a word in but he
just kept talking from the hip. However, I have always believed
that anyone who will stoop to speaking to fish is unfair.

This may give you some idea of the kind of person he is. One
time near the Congo when we were searching out the Pygmies,
we finally stopped for a picnic lunch many miles from anyone or
anywhere. After two gin and tonics and a sandwich, I thought-
lessly dropped a wax paper wrapping in the middle of the bush.
We got back into the Land-Rover to carry on the journey when I
noticed Jock get out of the vehicle and quietly pick up the wax
wrapper and put it in his jacket pocket. That's how much Africa
means to him. You see it is an immaculate country by the laws of
nature. Only man screws it up.

I just want to say before you read this delightful book that Betty
and Jock are two of my favorite people. And if they should ever
leave their home in Kenya and move to Nigeria, the Sudan, Mali
or even Nutley, New Jersey, I would never want to return to East
Africa again. *They* are an endangered species—free, and decent,
in love, and fun. For those who have not met them, their book in
their own words does them justice. They are super!!

What I feel about Africa and what I have seen after nine safaris
through it, is that much of what you have seen in motion pictures
and on television is a fake. I have not only never had a gun
in Africa, I have never seen one. Jock and Betty do not have a
gun—they just charm its animals and people with reasonableness
and understanding. Many producers, for lack of understanding
Africa, have been forced to invent things about it or to expand
myths. Perhaps they were incapable of observing for themselves
or feared the creativity of the truth.

Anyway, power to the people! Power to the animals! And in the words of that great philosopher, Jimmy Durante: "Leave everybody the hell alone."

Jack Paar

ELEPHANT HAVE
RIGHT OF WAY

Preface

Bagamoyo is the name of a little fishing village on the Indian Ocean in Tanzania where slaves were kept chained in dungeons before being shipped to other parts of the world. To get there they were marched hundreds of miles from the interior, and along the way they would pick mangoes from the trees, their only decent food, and after eating them they would toss the seeds away. Today, the old slave route is clearly defined because thousands of mango trees which sprang from the discarded seeds now line each side of the road. The last stop for the slaves before departing Africa, Bagamoyo, translated means, "Here I leave my heart."

I bet you think that I, too, am going to say I have left my heart in Africa. Well, I haven't even left it in San Francisco, but I think it is split in two, just like those migrating German storks, which I will tell you about later on, who don't know where "home" is either.

"And where is your home?" asked a stranger sitting next to me on a plane.

"I don't know," I answered.

"Oh," he said and looked funny, but after a few minutes of polite conversation he enquired, "Are you married?" and in all truth I replied,

"I don't know." I was waiting for a final divorce which could have been sent to me in the mail a day or two earlier, but I was not sure whether it was through yet. He stopped talking to me, and I was glad.

Anyway, I still don't know where home is. Is it Africa? Is it America? Does it matter?

I don't even know which I like better. There are different things to enjoy in both places. There are some things to enjoy here and other things there. My father told me a very long time ago that life was like a bottle—either half empty or half full—and it depends entirely upon how you yourself look at it. Life is just too short to regard it as being half empty. So when I'm in Africa I try to enjoy the things it has to offer, and when I'm in the States I try to enjoy the different things there. I'm afraid though, that sometimes it is like liking the summer in the winter and the winter in the summer because when I'm in the States I usually like Africa, and when I'm in Africa I like the States. (A typical Pisces swimming in opposite directions?)

In Africa I miss American women and Hershey bars with almonds. American women have an alertness and inquisitiveness, which I find, generally speaking, is lacking in other nationalities. The Colonial women—and many still remain in Independent Africa —are so dowdy, in dress and in thought. Their children are away at boarding schools, they have too many servants and nothing to do with their time but have "elevensies" (coffee) with the girls, then gin before lunch and "a little zizz" afterwards (this only means sleep), followed by tea and more booze with nothing sandwiched in all day but gossip with the girls. I just simply do not care who is sleeping with whom as long as it is not my husband. (I am very self-centered.) Also, it is bad enough that I have to cope with dentist appointments and measles and recipes—I don't want to talk about them, and I'm not interested in anyone else's children's teeth. In fact, I'm not even interested in my own children's teeth. At dinner parties I find it is usually the American women who mingle with the men and talk politics while the other women cluster together having girlie talks like Saturday afternoon dancing classes. The American woman has a mind and uses it. And that doesn't mean she is masculine. If you are really smart, you are smart enough to pretend you're feminine even if you really aren't. American women are interested in many things and have a great curiosity to learn. One proof of this is that nowhere in the world but in the States is there a lecture circuit, and lectures are usually sponsored and supported by women. American women are also altruistic. Yes, altruistic. They are the main ones here who teach the Africans how to dye fabric and print designs on it and how to weave baskets. The American women do a lot of good volunteer work helping the Africans to help themselves. I like American women's curiosity, energy, intelligence, drive and ability —and I miss them. Amen.

When I'm in the States I miss African things like the "Elephant Have the Right of Way" signs on the highways. And I miss servants. Servants buy time, and I love this time. People always say, "But you're sitting on a volcano living in Africa." Everyone is sitting on a volcano every place in the world these days, and I'd rather live on a volcano with servants.

People have said to me, "It must take a lot of courage to live in Africa." This is not true. It would have taken me more courage to live in the suburbs of Baltimore. But life should not be an endurance test. How can you give anybody joy—your husband, children, family and friends—if you don't have any yourself, much less any left over to give away? But if it had taken courage, I would still have tried it. If you don't do things you're afraid of, you'll never do anything at all. I was terrified of elephant and airplanes. But I got used to them, and I now sit in the midst of a herd of a thousand elephant feeling excitement but no fear, and I get on a plane today as I got on a streetcar yesterday. But in between was I afraid? Terrified. So what, that's part of life too.

A lot of people tell me I'm incident prone, and I guess I am, but probably only because I have tried most everything that has come my way because I believe you are only sorry for what you don't do. This has proved to be true over and over again. Oh, I've made many mistakes, but they can always be rectified, or at least

learned from. For example, if I hadn't liked Africa I could have
moved back. The only permanent mistake is not doing anything.
I know I'd be sorry if I were still sitting around Baltimore wondering what would have happened if I had gone to Africa.

Yet I absolutely love going back to the States, and especially
to Baltimore. I love it perhaps more than I would if I lived there.
I love change—the change of everything—the seasons, not only
because of the scenery and temperature changes, but because of
the different food and clothing as well. I would miss having no
seasons in Africa were I to live here permanently.

How lucky we are that we must go to the States for five months
each year. Routine and I are not symbiotic. I love doing unrelated
things—that is why my life fits me well. I like both worlds. And I
like going back and forth between them, too. We couldn't live
much further away from the States, for if we go further east, we
start coming closer again. It costs only forty-two dollars more to
go around the world than it does to fly from Nairobi to New York
and back, and one time when we had forty-two dollars we went
by way of India, Ceylon, Thailand, Japan and Hawaii. Usually
we go through Europe. If I need lipstick we go to Paris, if Jock
wants shoes we go to Switzerland. Or sometimes we go to London
for a maple-nut sundae.

In Ceylon we stayed with friends for a few days, and as we were
leaving I said to them, "I just don't know how to thank you," and
they said, "Well, try."

So I am writing this book to try to say thank you, Africa, for
all the joys you have given me.

My book is not about the serious but the joyful Africa. Mine
is just the cartoon before the main feature of Africa. I would like
you now to walk with me through a corner of this continent and
to share its smiles and joys.

I
Nothing of Value
or
Something of No Value

The only fan letter I ever got in my whole life was from a dog. Named Sniffles. With a ten dollar check in it too. The check was properly printed "Sniffles" with his name and address in Los Angeles, California. His stationery, too, carried his name and address and in addition, on the letterhead, there was a photograph of Sniffles standing on his hind legs going through his filing cabinet. In his letter he told me he had seen me on the "David Frost Show," and he was glad that I was a dog-type person too. He said that when he went to the movies he had to buy two seats—one for himself and one for someone to translate "human talk into dog talk." But he knew that *I* could understand dog talk without a translator. Sorry, Sniffles, I hate to disillusion you, but I am a people-type person. I felt so guilty about it that I gave the ten dollars to the Wildlife Society instead of keeping it for myself. I love my own dog, Shirley Brown, whom you'll meet later on (I sound like Sniffles now), and sometimes I even like my cat. But, generally speaking, people interest me more than animals.

Five months out of every year my husband, Jock, and I lecture in the States on Africa and its game, and for the rest of the year we run photographic safaris and make films about Africa and its animals—and here I am, a people-type person. I don't *dislike* animals; in fact, I enjoy the fact that they are nearby. It's like having the kids home from college—you never see them, but it's nice knowing they're around.

At every lecture I quote Mark Twain who said, "There is no such thing as immorality, vulgarity or war among the animals," and someone else who said, "Animals are punished for their sins by becoming man." I admit it *is* refreshing to be among creatures that have no immorality, vulgarity or war, and for a while I, too, had all these romantic thoughts that animals were superior to man. Then one day when I was extolling wildlife a friend said to me, "But an elephant will never whistle Beethoven's Fifth." It's just that once you have seen 42,000 elephant, and every wildebeest in the world, they do all sort of look alike and act alike. A million years ago an elephant was doing exactly what he is doing today, and he will be doing the same thing a million years from now. That can never be said of man. Animals have no choice. Man does, and although he may choose to do some outrageous things, he *is* interesting. I now find that having lived for thirteen years in Africa, after a week or two of being out in the bush, all this nature begins to decay me, and I long for neon signs, noise and that glorious rat race. To me, the only thing prettier than a river is a river with a bridge across it—especially if that bridge has lights. Socrates said, "Fields and trees teach me nothing, but men in cities do." I didn't read Socrates, but I read his quote in a New York City subway. See?

Please don't misunderstand me, I do everything in my power to preserve wildlife. I fight hard. I insult my friends by pointing to their zebra-skin rug and saying, "If it weren't for people like you . . ."

I truly believe that every single person in the whole wide world should be able to go on safari and see the animals. I truly believe that it is a beautiful experience, but an experience is a one-time happening, or a twenty-time happening, and then it becomes mundane. Finally, after twenty thousand times, I would rather go on safari in Bloomingdales than in East Africa, and I prefer the supermarket to any game park. In 1961 Tanzania's President Julius

Nyerere said, "Americans have a peculiar urge to see these animals, and we must ensure they are able to do it." I don't think it is a peculiar urge, but I now see why he thought it was.

Yet, I would hate to think our great-grandchildren would have to ask, "What was a lion?" or "What was a giraffe?" So I will continue to do all I can for the preservation of wildlife—but for the sake of people primarily, and for the sake of the animals secondarily. I like animals mainly because they give people so much joy. But how do I know if a hyena is happy—or can be? And I bet a leopard doesn't laugh. Maybe that's why I'm a people-type person —because I know people can be happy and can laugh.

Animals can make people laugh and cry—myself included. I still cry over *Black Beauty* and *Lassie.* My mother told me the story of how, when I was six years old, she took me to my first movie which was about a horse. At the end of the film the horse was running the most important race of its career, which it had to win or its life would be ruined forever. I stood up and jumped up and down and hollered and screamed, "Come on, OH, COME ON" at the top of my lungs in the theater, and when the horse lost, I collapsed in the aisle, sobbing and moaning. (My next movie was when I was fifteen years old—no one would take me for another nine years.) And just last week I was still crying over Elsa in *Born Free,* for the seventeenth time . . .

Lion are so trendy these days, and I've certainly been hearing a lot about them with all those TV shows, movies, books and lectures on scientific studies of lion—we always attend these scientific meetings in Nairobi to gather information for our own lectures and films. The only interesting new thing I've heard about lion in the last year is the fact that during the breeding season the male lion mates every eight minutes, twenty-four hours a day, with only two hours off for lunch and two hours off in the middle of the night. I like funny animal facts like that. In our own safari brochure there is a picture of an elephant and underneath the caption says, "Elephant." Do you think there is anybody in the world over six months old who doesn't know what an elephant is? In the old days, we used to tell our safari-ers, "If it's got a trunk, it's an elephant." But now the ecology craze has turned wildlife into a very serious business, and when we speak of these matters we wear our sincere shoes and earnestly say—"Note how the trunk is used both as a nose and a hand. There are forty thousand muscles in an elephant's trunk."

While making our wildlife film I found quite a few useless facts that intrigued me. For you, I list them here under the "So What Department" so that you can toss one or two of them out in the middle of a dinner party—especially if you want to change the subject.

1. Giraffe can't throw up. (Perhaps it is better to save that one until after dinner.)
2. The rhino's horn is not horn at all but densely matted hair and is believed, in the East, to be a powerful aphrodisiac. And, constant constipation is the cause of the rhino's ill temper.
3. One ostrich egg feeds eleven people scrambled egg. The male ostrich, which is black, sits on the eggs during the night for camouflage, and the female, which is brown, sits on the eggs during the day. (Be careful how you word this—our lecture pamphlet reads: "The male ostrich sits on the eggs during the night and the female during the day.")
4. Zebra are prone to heart attacks. That's why they can't be used for work.
5. The gestation period for a female elephant is twenty-two months and for a male twenty-four months. (That is, if the baby is a male, it takes twenty-four months.)
6. I saved my favorite for last, and that is the fact that a Blue Whale's tongue is bigger than an elephant, and it takes forty elephant to equal the weight of one Blue Whale.

I read about that in *Reader's Digest,* so I assume it's true. But all the animal books I've read on East Africa claim that a monitor lizard eats only crocodile eggs and insects. Yet in some film given to us by a kind friend, there is a long sequence of a monitor lizard very clearly eating a fish. I guess that lizard didn't read the book.

Be sure to say "elephant" instead of "elephants" and "lion"

instead of "lions." Other popular "in" animal vocabulary can be found in the "Tenthold Hints" chapter.

If your guests are retarded or drunk or children and *like* these facts, try the question game in the next to last chapter, "Safari Anyone?" But so that you won't have to turn there now, it contains questions like:

Q: "What is the only animal born with horns?"

A: "A giraffe."

Q: "What animal cannot chew?"

A: "A crocodile."

I learned all these things because I had to. At the close of our lectures, Jock and I have a half-hour question-and-answer period, and I just know that one day some wise guy will ask, "What is the incubation period of crocodile eggs?" (Ninety days is the answer, in case anyone ever asks you.) When we first started lecturing, I spent endless tedious hours trying to remember every historical, political and noteworthy event that took place in the history of East Africa. I wished I could get run over by a truck instead of facing the question-and-answer periods, but the only questions anyone ever asked me were, "Are there any snakes?" and "How old are you?" If I were an African and someone asked me how old I was, I could answer, "I don't remember the flood" and everyone would be satisfied (especially me), but not so in the States. Everyone always asks me how old I am. Sometimes I answer by saying, "Because the Julian Calendar is used in Ethiopia, everyone there is seven years younger. For example, in this year of 1973 it is still 1966 in Ethiopia. All car licenses read 1966, all business transactions are dated 1966, and if you can manage to have a birthday in Ethiopia, you are seven years younger. I've managed to have three birthdays in Addis Ababa, and I'm twenty-two years old— so get a pencil and figure it out. But sometimes I just tell the truth and admit "43½."

II
Are You Married,
or Do You Live in Kenya?

Often on the lecture platform or face to face with a rhino in the bush I get that what-on-earth-am-I-doing-here feeling. Why am I standing here on a stage in front of five thousand people telling them what it is like to live in Africa? Africa! Why on earth am I living in Africa? I mean, I was born in Baltimore and led a typical middle-class existence and had an uneventful but happy childhood and youth. I like all the usual things, such as camels and fudge with nuts and movies and massages and New York and beige and eating alone and mail and bathtubs and Jews and noise and ideas and pornography and P. J. Clark's cheeseburgers and the sound of tennis and leather. And I hate apartheid and bats and showers and Chinese food and movies with sheep and dams and sunrises and Queen Elizabeth's hats and criticism of me (especially constructive criticism) and Early-American furniture and people who have Early-American furniture. I have no interest whatsoever in sports or jewels or television, but I adore my children and being in love. I went to public schools, where other than reading and writing I never learned anything—much less where Africa even was. I went to the same high school as Spiro Agnew (much later, please note). Am I bright? I once tested myself from a "Know Your Own I.Q." book and scored "institutional level." Do you suppose there could be something funny about that school?

Why Africa then?

In 1951 I was teaching nursery school with a close friend of mine, Helen Harrison, who decided to marry a Roman Catholic boy. Since she was not a Catholic, she had to take the six-week instruction course that was compulsory then, and when she finished she said to me, "I'm not going to marry Joe after all."

I asked, "Why, don't you like Catholicism?"

And she answered, "On the contrary, I'm going to be a nun."

A nun! I would have been less surprised if she had said a stripper or a coal miner. And so, first she became a Catholic, then waited the required two years to become a nun, then joined the White Sisters, an international order that works only in Africa, and was sent to Kigoma in Tanzania (then Tanganyika), not far from Ujiji, where just over a hundred years ago Stanley met Livingstone. From there she wrote many letters to me.

Now there are two kinds of people in the world—those like my own sister who say, *"Africa!* Why on earth would anyone ever want to go there?" To them I say, "It is a form of insanity." They will agree, and that will be the end of the conversation because you will never be able to explain your longing for Africa to them. And then there are those who have a hang-over from Tarzan and a secret fascination and desire to see Africa. I, being in the latter category, had to go to Africa. I just *had* to. Although I had never been out of the country except to Bermuda for one honeymoon and Cuba for another, Africa was a must. At the time of my first trip I was married to Dan Bruce, who did not want to go because, "Damned if I want to spend two weeks in a convent." So I earned money by modeling in lunch-time fashion shows in Baltimore for a few years, saved my pennies and in 1958 set off with another friend from Baltimore, Bebe Rouse, to visit Sister Helen in Africa.

After a long trip, including an overnight ride in the caboose of a freight train, we reached the convent. Two weeks later, at the end of our visit I had fallen in love with the country and knew Dan Bruce would like it even more than I. When I got home he said, "Well, I'm glad you have got that out of your system." It

took me two years to convince him that he should quit his Baltimore bank job, which he didn't like anyway, and finally in 1960,
on borrowed money, we sailed with our three children from New
York to Mombasa, a thirty-five-day trip.

We went to the convent to see Helen, were helped by the nuns,
bought a Land-Rover, and set out for a month's investigation of
East Africa. By September we were back in America busily form-
ing the first non-hunting safaris to East Africa to be organized in
the States.

In June of 1962 we all headed back again, this time to live there
permanently and to operate our first safari for Mike Wallace and
his wife, Lorraine. He had signed up then and there while inter-
viewing me on his "P. M. East" show a month earlier. As we
crossed the ocean and headed for our new life in Africa, Sister
Helen was transferred to New Brunswick, New Jersey, and we
passed each other somewhere in the middle of the Atlantic. Ever
since I have lived in Africa and she has not, so now I write letters
to her about Africa and its joys and stop in convents in various
spots on the globe, wherever she has been posted, to visit her each
year.

And so it came to pass that Dan Bruce and I got a divorce, but
he still has his safari business and lives nearby and we are good
friends. (We always say we are related by divorce.)

Soon after our divorce, I met Jock who had just been divorced
after a long marriage of three months to The Lady Zinnia somebody or other. (I guess if you are The Lady Zinnia you don't *need*
a last name.) We met at the Indian Ocean, which is a very romantic place indeed, were married a year later and have had eight years
of happily ever after ever since.

But the lecturing—how this? Well, I was hired by mistake. It
was a result of my philosophy, "You are only sorry for what you
don't do." After my first trip to Africa to visit Sister Helen, I used
to bore people night after night with my slides. Very good friends
of mine in Baltimore are Linell and Marshall Smith. Linell is the
daughter of the late Ogden Nash, and one evening when he was
staying with them, I showed my slides. Mr. Nash, who was on a

lecture tour at the time said, "Betty, you should lecture. The next time you are in New York why don't you give my lecture bureau, Colston Leigh, a call." And so I did, because I knew I'd be sorry if I didn't try. If I had known then what I know now, I would never have had the nerve to telephone and say to Mr. Leigh, "I am a friend of Ogden Nash's daughter, and I would like to talk to you about lecturing on Africa." But I did, and he saw me, listened to me and said he thought what I had to say about Africa might just sell. We signed a contract then and there, and afterwards he said,

"How is your father?"

"My father has been dead for twenty-six years."

He was astonished. "I thought you said you were Ogden Nash's daughter."

"No, I said I was a *friend* of Ogden Nash's daughter."

"If I had known that, I would never have let you in here," he snorted, but by then it was too late.

So I started on the chicken-à-la-king circuit, and after one season of speaking on my own, I knew that Jock should be on the lecture circuit, too, because he is far more knowledgeable than I about Africa. I faked being sick, and Jock stood in for me. The reports to Colston Leigh were so good that Jock was hired, and ever since we have lectured together. It is much nicer than being up there on the platform alone, and in addition to the fun of being together, when I swallow a fly he is there to carry on. We both love taking our safari to the States each year and playing Tarzan and Jane in America.

I must tell you something about Jock, though.

He lived in Kenya and went to school here until going to Eton in England, followed by Sandhurst and the Coldstream Guards. He returned to Kenya in 1957 as aide to the Colonial Governor, and then went into politics, working with African Nationalist leaders in the move to independence for Kenya. After *uhuru* (independence) Jock gave up his British passport and became a Kenyan citizen because he has always regarded Kenya as home.

How did he get here? Jock's story of arriving in Kenya is very dull. He was born while his parents were on a trip to London and returned with them to Kenya when he was three months old, but his mother and father's story of getting here is a romantic one. Jock's grandfather in Scotland was the Earl of Leven and Melville. His father was not the eldest son and would not, therefore, inherit the title or castle, so he traveled around the world instead, which was not as easy to do in 1920 as it is today.

He decided to settle in Chile, but an earthquake there changed his mind and kept him traveling until he found Kenya, which captured him at once. A year or two later, on a ship between England and Mombasa he met Jock's mother. Theirs is a movie-like story. Jock's mother was married to a colonial civil servant who had been posted to west Uganda. She was not happy to be married to him and had done so under pressure from her Victorian parents who believed the marriage to be "appropriate," whatever that meant. After their first leave in England her husband sailed back to Africa and she was to follow three weeks later—which was fortuitous, for who should be aboard Jock's mother's ship but a handsome and dashing figure, son of a Scottish Earl, ex-cavalry officer, international polo player, former aide-de-camp to the King of Greece, world traveler—The Hon. David Leslie-Melville. Though they did not speak to one another until Suez, by the time the ship docked at Mombasa the marriage to the civil servant was already on the rocks. But Jock's mother set off, anyway, by rail, then on foot, to make her way to northwest Uganda. Her husband now appeared even more righteous and dreary than she had thought before. She decided to run away and sent a message to Jock's father five hundred miles east in Kenya. On the trip she contracted malaria, and a missionary doctor gave her an overdose of quinine to which she turned out to be allergic. She recovered from the malaria but the quinine had thickened her ear drums turning her almost deaf, and she has never regained her hearing. Jock's father, in response to the message from the damsel, who truly was in much distress by now, rushed to the rescue. The marriage to the civil servant was dissolved, freeing her to remarry, and the two started a farm in a remote and mountainous corner of Kenya.

Ask almost any European how he got here, and you are in for some strange story. It is a kind of magic question.

A former business partner of Jock's was piloting a light aircraft from London for delivery to South Africa just after the war. The plane crashed and when he extricated himself from the wreckage he found that he was in Kenya, and he liked what he saw—so much, in fact, that twenty-five years later he is still here.

Another friend of ours, a Swedish Baron who ultimately became Sweden's Ambassador to Kenya, told us of his arrival. When he was nineteen, he planned a trip with a cousin to Casablanca on the northwest coast of Africa. They celebrated their departure with much aquavit, and the ship duly sailed with the two still drinking toasts to each other. A little later they discovered that it was the wrong ship and was not bound for Casablanca at all but for Mombasa. He was so enchanted with the country that it was thirty-two years before he was to set foot in Europe again, and that was only because he had to visit his ailing mother.

During my 1960 trip I stopped in Arusha, Tanzania, to visit Henny Hemingway, another girl I knew from Baltimore, who married Ernest Hemingway's son, Patrick. I asked her how she had come to East Africa and this was her story: Right after she and Pat were married they decided to drive out West to see Pat's brother. Halfway there, to their surprise, they met the brother on a highway in one of those funny states which begins with an "I." They went to an all-night diner where the brother told them that he was sorry not to wait for their arrival, but he had had this magnificent idea which just couldn't wait. His plan was to go to Kenya and raise coffee and call it "King Kong Koffee." Henny said she didn't know if Kenya was something to eat or step on—she had never even heard of it.

By dawn, the brother had convinced them it was the only thing for them to do with their lives, too, so they turned the car around and got on the first boat to Kenya, with plans to meet the brother there after he had acquired a bank loan for their new business project. They finally docked in Kenya and there was a message waiting for them from the brother saying he could not get the bank loan and perhaps it wasn't such a great idea after all. He never showed up. Pat and Henny didn't have money enough to go back home, so Pat got a job with the Game Department. Unhappily, Henny died of diabetes a few years later, but Patrick Hemingway is still with the Game Department today—teaching Africans to become game wardens.

After I had been living in Kenya a few years, the phone rang one day.

"Will you come to our wedding on Saturday?" asked a very meek friend whom I would describe as plain vanilla, a perfect housewife and mother of three.

"Whose wedding?" I asked.

"John's and mine."

John is her husband—or so I had assumed for many years. As I stood there with my mouth open, she explained that they had lived together for thirteen years, had three children and were legally John and Mary Thompson, as I shall call them, but only because she had changed her name to Thompson for $1.00 instead of getting married.

I have ceased being surprised by this since it has happened so many times. People have been living openly together here for years —long before our American youth thought of it—and no one even notices. Perhaps this is why everyone asks, "Are you married, or do you live in Kenya?"

When Jock and I went to tell his mother that we were going to get married she looked absolutely horrified and said, "MARRIED!"

I thought, "Oh dear god, she hates me."

But she continued, "Why don't you just live together?"

Sweet little old lady. But I explained that I have a hang-over from Sunday School and I *have* to get married—that I just wouldn't feel comfortable living with anyone. And so we got married. Or at least I think we did. The District Commissioner married us, and since there are Muslims, pagans, Hindus, Christians and Jews all living in Kenya, all of whom have different marriage customs and divorce laws, each couple is married according to his belief.

Our wedding ceremony went something like this. D.C. to us: "What marriage laws are you going to be wed by?"

"Christian," we answered, feeling more familiar with that than any of the others.

D.C. to me: "Do you, Betty, know that if you take another husband while this one is still alive or if you haven't divorced, it will be bigamy?"

"Yes I know that."

"Do you, Jock, know that if you take another wife while this one is still alive or if you haven't divorced, it will be bigamy?"

"Yes I know that."

"I now pronounce you man and wife."

I keep wondering if we are *really* married?

Anyone married by the British law (which Kenya largely adopted) must be divorced by the same law. If we had been married under Muslim law, for example, Jock need only to go to the top of a hill and say "I divorce thee" three times, turn around four times or something, and it would all be over. But British law calls for the couple to be married for three years before they may even apply for a divorce, then once it is granted they have to wait another three months before the decree becomes "absolute" and they can remarry. This presents difficulties. We had friends who decided to get divorced one year after they had married, but had to wait the three years before they could even apply for divorce. By this time the man's new girl friend was pregnant, naturally. He got his divorce, but it was apparent that they would never make the three month wait before the baby was born, so they applied to the D.C. and got a special dispensation to get married earlier, in order to make the baby legitimate. Then the baby came early. The day after the baby was born she got out of bed and went to the D.C.'s office to get married before she filled in the birth certificate so the baby could be legitimate.

But the D.C. said, "We can only marry you because you are pregnant, and you are not pregnant."

They could just see themselves at another D.C.'s the next day with a pillow on her stomach, but he very kindly understood, married them anyway, and she went back to the hospital and filled in their son's birth certificate with glee.

III
Tarzan Doesn't Live Here Any More

What is it like for an American woman and her three children to live in Africa? That's an impossible question to answer. There are currently forty-eight countries on the continent of Africa, between Cairo and Cape Town, with politics and topography as diverse as would be found between Canada and Chile. Africa is vast—you can put the United States into Africa three and a half times.

Most Americans assume that living in Africa must be exotic, but unless you are some kind of bush buff or work on tsetse fly or locust control, are a game warden or missionary, or have a peculiar desire to live with lion or gorilla, there is little difference in day-to-day life between living in suburban Baltimore or suburban Nairobi. The majority of men here go to work from 9 A.M. to 5 P.M. and play golf or meet for a drink afterwards. (Greens fees are fifty cents.) The women drive car pools, play bridge and go to the *supah*market, as the British pronounce it.

Many of our friends who live here, Africans and expatriates alike, have never spent a night in a game park, and one fortyish British friend who was born in Kenya just saw his first elephant while on holiday in London's zoo. Jock, who has lived here all his life and was raised in the Aberdare Forest just a few miles from the famous Treetops, never went "up the Tree," as we say, until a

few years ago when I suggested it really was worthwhile. It is like
New Yorkers not going to the Empire State Building. It is also a
sort of reverse snob thing.

Few people here have Africana in their houses—no African
carvings, no masks, statues or bookends, zebra rugs or Masai
beads. Not even the modern Africans have many such things in
their houses. These curios are bought by the tourists, and I've seen
them mainly in houses in the States.

I wouldn't be caught dead in a bush jacket. I buy all my safari
clothes in Bloomingdales or Korvettes, and when people ask,
"What kind of safari boots should I buy—what do you wear in the
bush?" my answer is, "Tennis shoes when it's cool and forty-two-
cent rubber-thonged beach sandals when it's hot."

Life here need not be exotic, and often it can be mundane. Many
visitors who come here on safari are sure they have found Utopia,
but no matter where you live, you have to take your clothes to the
cleaners and fill your car with gas—or at least arrange for these
tedious things to be done.

The area in which we live is a suburb called Karen, after the
famous Danish writer Isak Dinesen (one of my favorite authors),
whose real name was Baroness Karen von Blixen and who lived a
few miles from us. She was a friend of my mother-in-law's, and
when she left Kenya she gave my mother-in-law a lot of her furniture. I walked about touching the chairs and vases and bureaus
reverently saying, "So this was Isak Dinesen's?"

My mother-in-law looked puzzled that I should have heard of
her and said, "Oh, that's right, Karen did write a book once—I must
read it one of these days."

Ours is the last house in suburban Nairobi and at the bottom of
our garden is the Masai reserve stretching into hundreds of miles
of Africa. Recently we had three buffalo grazing on our lawn,
right by our terrace—they had walked down the tarmac road and
onto our property. Steinbuck (antelope) eat all the rose shoots—
their favorite food—and a troop of about thirty huge black monkeys with white faces swing in our trees and walk across our lawn
once or twice every day. Our next door neighbor's dog was taken

by a leopard, and every night we have to bring our Labrador, Shirley Brown, inside because dogs are leopards' favorite tidbits. Near another house we have by the sea, a python ate a Labrador—so Shirley Brown has problems wherever she goes. Or rather we do —she acts mentally retarded most of the time.

One rainy night we noticed Shirley Brown wasn't in the house whereas she is usually right under our feet. Sometimes she goes into the forest to chase monkeys, but she always comes bouncing back immediately when called. This time she didn't. Our cook said he knew of some wire snares in the forest, so with flashlight and wire cutters we stomped through the rain and mud in the dark in evening clothes (we had been on our way to a dinner party) and finally found Shirley Brown with a wire noose around her neck choking to death so that it was impossible for her even to bark. We clipped the snare and freed her, and fortunately she was fine. Shirley Brown ranges from being Shirley Temple to Sarah Bernhardt six times every day—so you can imagine how she enjoyed the episode, extracting all she could from it with days of feeling sorry for herself. If our cook hadn't known about the poacher's snares, she would have died in another hour. I didn't really thank him because he was most likely the one who had set the snare in the first place —not for Shirley Brown, but for antelope for him to eat.

Our servants work five and a half days a week, and we pay them thirty dollars a month and provide housing, fuel and water. This is good for us and good for them.

Since there is over 90 per cent unemployment in Kenya, the more help everybody can hire the better. Unemployment in this sense means earning money as a sole means of staying alive. As in most developing countries, the bulk of the population live off the land, eating what they grow and doing without much cash. But in the cities there are many who badly need work, so in Nairobi we always employ four, though for much of the year we really need only two—a practical means followed by many employers of trying to help out.

Now I don't want any guff from anyone about my "servants." My cook is my cook because he is a much better cook than I'll ever be. He has pride in his work and does not mind being a servant or being called one. He works for us as I work for the lecture bureau, or Jock works for Percival Tours. Shouldn't the African be working in an office and making more money and living in a house like ours? Of course he should, and many thousands already do, and through increased education and a better economy these things will come to pass. But right now, realistically, there *aren't* any other jobs for our cook, nor is he trained to do anything else, so instead of being jobless altogether, he is glad to be "our servant," so judge him by his standards, not yours, please.

We employ men in the house. Below a certain educational level the African women here do all the heavy labor—they cut down trees, carry the lumber, build the houses, take the night guards, and the men sit under trees all day and make decisions—just like the United States; no difference. Usually it is the men who are hired to do the washing, ironing, cooking, sewing and cleaning. Our servants live in a house on our property, and when their wives have finished doing all the tilling and planting on their own land some miles from Nairobi, they let the wives and children come and stay with them for a while. So, sometimes their families are with them and sometimes not. This is entirely their business, not ours.

A popular story in Africa is the one about a tourist who saw a woman bent into a right angle carrying lumber and a baby on her back and a water container in each hand. In front of her, her husband rode on a donkey carrying nothing. The tourist called to the man, "Why doesn't your wife ride the donkey?" and the man answered, "She doesn't have a donkey." However, things are improving for the women here. Only recently I read in the paper that a bus did stop and wait a few minutes while one of the women passengers got off and had a baby behind a bush, then she and the child got back on the bus and continued the journey. African men and women seem either to live like peasants or are very emancipated—nothing much in between.

Our staff come to work at 6:30 A.M. Every day they wax and polish the floors—I've never had floors shining like mirrors before. To do this, they stand with each foot on a sheepskin and skate around the floors. They wash clothes by hand, hang the laundry on sisal bushes outside to dry, and iron every afternoon. Our cook, who speaks no English and can neither read nor write, graduated from the Cordon Bleu cooking school, which is taught in Nairobi in Swahili. He memorizes every recipe and cooks beautifully—his cheese souffles are so high he can hardly get them into the dining room. He won't touch our food or any of the good things he cooks. If we have food left over, or if we are going away, we offer it to him but he says no, he wants his *posho*—ground corn meal. I know just what it tastes like because one time when Jock and I were lecturing in South Carolina, Jock went out for breakfast alone. He came back astonished, "They gave me *posho* for breakfast along with my eggs and bacon." Hominy grits. This is the African's staple diet. When you see pictures of Africans pounding things, they are either pulverizing mohogo root into a meal, which is made into a cream-of-wheat-type mess, or they are pounding corn into a flour called *posho*, which they eat along with cabbage or beans or sometimes meat. The average African eats once a day. Most servants have four or five hours off during the afternoon, and it is then they eat—about 2 P.M.

Jock comes home every day for lunch and we have our big meal then. For supper, at about 8 P.M., we eat yoghurt or an egg or something light, and I have found I like this very much better than eating a big meal at night. Many husbands in Nairobi go home for lunch, since all business offices and many stores close between 12:30 and 2 P.M. Someone once said she had married her husband for better or worse but not for lunch, but I like Jock's coming home. Unless we have a dinner party, we are in bed by 9:30 P.M., but everyone gets up very early and is running around in his office or store between 8 and 8:30 A.M.

If we give a dinner party, I merely announce to the cook that fourteen guests will be coming and then I attend the party. I buy the food, but as I drive up to the house the servants come out to carry all packages into the kitchen. Every day one of them washes the car, but they won't wash women's underpants or clean the toilet bowls. This is something that Africans just won't do for other people. They believe that each person should take care of his own personal matters, and I not only respect this attitude but am inclined to agree with it.

The cleaning of toilets in hotels or public buildings is undertaken by special men called "sweepers," who have chosen this menial vocation, eschewed totally by the vast majority of Africans.

Our gardener, whom we pay seventy-five U. S. cents a day, takes total care of the garden (since I could write a book on what I don't know about gardening). I have a black thumb and have only to water a plant for it to wither and die within the hour. Our house stands on five acres, which is really embarrassingly small in Kenya. When I first went to where Jock's sister lived upcountry, I asked how many acres there were since the estate seemed vast, and she answered, "Very small, only fifty thousand acres." However, in our garden poinsettias grow wild, I pick about a hundred gardenias every day, roses grow like potatoes, and it is like living in a technicolor world. And I do hope when you get here the marijuana is in bloom, too.

We have no garbage collection, just pits dug way out back, into which we put the garbage and trash and burn it once a week. When it becomes filled, the pit is covered over and then another is dug, which to me seems a much easier arrangement than the U.S. garbage collection system—all you need is land and diggers.

We have no mailman, we must go to the Post Office every day to collect our mail from a little box to which we have a key, but we can get it on Sundays, too, because mail is sorted seven days a week. Since there is no delivery of any kind, urgent telegrams can sit in your mail box for weeks if you are away.

Our milk comes straight from the cows just down the road, unpasteurized, and the cream is so thick you have to bang the bottle like catchup to get it out. Since there is no skim milk, I telephoned our diary neighbor one day and asked her what she did with the milk after taking the cream off, and she answered, "Oh, we give it to the pigs." So I asked if she would give it to the pigs and us, which she now does. I was worried about no pasteurization until I learned that the object of pasteurization is to eliminate tuberculosis from milk, but because the cattle in East Africa are tuberculosis-free, there is little point in pasteurizing—it would be a wasted exercise.

It is unnecessary to wash the lettuce in Tide as one American newcomer did. Human fertilizer is not used here, and only a little DDT. We have negligible pollution, the chickens are free-range feeders and vegetables are grown naturally. Rejoice, ye microbiotic enthusiasts.

Some people employ night watchmen to sit outside their houses all night—usually people who are sent here by their governments or Shell or other temporary people who haven't time to grow secure. I know of no local people who hire night watchmen, but many businessmen have night guards for their stores and factories. One factory in Nairobi is guarded by a man who sits there with a bow and arrow, and last year he had occasion to use it.

But personal safety is not a thing we normally have to worry about much. The ordinary African is a gentle, kindly person. Burglars are interested in stealing things but not at the expense of hurting people. When you get away from the cities, what little violence there is almost vanishes. I would happily walk through an African village at night alone, but I am not about to risk walking the streets in large American cities—New York or Washington, D.C.—by myself at night.

I think some of our house guests wish we did have night guards. In the trees on our property live hyrax (pronounced like "pyrex"), little furry animals like squirrels without a tail, whose closest relation is the elephant. I must confess I don't instantly recognize the startling similarity between an elephant and a little furry tree animal, but I am told it has to do with "skull formation" or something unarguable like that. At night, these little nocturnal hyrax make the most horrific noise. First it sounds like rapid gunfire—eh-eh-eh-eh-eh-eh—or a coffin lid creaking open, and then EEEE-EEEEEEKKKKKKK—a ghastly screech as if someone is being murdered. But, like sirens in New York or a regular train passing by, after a while we stopped noticing them. Sometimes we forget to warn our house guests, and we've had many a panicked visitor sitting bolt upright in his bed awaiting his African death.

There are no "department stores" in Kenya, and when anyone furnishes a house here, the furniture must either be sent from Europe or the United States or made locally. I tore a picture of twin canopy beds from a *House Beautiful* magazine and took it to an old turbaned Sikh wood carver who squats on his haunches and carves by hand all day long. We agreed that the beds would be carved from mahogany (since mahogany grows here), and he said it would take a long time because there was very intricate carving to be done. Six weeks later they were finished and when I saw them I was delighted—they were so perfect I was afraid to ask their cost. "Oh," he hummed and hawed, "I'm afraid I'll have to charge you quite a bit of money for these beds—a lot of work. Um—they'll be fifteen dollars each." I tore more pictures out of more magazines and took them to him, and that, basically, is how we furnished our house. We had a painter who painted the entire outside of our house for five dollars. I think he stole the paint.

A British friend of ours, Lady Lindsay, has an interior-decorating shop in Nairobi, and she once asked me if I would help her decorate a few embassies and African politicians' houses. "I'm no interior decorator," I told her, but that didn't bother her at all and soon I learned why. In Nairobi, to be an interior decorator all you have to know is, "Take the refrigerator out of your living room."

I think we Americans tend to judge other peoples by our standards and values, not theirs. I am no exception. I merely assume all kinds of things—such as that everyone in the world has been in an elevator or at least knows what one is. We hired a gardener from "up-country," which means he was no city kid, and one day he was helping me carry something or other into Jock's town office, which is on the tenth floor, but is called the ninth floor because we call the ground floor the first floor, and all of that. (And did you know that the British billion is different from the American billion? I didn't know that. The American billion is a thousand million and the British billion is a million million. Don't admit it, but theirs is the logical way—following the same procedure as thousands to millions.) Anyway, my gardener was following me through town—he had not been to Jock's office before—and I simply turned into the building and got on the elevator and he followed. The doors closed and we started up. Suddenly I heard these loud terrified cries and saw he had dropped the packages and was clinging to the walls. I then realized he had never seen or even heard of an elevator before. What a terrible shock it must have been. Imagine trying to explain in Swahili what an elevator is to a terrified person traveling in one for the first time? He walked down. He said he thought we had gone into a closet (I don't usually take people into closets) and that the floor was falling away.

A few weeks later Jock and I saw a very modern black-and-white painting in the art gallery in Nairobi, which we couldn't afford but which we bought anyway. We left it rolled up in the back of our station wagon, waiting to be taken to the framer the next day. The following morning I couldn't find it and asked our gardener if he had seen it. "Oh yes," a big smile signifying much pleasure at a job well done, "someone had spilled black paint all over that paper, so I threw it out and burned it." Although it almost killed me, and I almost killed him, I soon (three years later) saw the humor in it and nearly wrote the artist to tell him what our gardener thought of his painting. But why should I expect him to know about modern painting any more than I would know about the things he uses to hunt with? On the whole, African servants probably get along better in our world than we would in theirs.

Sometimes you just can't rationalize though. For twenty years our cook has been cooking poached eggs. Every morning of his life Jock eats a poached egg on toast. One morning Jock looked at his breakfast plate and asked, "What's this?" pointing to a *raw* egg on the toast. The cook looked at it and answered, "Oh, I forgot to cook it." How could you forget to cook an egg?

These total lapses of memory are fairly common, and to me, completely incomprehensible. Our Swedish friends, Baron and Baroness Akerheilm, are gourmets. Their cook has been with them so long that when people ask him what tribe he is, instead of saying, Kikuyu, or Luo, or whatever he is, he says he's a Swede. For thirty-seven years he has been bringing the Akerheilms five-course meals every day. One time when they had driven four hundred miles to their beach house, and arrived late and tired, Baroness Akerheilm asked her family if they would mind just having fish and potatoes for supper, which in itself is funny if you had ever eaten the elaborate meals at their house. The family agreed, and when they sat down at the table their cook brought them mashed potatoes only. They waited, then rang for him, "Where's the fish?" He, too, had forgotten all about the fish. This forgetting is just something I'll never be able to fathom. After living in Africa for five years I thought I knew the Africans well. Now, after thirteen years, I know I don't know them at all. I like them very much, but I don't understand them. I feel certain, too, that this is a mutual feeling—our behavior must often be incomprehensible to them.

It is understandable when they "kill" your eyelashes—which you have left on your dressing table—by banging them with a shoe, thinking they were bugs because they have never seen false eyelashes. Many are the times I've picked the tuna fish out of my eyelashes, which had been thrown away in the garbage pit, having been mistaken for bugs. Even after an explanation it is hard for them to grasp because, with icy logic, they can see that you have perfectly good eyelashes anyway.

It is also understandable that after you've told them that you want lemon in your tea (the British for whom they may have worked before like milk) you also get lemon with your coffee and hot chocolate. This actually shows commendable initiative.

A very elegantly dressed friend of ours from the States, Ray Bates, was staying with us in Nairobi, and one night when he was going out to a dinner party he asked if our servant, Petro, could press his fancy new initialed shirt. An hour later I went into the kitchen and there was Petro, standing over the ironing board working away at the shirt, and to my amazement, he was carefully picking out every thread of the initials. He had never seen initialed shirts before, and being unable to read or write, he feared that something on the bottom of the iron had marred the shirt. The next day Ray flew by private plane to our coast house and took Petro with him for his very first plane ride. The poor man was excited but terrified, so Ray sat next to him and held his hand to calm him and to show he wasn't mad about the shirt.

A friend of ours told us she was having such a difficult time trying to get her cook to boil eggs for just three minutes, so she bought him an egg timer. She explained to him that it was for timing eggs and that when the sand went from the top to the bottom, the eggs were done. She sat at the dining-room table and waited happily for her "just right" eggs. Ten minutes passed, so she went into the kitchen to see what the trouble was an saw the cook standing over the stove looking into the pan which held the egg *and* the egg timer—both of them boiling away together.

A friend of ours arrived from the States with a present for us. It was the newest rage, he said, and was called a Frisbee. We had a super time, like the kids on thousands of blocks in the States, throwing the Frisbee to one another, and the hands-down winner who never missed a catch (though she had not actually been invited to play) was Shirley Brown. When we tired, we wandered back into the house through the kitchen and tossed the Frisbee onto the counter.

A few days later we had guests for lunch—safari clients whom we hardly knew. The cook had done a good job and we particularly looked forward to a strawberry-and-meringue concoction for dessert. It was presented with a flourish—in the Frisbee.

To offset the exasperation there are many laughs and touching moments, too. When returning from his leave, our cook will carry a little gift of eggs, or fruit, or a chicken for us—once a live chicken, when we lived in an apartment in the city. We had nowhere to put a chicken, so with a long string he tied it to the refrigerator, which was just too sordid for me, so I untied it and it sat on the living room sofa, which was even more sordid. Finally, we gave it to Jock's mother, who served it to us for lunch the following day. I could not eat it—after all, I had sat next to it on the sofa and looked into its eyes.

Entirely on his own initiative, the caretaker at our coast house will pick flowers in readiness for our arrival—although once we found a green mamba curled up in one of his arrangements. And once in Nairobi when we were away our servant fought off single-handed a gang of burglars. I am not sure that I would risk being beaten up in defense of someone else's possessions.

There is a close servant-employer relationship. They are almost part of the family, and we share their joys and their sadnesses. They want to know what our children are up to. We are forever taking their wives to the hospital to have babies, giving them medicine for their colds and cut fingers, or showing them slides of America. Because they have seen pictures of the riots, etc., they worry about us when we go to the States and say, "Please don't go to the States, it is very dangerous there." (We seem to spend all our time in America telling people Africa is not dangerous and all our time here telling Africans the States is not as bad as it appears.)

Some years ago I threw the Mickey Mouse comic books away after the children had read them forty-seven times and had gone on to adult things like *Mad* magazine. A few days later my oldest son, Rick, noticed our cook was sitting in the kitchen reading the comics —looking at them, I should say, because he can't read. Rick asked, "Do you like Mickey Mouse?" and he answered, "Oh, very much. One day I would like to go to America where the mice wear clothes and talk."

IV
God

Some years ago I went to Singida, in Tanzania, to film a documentary on leprosy. I was to spend about five days in the leprosarium, but I knew nothing about leprosy or what to do about not catching it. So, when I arrived I asked the missionaries what precautionary measures they took. They answered, "Oh, the Good Lord sent us and He will take care of us." "Yes," I thought uneasily, "but it was only the TV station that sent me."

There are eleven million people in Kenya. Less than 1 per cent are white. There are six times as many Asians as there are whites. The majority of the Asians in East Africa are Hindus. We asked a Hindu friend once what his religion was all about and he answered, "It is a combination of sex and mathematics." That is all I have ever learned about the Hindu religion.

Among the Asians, who originally came from India and Pakistan, there are also Muslims and Sikhs. Scattered along the coast live about sixty thousand Arabs who have been there for centuries. Although the missionaries arrived in 1844, today only 12 per cent of the eleven million population are Christians, and the majority of the Africans are Muslims or pagans. In Nairobi, there are mosques and temples and cathedrals and churches and synagogues and Christian Science reading rooms and other edifices erected by man, each advertising, "This way to Heaven."

I long ago gave up trying to pick the winner—after all, difference of opinion is what makes horse racing. I believe there are many rights, and each person must follow whichever path suits him best. I tried a few religions on for size, but none of them seem to fit me, so I practice "Bettyism." An unkind friend said, "Does that mean that everyone should worship Betty?" That would be nice, but I can't get anyone to do it, and so I content myself with my own private religion and respect the idiosyncracies of others, too.

Neither strict Muslims nor Hindus drink anything alcoholic, and the Hindus won't eat beef because of the holy cow thing. The Muslims won't touch pork and only eat other kinds of meat when the throat has been slit. Dinner parties can thus get very complicated, so when Hindus come to dinner I lie and tell them it isn't wine in the lobster sauce, it's vinegar. But it is difficult to convince them the rum in the rum cake is vinegar.

To accommodate the Muslims throughout East Africa and those in the Middle East who buy meat products exported from Kenya, the government-controlled meat packing factory has cunningly tailored one important part of its production line. The law requires here, as in the States, that a humane killer be used to despatch the steers on their final journey. This machine plunges a bolt into the brain of the beast and although it kills it instantly, the animal continues to twitch and kick as it slides down a chute to be picked up by the conveyor belt. As it arrives at the bottom of the chute, dead but kicking, a fearsome Muslim figure, wearing turban, loincloth and beard, leaps upon it and with religious fervor slits its throat with a razor-sharp curved dagger. Honor is satisfied, and the resulting corned beef can be eaten happily by all god-fearing Muslims.

Many people in Kenya hire Muslims in preference to Christians because Muslims won't steal—at least, that is the theory. Christians believe they can be forgiven, but this is not so with Muslims. Once we had a good servant named Juma who was a Muslim, but our problem was not Juma, it was Shirley Brown, our Labrador who loves everyone and especially Juma. Muslims believe dogs are unclean and cannot be touched, but if accidently it should happen, they must wash their clothes seven times—once in the earth. Juma spent his entire day washing his own clothes, after unsuccessfully backing away from Shirley Brown who wanted always to kiss him and loved the game he played of running away from her.

When we go to a mosque or a Hindu temple we take our shoes off, but we have never been as unfortunate as a former Mayor of Nairobi, a Protestant, who once made a formal visit to the mosque and dutifully slipped off his shoes outside. When he left, he found that his shoes had been stolen, and he completed the dignified procession of the city on stockinged feet.

God causes quite a bit of confusion in East Africa, or perhaps I should say religion does. For example, think how difficult it must be for a pagan who has never heard of Christianity to suddenly find a Seventh-Day Adventist Mission on one side of his village and a Roman Catholic Mission on the other. The Catholic priest will tell him that he must go to church on Sunday, and that it is all right if he smokes and drinks. The Seventh-Day Adventist will tell him he must go to church on Saturday and that he may not smoke or drink. This is confusing enough for us who profess to be Christians.

The pagan is inclined to take Christianity very literally. For example, our servant Petro was converted by the Pentecostals, and he worked for us five days a week, including Sunday. One Sunday, after he had washed, ironed and cleaned the house, he cut down a tree out of which Jock wanted to make a garden bench. Petro had split the tree and put one half on little legs, which was fine except for the fact that the bench wobbled, so Jock asked him to dig away an inch of earth under one leg to steady it. Petro answered "No." We looked at him in astonishment and asked why not, to which he replied, "The Lord saith 'Thou shall not till the soil on Sunday.'" "Oh," we answered, and tilled the soil ourselves.

The Lutheran missionaries at the leprosarium told me that after they had been teaching Christianity for a few months, one young man kept coming to them for money for clothes and for food, until finally they said to him, "You must go out and work for these

things, you just don't come to us and ask for them." To which he
answered, "That is not what you told me. You said, 'Ask and ye
shall receive.'"

One day my nun friend who had been teaching school way out
in the bush, heard that the Bishop was going to visit all the primary
schools in her area. She wanted him to see what a good job she
was doing, so she announced to her class that the Bishop would
arrive the next day and for them to be sure to wear clothes to school
—which sometimes they did and sometimes they didn't. One child
was absent that day, and the next morning he arrived at school
completely naked. Since he didn't live far away, she asked him to
please go home and put some clothes on in honor of the Bishop's
visit. With great enthusiasm he dashed off, and when he returned
he had on a pair of sunglasses, a hat and a necktie.

I must say that religion seems to be as confusing to my children
as it does to the Africans. Religious studies are a required subject
in British schools, and on my ten-year-old son, McDonnell's, report card the teacher wrote in the space for his first "Sacred
Studies" mark, "He sews not neither does he reap." I asked Mc-
Donnell what his problem was with sacred studies, and he answered, "I just can't understand the Bibble."

Later on in the year he fell down and the school was afraid
he had broken his arm, so they sent him to a nearby hospital and
telephoned me. I got in the car and drove the 125 miles to the
hospital to find him riding on the food carts all around the ward,
perfectly happy, with his arm in a sling but unbroken. I asked
him if he had had any trouble with all those dreary questions they
ask when you enter a hospital, and he said no, he could answer
them all but one. It seems that when they asked him what religion
he was he didn't know, so he said he wasn't quite sure. Horrified,
I asked him what happened then, and he said, "Well, the nurse at
the desk said if she read off a few religions did I think I would
recognize the sound of one, so I said I'd try. She read, 'Catholic'
and then 'Protestant' and I said yes, I thought Protestant sounded
familiar, so she checked that."

A few weeks later I was repeating the story in the presence of our daughter, Dancy, who is just eleven months older, and in total disgust she turned to him and said, "McDonnell, don't you know that you are a Piscopalian—P-I-S-C-O-P-A-L-I-A-N."

One time at dinner before a lecture in the Bible Belt of our United States, a woman attacked me saying, "What denomination are YOU?"

Being a coward I answered, "Episcopalian."

"Just like the Catholics except you don't worship the Pope!"

Uh, oh, I thought, I'd better find out what battleground I'm on. "What religion are YOU?" I asked.

"Disciples of Christ," was her reply.

A friend in New York said I should have asked, "Disciples of *whom?*"

It is just that so often I find this quote to be all too true about so many religious people: "They pray to God on Sundays and on their neighbors for the rest of the week."

God is actually warm and fun and has a great sense of humor. I know—I often hear Him laughing when we sit down at our dinner table, for instance, and Jock says grace, "For this food we are about to receive, let us give thanks to Jock Leslie-Melville."

We have seldom enjoyed two more delightful and amusing safari companions than Cy Feuer and his son Jed. Cy produced *Can-Can, Guys and Dolls, How to Succeed in Business* and many other Broadway shows and told us that in Hollywood a cartoonist he knew named "Doodles" had in his office, instead of the usual signed life-sized cut-out of Gina Lollobrigida or Raquel Welch, a cardboard full-sized picture of Jesus on the cross and written on it was, "To Doodles, from J.C."

If God isn't laughing about that, then I don't want to go. Robert Frost's poem says it all for me. "Forgive oh Lord, my little jokes on Thee, and I'll forgive Thy great big one on me."

V

Woolworths and Witch Doctors

Although we spend most of our time in Nairobi, Jock and I also have a house at Malindi, almost *in* the Indian Ocean, which we designed and built ourselves with the aid of twenty-five African masons, carpenters and painters—and it looks as if we had made it entirely by ourselves. From the Arabs we stole the idea of the arches, from the Zanzibaris the concept of the shuttered doors and windows, the coconut-palm thatched roof we copied from the Africans, and the idea of leaving a huge tree growing in the middle of the living room we stole from F. Lloyd Wright. The sunken tub and "A frame" are American-inspired, and the mosquito nets are by courtesy of the British. Then we added a few ideas of our own —such as using the top of a birdbath as an outside footbath in which to rinse our feet so that we don't drag sand into the house, and also an open-air bathroom with a sunken tub. When our gardener saw the sunken tub, he said, "Oh, too bad they put the tub in wrong—what a terrible mistake."

About every other weekend we drive the 378 miles from Nairobi to Malindi. Since there are no speed limits in Kenya, we drive too fast and make it in about five and a half hours. (I always fasten my seat belt because I'd rather die in the privacy of my own car than out there in public on the road.) At Malindi we lie in the sun eating bonbons and mangoes and fall apart in little pieces. The twelve-foot tide gives us different sounds and views all day long, and as the sun rises over the ocean it turns our world bright orange. The naked African fishermen perform a ballet in silhouette as they pole their fishing boats out to sea in unconscious unison. Later they come to the house selling lobsters and crab and shrimp all alive and glistening.

My only sport is sunbathing, but sometimes I do enjoy goggling. I asked Jock's Scottish cousin once if he had ever goggled, and he looked funny and said yes—but only for a sore throat. He thought I had said "gargle." We Americans call it snorkeling, I think. Anyway, you put on flippers and goggles and go swimming among the fish. Two thirds of the world is under water, and we know so little about it. Jock and I are becoming as interested in the animals under water as we are in those above it. It is a silent world of modern paintings that suddenly come alive and move.

You swim under water among darting zebra-striped fish, and creatures like weird undulating demented pancakes and fried eggs gliding among paisley jellyfish in pink-coral castles.

In fact, these underwater creatures are about the only things that move with any vigor at the coast. When a night club first opened in Malindi, African dancers and drummers were featured. They had been rehearsing for weeks and were excellent. Came the big opening night, and the Minister of Tourism and the Minister of Information and a lot of other VIPs arrived all the way from Nairobi. It was a very important event indeed, and things were going beautifully through dinner, but soon afterwards we saw our friend, the manager, getting nervous. A few minutes later he confided to us that the dancers had not shown up and an hour later when people were beginning to get restless and wanted entertainment, they still hadn't arrived. So the manager excused himself and left. About a half hour later he returned and whispered to us that he had gone to the dancers' village and found them all in bed asleep. He screamed why hadn't they come as had been planned for three weeks, and they answered, "Oh, we thought we'd come tomorrow night instead."

Vasco da Gama discovered Malindi in 1498, and it hasn't changed since then, at least not enough to notice. It is sometimes referred to as the Florida of Africa, but Miami Beach doesn't look like a tiny old Arab town to me. There are only four hotels in all of Malindi, one of which is so filled with German tourists that it is referred to by Malindi's residents as "Stalag 17." The German tourists march up and down the beach, and when you tell them to beware of sunburn since they are exposed to equatorial sun, they shout, "Vee Germans can endure anything."

A British comedian whom Jock knew in England was flying on a German plane and when it landed in Munich, instead of the usual "Thank you for flying Pan Am" and "We hope you enjoyed our flight," etc., the intercom switched on and a voice barked, "You vill now proceed to the immigration authorities! Zhere you will present your passport and health documents for scrutiny! Zhen you vill leave zee customs and turn right vere you vill vait in zee room until your name is called!" Then the intercom clicked off. The British comedian jumped to his feet and shouted throughout the plane, "Und zen you vill be shot!"

Although four hotels have been built in Malindi since Vasco da Gama's day, nobody has bothered with a movie theater. However, for culture and entertainment, every Sunday night you can go to one of the hotels and sit outside and watch Freddie Bartholemew on 16 mm in *Captains Courageous,* or Fess Parker in *Davy Crockett* and other such modern films. Since it is projected on a sheet that blows in the wind, we call it "Ripple Vision," and "Fungus Color" because things get green with mold at Malindi. Everyone sits outside on uncomfortable chairs for eight reel changes, and perhaps as many film breaks, during which time members of the audience go to the bar for another drink. (I think the film's constant breaks are just a decoy to sell drinks.)

For those who don't drink all day, marijuana is delivered on a bicycle along with the milk and the morning paper. I wish the entire marijuana syndrome had never arisen. If only it had been left with the Africans and Asians—the people who have been smoking it for thousands of years. But no, it had to become the trendy thing to do among the Europeans in East Africa, and lots of our friends are running to the bus stop or the chicken market or the gas station and buying their joints along with their chicken breasts and five gallons of gas. It is said to be very pure here and of the top quality.

Soon these friends were saying to us in astonishment, "You mean you NEVER even TRIED marijuana?" and I felt as I hadn't felt since I was thirteen years old and the only girl among my friends who hadn't menstruated yet. For many months I listened to sensible contemporaries raving about the joys of cannabis, and I heard them giggling away as I would leave the party exhausted and not nearly as delighted with life as they sounded. The next morning I felt dreadful from too many cigarettes (plain) and too many drinks, and they bounced around full of vigor and health.

After some months I got the most terrible feeling—suppose they were right? Suppose marijuana was as good and as harmless as sex, for instance? Suppose I was thirteen again and they were trying to tell me about an orgasm. Didn't I then sound ridiculous saying things like, "I have no interest. I'm happy enough without it. I don't *need* it." Wow. So, finally I decided not to keep off the grass any longer and tried it. I did not like it. So now things are worse—can you imagine having an orgasm and saying you didn't *like* it? Before, to them, I was just some kind of religious fanatic, but now I am totally unacceptable as a human being.

But the fact is that when we smoked, Jock withdrew into a private world of his own and was no fun, and I became obnoxious even to the point of tap-dancing. But that was an outward manifestation. Inside it made me paranoid—was everyone playing a trick on me?—and very dopey. My mind went, and although food tasted more delicious and music sounded better and colors seemed much brighter—I admired the whiteness of the toothpaste for what seemed like a half hour—I kept wanting my mind to come back. I would start a very important sentence, but by the time I got two words out I couldn't remember what I had started to say. A baboon can count to four, but I could only get to two. Or if someone was telling me something I was intensely interested in, I couldn't

remember the first part of the sentence. I had no past and no fu-
ture—grass is a very now thing. I felt like an animal and this bothered me—senses sharpened, mind less. I like possessing all my
faculties, and I seem to have a built-in happiness generator that
resents any outside help. I guess I am lucky. And so we put the
marijuana away in the china jar which has "Marijuana" embossed
on it—given to us by a friend—and there it has remained untouched
for the last few years.

I am opposed to young people getting stoned but no more, I
suppose, than their getting drunk. Remember, we Americans live
in an alcoholic supportive culture, and it takes awhile to equate
the two. I am violently opposed to LSD, amphetamines and all
hard drugs, yet I am inclined to believe, because I have been told
by doctors who have been around marijuana supportive cultures
for years, that grass is certainly no more harmful and addictive
than alcohol and regular cigarettes, both of which can be disas-
trous but which may be all right if taken in moderation.

I think old people should smoke grass. After one *has* coped with
life, and has known the joy of accomplishment but has little left
to look forward to, why *not* smoke if it makes you hear music
more beautifully, see colors more brilliantly, taste food better, and
generally improves the declining state of being? When the only
realities left are loneliness, illness, pain and death, then it's time
to ward them off. Jock's mother should smoke marijuana all day
long. He says he's going to get his own back by going there every
day and saying to her, "It's time for potty!" We plan one day to
open an old folks' home and call it "Marijuana Manor."

In Switzerland, at the school my children attend, the authorities
had what is called a "drug bust," or sudden search for hidden
drugs. They found no hard drugs, only cannabis. Some children
were expelled from the school, some were even deported from
Switzerland (the Swiss really frown on marijuana)—so it was a
nasty business. A few weeks after the big drama, it was prize-
giving day at school. During the awards at the assembly, the Headmaster got to the literary prize and announced that since it was a
tie, there would be a joint prize. The entire school broke into ap-

plause, stomped their feet and whistled. Wouldn't you hate to be a Headmaster of a school anywhere in the 1970s?

A few years ago census taking in Kenya went like this: Two schoolboys arrived at our Malindi house—one was an Arab and the other an African. They were taking the census of everybody in the house, and after we had answered all their questions about ourselves they called our staff. After the census takers had written down our servants' names, whether they had gone to school, how many children they had, etc., it came to the question of age—but none of our staff knew how old they were. Many Africans do not know how old they are because their births have never been recorded—even our President is not sure of his age. Now, of course, births are beginning to be registered. So the census takers took out a little piece of paper and started asking questions like, "Do you remember the D. C. Matthews?" "No," our cook would shake his head. "Do you remember the day the elephant was washed up on the beach?" "No." "Do you remember Chief Ali?" Again, "No." "Do you remember the flood?" "No." "Do you remember the D. C. Wilson?" "Ah! yes," said our cook. "How tall were you then?" asked the census takers. He held his hand up about the height of the table and said, "Oh, I guess I was nine." "You weren't nine," I interrupted, "You could only have been five or six." The census taker said, "We will say six." He then looked at the date when the D. C. Wilson held office, did some adding and subtracting, calculated the year of our cook's birth, and marked it down on the census form. (I guess they must figure those with bad memories aren't born.) This tedious procedure took ages, but finally everyone had finished with the exception of an old servant of ours whom I had assumed was somewhere between seventy and a thousand years old. He shuffled out on the veranda where all this was going on, and when they got to the part, "Do you know how old you are?" unlike the three younger ones he answered, "Yes, I know how old I am." "How old?" the census takers asked. Bent over and voice quivering he answered, "Thirty-nine." Another Jack Benny. So they wrote down thirty-nine and off they went. You can see how accurate the census taking is in East Africa.

Out in the bush when the children don't know how old they are, they line up and those who can touch their left ear by reaching over the top of their heads with their right hand can go to first grade. This is because you are not able to reach your left ear in this manner until you are about six, so now if you come to East Africa you will know what all the children are doing lined up with their right arms over the top of their heads. Those who fail to reach their left ear go away and come back next year to try again to see if they can enter first grade.

Many interesting people live at the coast, and at the top of the list I would certainly put Zoltan Rosinger, Esq. Zoltan, an Austrian, was a pupil of Sigmund Freud's but switched camps to follow Adler.

Though a trained psychiatrist for the last twenty years, he has been responsible for the health of eighty thousand people and until recently was the only doctor in the Coast Region of Malindi. I would as soon go to Dr. Rosinger as any doctor I know.

A friend of ours, Myles Burton, had been spear fishing about thirty miles north of Malindi and shot the harpoon right through his own hand where it lodged. It was miles back to his car and many more miles still back to Malindi to find Dr. Rosinger. Hours later, when he finally succeeded in getting there, he was afraid he was going to faint. Dr. Rosinger took one look at the spear through his hand and said, "Very interesting, very interesting," then ran off. Myles was sure he had gone for morphine, but Dr. Rosinger came back with a camera and promptly took a picture of the spear through his hand saying, "Never have I seen anything like this before—very interesting." He then removed the harpoon and set the broken finger by using a strip of chrome from a refrigerator as a splint. Zoltan told him to fly the next day to Nairobi to see an orthopedic surgeon, since he did not have X-ray facilities at Malindi. The orthopedic man took one look at what Rosinger had done and said, "I cannot improve upon this. It is absolutely perfect."

Going to Dr. Rosinger's clinic is an experience in itself. Everyone sits outside on a bench under a tree waiting his turn to see him. One day when I was there, an adorable little African boy in a white Eton suit with white shoes and socks appeared with his mother and father. Dr. Rosinger came out and said to me, pointing to the child, "This is Zoltan Rosinger, Esq." He went on to explain that after nine miscarriages the mother had finally come to him and he told her that this time she *would* have a baby, because after examining her he found out it was necessary for her to have a Caesarian, which he performed with success. They were so pleased and indebted to Zoltan that they named their child, Zoltan Rosinger, Esq., copied from an envelope addressed to Dr. Rosinger.

The doctor and his wife have no children, and he laughed about this knowing the African custom that a man is called "Charo, son of David" or "Mwangi, son of Kamau." Zoltan said he can just see in years to come when this child grows up and has a son, Zoltan's relatives from Austria will appear and will be introduced to "Ahamed, son of Zoltan Rosinger, Esq.," and will assume that Zoltan had had an amorous past about which they had not heard.

Another character at the coast is the witch doctor named Kabwere. (Having both a witch doctor and a Woolworths just a few miles apart amuses me; and I haven't spelled Woolworths wrong. It actually has nothing to do with the F. W. Woolworth's Company in the States, but was a name deliberately chosen by an astute Asian businessman who figured that he was not violating the patent laws and by merely leaving out the apostrophe could still cash in on a name known throughout the world.) Kabwere is a good witch doctor. There are good witch doctors and bad witch doctors. The bad witch doctor casts a spell and the good witch doctor removes it. (I am sure they must work in cahoots.)

Whenever Kabwere has a sore throat he sneaks out to Dr. Rosinger and after the latter has painted it, he always asks, "How much would *you* have charged for this treatment, Kabwere?" and whatever amount the witch doctor replies, Dr. Rosinger charges one shilling more. If Kabwere were to answer, "Six shillings,"

Dr. Rosinger would say, "I then will charge you seven shillings because I am a better doctor than you."

Over the years their friendship has developed, but as far as I know Zoltan has not passed on to Kabwere a bit of witchcraft which he thought up some years ago and which was once used to great effect by a colleague of his. It is not uncommon for the youths, especially girls, to get into a hysterical frenzy and be unable to stop dancing—even risking death from exhaustion by dancing for days on end. Zoltan discussed his idea with his friend, a psychiatrist who worked for the Government, and when a few months later the frenetic dancing started in an African village the man went to the scene fully briefed and prepared to execute Zoltan's plan. He told the young people, yes, they were possessed by a *Shaitani* (a corruption of the word Satan). Evidently it is important to agree that there is a problem because witchcraft is no more than applied psychiatry, and when reasoning will not prevail you must let people believe that they are guilty and are possessed by the devil because that is what they want to believe psychologically, and they subconsciously wish to be punished. The doctor said that he had the medicine to cure them, and he gave them each a pill containing an acid that was quite harmless but made the blood flow through their veins with a burning sensation. Later the pill would make them urinate red, and he told them that first they would feel the burning and then they would see the devil pass, thus exorcising them. And this is exactly what happened. I bet Kabwere would give a lot to know the secret of Zoltan Rosinger's magic potion.

For the past few years Jock and I have acted as Jack Paar's consultants and organizers for his "African Special" programs. We have loved working with him—many laughs, as you can imagine, and the association has led to a number of interesting encounters, one of which was with Kabwere. Jock and I thought that perhaps Jack might like to interview the witch doctor and Dr. Rosinger for one of his programs.

Myles Burton knew Kabwere because he had sold a minibus to the witch doctor for eight thousand shillings. He said he got to know him very well because when he delivered the bus, Kabwere paid him by digging into the ground and hauling out a big metal box, out of which he counted eight thousand one-shilling coins! Kabwere gets paid by his patients in small change, and this is how he in turn pays for everything that he buys. Anyway, Myles took us to the village and introduced us to Kabwere.

At the entrance to his driveway there is a sign that reads "ALL TOURISTS ARE NOT ALLOWED" and another sign on the opposite side of the driveway advertising "ANTI-WITCHCRAFT MEDICINE." We had noticed only this latter sign and drove on into the property. Kabwere has 123 wives and goodness knows how many children. In the center of the little village stood an old man with a big pot belly, looking very scruffy. Myles, knowing the custom, got out of the car, went up to Kabwere and said, "I would like to see Kabwere." He answered, speaking of himself in the third person, "Why would you like to see him?" and Myles said, "I would like to see him about a business matter." Kabwere then said, "Didn't you see the sign coming in?" and Myles asked, "The sign that says 'ANTI-WITCHCRAFT MEDICINE'?" Kabwere said, "No, the other sign." Myles admitted he hadn't seen it, so Kabwere got into the back of the car with me, and we turned around and drove to the entrance where he pointed out the sign which read "ALL TOURISTS ARE NOT ALLOWED." Myles explained that he was not a tourist—that he lived here— that he had sold Kabwere his minibus at one time, and that the sign therefore did not apply to him. This seemed to satisfy him, so he said, "If you want to see Kabwere you must go across the street and make an appointment with his son." "Where is his son?" asked Myles. "His son is in the bar." So we went to the bar across the street and met his smiling son. Myles explained about the television interview, to which the son said that he would have to ask his father, and that if we would come early next morning at seven o'clock, with a case of beer as an entrance fee, we would indeed be able to have appointment to see Kabwere. Then he added, "I and my colleges (he meant colleagues) will be there too."

So the next morning Jock and I went along with Shirley Brown and a case of beer to see Kabwere. Because I am but a lowly woman, it was proper for me to stay in the car, which I did while Jock went into the main hut.

Immediately the car was surrounded by some of Kabwere's wives and about sixty-two of his children, who pointed to Shirley Brown and said in Swahili what a nice goat she was. Shirley Brown was very offended, so I explained she was not a goat but a dog. No, they said, she couldn't be a dog for their dogs were never plain black, only their goats. I then asked Shirley Brown to give me her paw and to do a lot of other tricks, which she performed in a resigned fashion but which astonished the children.

Meanwhile, Jock was inside talking to Kabwere in Swahili about his possible television interview. Kabwere agreed readily, and then the discussion of a price began. Finishing his cake and beer Kabwere got up, wandered over to the window and stood there, looking out thoughtfully. Jock thought he was trying to figure out how much he could ask, which indeed he was. After a moment or two he said, "Yes, I will do it for one hundred shillings ($15) and that dog." (*He* knew Shirley Brown wasn't a goat.) Jock explained that he couldn't have that particular dog, but that he would bring him one very much like it. (Now every time Shirley Brown misbehaves we threaten to send her to the witch doctor.)

There was an interesting by-product to this encounter with Kabwere. While negotiating in the hut, Jock had noticed a quiet, nice-looking young African who was well dressed and seemed strangely misplaced. Finally the young man spoke, in flawless English, and Jock chatted with him for a few minutes. He had gone to the States six years before as a medical student but had left medical school after four years and switched to an economics course. Shortly after, his health had deteriorated and he had spent the next two years studying economics and going in and out of hospital. Finally his doctors in the U.S., failing to diagnose the trouble, advised him to return home since Nairobi is a great center for tropical medicine; but they were unable to help him in Nairobi either, and he still felt sick and listless.

In desperation he switched tactics completely and abandoning any hope of a cure from scientific medicine, he presented himself to

Kabwere, the witch doctor. (This reversion to tribal or traditional ways is not uncommon, even among supposedly sophisticated Africans—or even among supposedly sophisticated Americans, for that matter, only we don't call it tribalism. When the news came that Robert Kennedy was assassinated I was shopping in Nairobi. Suddenly I found myself in the American Embassy—I never go to the American Embassy, but there I was with a lot of other Americans who had also wandered there because they wanted to be with their own kind. At least we all knew how the others felt but there was not that same communication with different nationalities. Tribalism?)

Nearly a year later Jock picked up an African who was thumbing a lift and who remembered him, since he, too, had been at the witch doctor's that day. Jock asked him about the sick student and was told, "Oh, he recovered completely after a couple of months and has returned to his studies." Herbalism? Psychosomatic illness? Mind over matter? We will never know.

Kabwere does not have a monopoly of unusual cures, however. One English patient of Dr. Rosinger's, who had stepped on a sea urchin while goggling, grew impatient waiting outside in the long line because the spines in his foot were terribly painful. As Dr. Rosinger hurried by he called, "Doctor, Doctor, can't you help me now—I'm in such pain?" Dr. Rosinger paused a second, glancing at the outstretched foot, and said, "Oh, go home and put your foot in paw-paw" (papaya), and with that stomped off. The visitor, angry at being brushed off like this, went home, nevertheless, and feeling rather foolish but desperate because of the pain, took a large paw-paw from the refrigerator, cut it in half, and when no one was looking, put his foot in the fruit. Sure enough, in just a few minutes the spines were dissolved and the pain had gone. Maybe the use of paw-paw is something that Dr. Rosinger learned from his friend Kabwere.

One evening a friend of ours got a moth in his ear. He thought the moth would either fly out again, not liking those crowded conditions, or he could get it out himself. But by 2 A.M. his efforts had failed and the moth was boring deeper and deeper into his ear and making such a noise inside his head that he decided he had to drive the twelve miles to Dr. Rosinger's house. Much as he hated to do so, he awakened the good doctor in the middle of the night, who with his blunt bedside manner, commanded him to, "Go in the living room and sit on the sofa." Then he disappeared. In a few minutes Zoltan was back with a bottle of Le Roux Brandy and a small glass. "I don't want a drink, thank you. I'm O.K.—I don't need brandy, just get the moth out," he protested. (Besides, our friend, who was something of a connoisseur, would never have been caught dead drinking Le Roux Brandy.) "It's not for you—it's for the moth," barked Zoltan. "I'm going to put it to sleep and you can come back in the morning and we'll get it out then."

In another minute, our friend was driving home with a drunken passed-out moth in his ear, wishing like hell he had thought of that and saved himself his midnight journey.

Because Malindi is a popular tourist center, much of Dr. Rosinger's time is spent looking after the health of travelers. There are many German tourists as well as French and English and a number of Americans. More so than other nationalities, the Germans who visit East Africa seem preoccupied with sex, and indeed until the Government intervened, one German tour company was advertising "Sex Safaris to East Africa."

Many of those who visit Malindi's Red Light district show up a few days later in Dr. Rosinger's clinic, and he told us that it is astonishing how many V.D. patients use the excuse of catching it in a toilet. But as Zoltan says, "Of course you can catch V.D. in a toilet—but it is extremely uncomfortable."

Another interesting character at the coast is an Englishman who looks just like Jesus. He has piercing blue eyes and wore his hair shoulder-length long before it was fashionable. He is tall and thin and very ethereal-looking, and everyone says he is a mystic. He became a Muslim many years ago and ran a shark fishery way north of Malindi in a little tiny fishing village where nobody ever went. One day the Shifta, the bad guys from Somalia with whom Kenya were having a border dispute, swooped down and captured him. They marched him through the desert making him carry their baggage for five hundred miles and, of course, they planned to kill him.

Every day he knelt on his mat and prayed facing East to Mecca and recited from the Koran, proving he was a Muslim, and saying to them, "You would not kill one of your own brothers." Since he spoke Arabic fluently and obviously knew the Koran, they did not kill him but set him free, and he returned to Kenya and wrote a book about his experiences.

Soon afterwards he decided to give up his job as shark officer, and he bought a tiny island right in the Indian Ocean about thirty-five miles north of Malindi. He called it Robinson's Island and grew vegetables and shipped them to Malindi. The only time I ever spoke to him was in his vegetable market where I asked penetrating things like, "Do you have any parsley?" but I always felt very eerie around him. One day a notice was put on the bulletin board of the hotel at Malindi, saying that anyone who wanted to go to Robinson's Island could do so for a Shs.12/– ($1.70) lunch, so Jock and the three children and I drove the thirty-five miles, and there on the right-hand side of the road we saw an arrow made of twigs pointing to the sea and a little cardboard sign saying ROBINSON'S ISLAND. The track led us to a little estuary among the mangrove swamps, where it petered out. We blew the horn of our car a couple of times and waited. It seemed silly blowing a horn in the middle of nowhere, but this is what we had been told to do.

In about twenty minutes, around the bend of the estuary there appeared an African standing up and punting a boat, into which we all climbed. It was a perfectly beautiful spot, the river twisted and turned, trees were growing in the swamps, birds of all kinds were singing. Finally we stopped at a sand dune. The African gestured, and we got out and ran up over the hill where we saw a palm-thatched hut straight out of a desert island movie. The walls and the roof were of palm thatch and the floor was simply sand. This was his house and also the restaurant.

Way out in the middle of the ocean I saw a tiny black dot. "What's that?" I asked, and was told it was the cook. When he heard our car horn blow, he went out into the ocean to catch our lunch, and his assistants went to the creek to net shrimps and dig oysters. Fishing was difficult that day, and our lunch wasn't caught until 3:30 P.M., but the mood of the place was so tranquil, so timeless, that we didn't mind.

Lamu, still further north, is a tiny remote island off the Kenya coast. It used to be an Arab sultanate and is so behind the times it makes Zanzibar look like Chicago. There are no wheeled vehicles on the island of Lamu, not even a bicycle. To get there, you fly from Malindi to a nearby island, then cross to Lamu by canoe. All the women are in strict purdah. I wish purdah would become fashionable in the States. How easy it would be just to throw a black robe over yourself—no girdles, clothes, hair-styles. In fact, since the only thing that shows is your eyes, all you'd need is a few tablespoons of mascara each day.

Beautiful Arab dhows (*Arabian Nights* type sailing vessels) with their billowing single triangular sails still ply to and from Lamu as they did in Biblical times—sailing back and forth from Arabia with the monsoons. To find yourself in a world that has not changed in a thousand years is a weird and vaguely unsettling experience. If you like Lamu and want to spend a few days way back in history, there are two hotels there, one of which is known affectionately as "The Dysentery Arms." It looks just like Humphrey Bogart's hangout, and you expect to see Sidney Greenstreet and Peter Lorre lurking about the entrance. Many years ago, the Headmaster of a good boys' school in Kenya decided to hell with convention—he would do what he wanted. So with his boy friend he went to remote Lamu to open a hotel and live happily ever after. But, soon after the hotel opened the two homosexuals had a fight and didn't speak to each other for the next twenty-five years. During that time if you wanted a drink before a meal but had gone into the dining room upstairs instead of the bar downstairs and asked for gin and tonic, the ex-Headmaster would pout and say, "I'm sorry, but you can't get a drink here. I *think* there is a person downstairs who *may* be able to get you one." So you would have to get your own drink downstairs and carry it upstairs yourself.

Similarly, if you wanted some hors d'oeuvres or a sandwich while you were having a drink downstairs and asked if you could have something to eat, you'd get the same abrupt reply, "NO food here. If you HAVE to have some, ask that dreadful person upstairs." And so they lived for twenty-five years, until the ex-Headmaster was murdered by his young Arab servant, who had become his new boy friend.

I've always said that if I ever wrote a book about Africa, it would not be about the animals but about the people here. But I can't do that, I'd lose all my friends. A distant relative of Churchill's lives here and married a black Seychellois night-club singer and dancer who had four illigitimate children before they were married and at the time of their marriage was very pregnant (not by him, but she wasn't quite sure by whom). The marriage must have pleased his family in England. The couple lived in marital bliss for two months, and then she stabbed and wounded him on the dance floor.

One of Churchill's granddaughters also married and lived here for a little while. When she first arrived in Kenya a few years ago, she sat in someone's drawing room one evening and shot the light bulbs out with a pistol. Which takes us to wildlife in Nairobi.

VI
Wildlife in Nairobi

Nairobi is a city where you can't get douche powder but you might get a turtle in your Coke. It is also eighty-seven miles south of the Equator, one mile high (which makes my stomach growl), and is inclined to be cold rather than hot. In January and February, our summer, the thermometer might rise to 78° at mid-day, but nights are always sweater cool. In July and August, our winter, the temperature frequently goes down to 40° at night, and 40° without central heating is very cold indeed. I am vague on the temperature because no one ever talks about it. In the States people always say, "Do you *know* what the temperature was at noon?" and of course everyone *always* knows what the temperature was at noon—except those in a coma—because you hear it over the radio and on television every five minutes. Temperature is not announced here and no one ever mentions it. This does not mean to say they don't complain about the weather. They do so constantly, especially the British, who on a beautifully balmy day say, "Isn't this dreadful? I've never been so hot. Ghastly." The thermometer might read 79°. Obviously they have never been to Baltimore or Washington, D.C., in the summer. By American standards it never gets hot or cold in East Africa. The mean temperatures are given in an obscure place in the newspapers every day, but it always says "13° C." Finally one day when there was nothing pressing that had to be done immediately, I looked up how to change Centigrade into Fahrenheit and found you must first multiply by nine fifths, then add thirty-two, so I have never known what 13° C is. Suffice it to say that every evening I put on a sweater, sheep-skin slippers and slacks for warmth (in July and August during the day as well) and that all visitors are astonished at how chilly it is here and wonder where the hot, steaming jungles are.

Nairobi, a Masai word for "place of cold water," is an exceptionally pretty city. Palm trees, Jacarandas, cassias, flame trees and Bougainvillaea line the streets and highways and each traffic circle is a beautiful rock garden. Pessimists feared the African Government would allow the beauty of the city to deteriorate; instead they have improved it with more shrubs and flowers and parks and lakes, all beautifully planned and kept.

I think many tourists are disappointed when they first arrive in Nairobi—they expect to get off the plane and onto a vine and swing through the jungle, but all they get are highways, neon signs, Woolworth's, the supermarket, and Hilton and Intercontinental hotels complete with swimming pools and sauna baths. There are about five good hotels in Nairobi and at least five unacceptable ones. Our friend Ray Bates, who arrived from the States once in the middle of the night when we were at the coast, was to take the first plane out in the morning for Malindi. Since all the decent hotels were fully booked and he needed a bed for about three hours only, he took a room (no bath) in a grotty hotel in the center of the city. He was intrigued with the place and said he hadn't spent a night like that since he had been in jail in Alabama.

Nairobi is a modern city with half a million people and more cars than any other city of its size in the world, and probably the largest assortment of makes of cars as well as the largest assortment of makes of people. As I mentioned before, in Kenya there are eleven million people, less than 1 per cent of whom are white. All whites are classified as Europeans—Americans are called Europeans, too. The largest European community in Nairobi is British, then Italian, then American (three thousand, mostly missionaries),

Scandanavians, Greeks, Germans, French and every other nationality you can think of live here too. There are six times as many
Asians as Europeans. Most of them came over from India in the
1890s to work as "coolies" on the railroad, settled afterwards,
and have been here ever since. Among the Asians there are Pak-
istanis, Hindus, Muslims, Sikhs and Goans, who are Roman Catholics. Arabs have lived along the coast for thousands of years, and
a few have gone inland to Nairobi. Every community has its own
customs which are maintained. We skål with the Swedes and down
Vodka and smash glasses wth the Poles. In Greek households
we drink ouzo, with the Hindu men we drink grape juice (the
women are not allowed to be present), and with the British and
Africans we drink scotch or gin or beer.

Nairobi is also known as an Embassy City and as well as the
United States, Russia and Red China are represented, too.

The city has a lot of character but very little flavor. By that I
mean that in Paris everything is very French—French food and
fashion and everyone speaks French; and Tokyo is very Japanese.
Most cities in the world have their own people, food, language
and culture. But Nairobi has nothing that is obviously its own,
yet it has everything.

There are authentic French, Italian and Chinese restaurants,
Asian ones which feature samosas and curries that always make
my ears hurt, and of course a Wimpy's hamburger joint for Americans. People often wonder why there is no place you can buy game
meat—elephant trunk steaks and zebra and antelope—but the reason is that it is illegal in Kenya. In Uganda there is a national dish,
matoke, which is bananas ruined. Bananas are delicious raw or
fried or baked, but by boiling them the Ugandans have certainly
discovered the secret of Banana Disaster. As I mentioned before,
posho is what the majority of Africans eat and barbecued goat is a
favorite for parties, but fortunately there is no restaurant in
Nairobi that serves this. The Africans in the main parts of the city
eat the same foods as we do—sometimes in the French restaurants,
sometimes in the Italian ones, and sometimes in Wimpy's.

Nairobi is a sophisticated, international city and has more than its share of elegance—elegance through people though, not through culture. It has, in fact, been called a cultural desert, but then so have many cities in the States. Nevertheless, there are a few art galleries, an excellent natural history museum and a Conservatoire of Music. There is a superb theater with a good repertory company with actors from London, and another large theater where visiting musicians from Yehudi Menuhin to Satchmo have appeared. Many people often attend these functions, as well as private dinner parties, in evening dresses and black ties.

There are about five movie theaters and two drive-ins. There is a Film Society that screens such movies as the Russian *Hamlet* and the Japanese *Macbeth*. The latter was just too Japanese for me—the castle was pagoda-like with curly roofs everywhere and an almond-eyed Lady Macbeth shuffled around in sandals and that cushion-thing on her back, and all the men rushed about like Samurai warriors. (That was the night McDonnell found a turtle in his Coke bottle.) The next film at the Film Society was *Ivan the Terrible*, which should have been called "Ivan the Terrible Movie," so we stopped going to the society and now have only the regular movies to complain about.

We see modern art films—like every one of Doris Day's and Rock Hudson's and Lana Turner in the *Three Musketeers*. Some theaters specialize in Asian films—which do not allow filthy things like kissing. Fortunately, they are shown without sub-titles, so we are spared being asked by our Asian friends. It is partly because of the puritanical Asian women on the censor board that we have films such as the ones I just mentioned. On television "Bonanza" was banned for being too violent. Occasionally we do get a good film and frequently a fair one, and we are always there—even for the deplorable ones.

I have very bad taste in movies, among other things. In Baltimore, a good friend, Hal Gardner, the drama critic for the Baltimore *Sun,* always telephoned me and said, "Betty, there is a terrible new movie in town—it is just awful—don't miss it, you'll love it." And he was usually right. I do love bad movies. I love the escape, just to hunch up in my seat and eat Hershey bars with almonds, or

Goldenberg's Peanut Chews—oh wow, what I'd do right now for a
Goldenberg's Peanut Chew. Anyway, I love movies with beginnings and endings and even middles, and all those old-fashioned
things. I love B-rate films with corny dialogue and Elizabeth Taylor
screaming or collapsing. I want to laugh or cry in the movies. It
is much easier to make people cry than laugh—I hardly ever laugh
in the movies. I just don't think walking through screen doors is
funny, and throwing a pie in someone's face irritates the hell out
of me and as for those British slapstick things like *Those Magnificent Men in Their Flying Machines*—when I die and go to hell
the only movie they show there will be that one. But sometimes
Jock and I sit in the movies and we laugh but no one else in the
whole theater does.

I tell you when I did laugh. Twentieth Century Fox sent us a
nicely printed booklet of all the 16-mm films available here to
be shown at home. One movie on the list was *The Horse in the
Grey Flannel Shit,*" which I would much rather see than *The Horse
in the Grey Flannel Suit.*

Just going to the movies in Nairobi is an outrageous experience.
First you buy your seat at the box office, choosing either the "circle" or the "stalls"—one is upstairs and the other is downstairs,
and I still can't remember which is which (I've just asked Jock,
and he tells me for the 457th time that the circle is *upstairs*). The
circle seats are more expensive than the stalls downstairs. You
choose which of the three priced tickets you want and pick your
very seat—just like the theaters on Broadway, only movie tickets
here range from sixty cents to a dollar.

The first thing that comes onto the screen is a picture of the
Kenya flag waving in the breeze, and as the Kenya National An-
them is played everyone stands up. Before Independence in 1963,
the British flag waved in the breeze, "God Save the Queen" was
played and everyone stood up. Then the commercials start. Because few people have television, advertisers find this a good way
of reaching the public, and so you sit there and watch two- or
three-minute commercials, one after the other, of cars, dry cleaners, shoes, booze, paint, airlines, cigarettes—anything. The toilet

paper commercials always bring applause. Every movie theater has a bar, so you can stop there before the commercials, or
during the intermission and again after the film, and I suppose
during the film, too, if you can't wait any longer. You can smoke
throughout the performance anywhere in the theater and ash trays
are provided on the backs of the seats in front of you. After the
news and coming attractions, which they call trailers, there is an
intermission, which they call an interval, and everyone races for
refills of booze or popcorn, but if you are too lazy to move, men
carrying boxes slung by a strap from their necks walk up and
down the aisle selling ice cream and things—just like burlesque
houses, except you are not promised a free watch in each and
every package. People pass the intermission time by reading newspapers or magazines which they have brought with them just for
this purpose—I don't remember ever seeing people in the States
reading in the movies. Anyway, the bell rings for more commercials, and after you have been in the theater for about fifty minutes,
the main feature starts. If you are unlucky, a turbaned Sikh may
sit in front of you, and since you can't ask him to take his hat off,
you just have to move. I have never minded because I love those
turbans—especially the bright pink ones. Sikhs are often very good
looking—very virile and strong and masculine despite their feminine turbans and little hairnets over their beards.

In addition to the movies, we enjoy the discussion groups held
in Nairobi every other Thursday night at the house of our Muslim
friend, Abdul Gafir Sheik, known to all as "Gaby." Anyone who
wishes to speak just says so, and everyone traipses off to Gaby's
to argue. The speaker has about forty-five minutes to present his
subject before it is thrown open to the listeners for discussion.
The topics range from Pollution to Apartheid to Intelligence in the
Universe. Once a man spoke on "My Faith and Its Importance"
and at the end of his talk someone in the audience stood up and
said he would like to give a speech, too, on "My Lack of Faith
and Its Unimportance." (I can't remember much of what either
of them said because I was so distracted by the fact that one of
them looked just like Dopey in *Snow White,* who had grown up

and old—a big, seventy-seven year old Dopey—and the other one looked as if he hadn't been born at all, but had been blown out of a bubble pipe.) I do remember laughing a few times. One of them said, "Always succumb to temptation lest it should cease to assail thee," and the other one said his conscience never stopped him from doing anything—only from enjoying it, and claimed he needed not moral but immoral support. A friend of ours claims the discussions are nothing but mental masturbation, but as I tell him, that's better than no sex at all.

Anyone can come to Gaby's group, it is open and free and coffee is served. A potpourri of forty to fifty people spill onto the floors after the chairs are filled, and every time I marvel at this mixed group and wonder if you could ever get such a wide selection so spontaneously anywhere else in the world. Frequently I am appalled or furious or dismayed at views expressed. Being a filthy capitalist, the Communist view put forward by a Russian may upset me, or an African will say that birth control is the white man's plot to limit the Africans, or an American black will say the entire Vietnam war is a Russian-American plot to get rid of the black American. But I *like* being furious and appalled—it is certainly better than being bored.

Outside of dinner parties, here endeth our wildlife in Nairobi. We don't go to cocktail parties because we find it more fun to stay home by ourselves, and we don't play golf or tennis or bridge or ride horses. Nor are we joiners, but all of that is available in Nairobi—the Rotary, Masons, Lions clubs, country clubs, stamp clubs, nightclubs and so forth.

Although people are inclined to stay in their own groups out of preference, especially the Asians, anyone can belong to anything regardless of race or color. There is no segregation in Kenya other than a self-imposed intellectual segregation. We have horizontal as well as vertical integration. Many of our friends have married people of other races. Quite a few Asians we know are married to Europeans; and an African, who was Vice-President of the country, is married to an English girl. Another African, who is a friend and business colleague, was Kenya's United Nations representative in New York and is married to a Swiss girl and their children are particularly gorgeous. If you are considering marrying someone of a different color, Kenya is the place to live. No one even notices. In fact, we have had mixed couples for dinner with American visitors and have forgotten to tell the visitors beforehand that our friend Jim, whom they have heard so much about, is black and that his wife is white.

I am color blind, and coming from Baltimore and never even having had dinner with a black until I was thirty, I never thought I would be. If someone asks me now if I think the blacks are right or wrong, the question is as meaningless as asking me if I think blue is right or wrong. Only the issues matter. This works both ways. I am in no way against a black person, but neither am I for him. A color-blind person will throw a rude loudmouth out of his office be he black or white. Recently in the States, I told an American black I thought he was being stupid about something or other, and he said I said he was stupid because he was black. But I had said he was stupid because he was stupid. Africans are not as sensitive as American blacks, and why should they be—they have what they want—they govern, they *are* boss. Black power is totally different from blacks in power. The African and the black American are a long way apart. I don't understand why the American blacks want to learn Swahili when no American blacks came from East Africa anyway—they all came from West Africa where Swahili is not spoken. Swahili is not anybody's mother tongue, but a lingua franca learned by all Africans in East Africa and spoken in order to communicate with the other tribes.

People often ask, "What is the African like?" This is as impossible a question to answer as "What is the European like?" Whom would I describe, the peasant or the king, the Yugoslav or the Frenchman? At least they would both be Caucasian, but among the Africans in Kenya, in addition to social differences, there are four distinct ethnic groups that are further divided into forty-two tribes. There are 220 tribes in all of East Africa. The different ethnic groups are as different from one another, in terms of language, custom and mode of life, as an Irishman is from an Eskimo.

The only thing they have in common is the color of their skin and the fact that they live in Africa. This surprises most visitors because they have assumed the Africans, at least the Kenyan Africans, are homogenous. If you looked all over the world, you couldn't find more dissimilar people. During a constitutional conference preceding Independence, the British Colonial Secretary, becoming impatient with the slow progress of the Africans in reaching agreement said, "Why can't you black men get together?" One of the African delegates replied, "As we see it, Mr. Khrushchev and Mr. Kennedy are both white."

Most of the troubles which beset Africa stem from tribalism. The never-ending political coups, the Congo, Biafra, the Sudan—all of it is directly attributable to tribalism. The European powers at the end of the last century are largely to blame. When the great carve-up was on, Britain, France, Belgium, Germany and Italy all tried to grab what they could.

Expeditionary forces, led by unlikely generals, would demarcate territory by marching in straight lines, paying no regard to peoples. New countries were defined at the expense of tribes being split in two and hostile groups being lumped together. For half a century the colonial powers kept the peace, but with their departure the tribes tried to reunite across what by now were accepted national boundaries and those who had hated each other all along found themselves sitting in the same legislatures—and not liking it.

The ingredients of instability were carelessly mixed many years ago. Only time will tell if the leaders of present African countries can create unity or can overcome the tribalism in their own hearts.

African girls and boys are as difficult to tell apart as American youth are, not because of the long hair but because the African youngsters of both sexes have crew cuts. McDonnell, whose long hair reaches just below his ears, was standing in our kitchen once when an African woman outside, who could only see him from the neck up said, "Jambo, *mem-sahib*" (Hello, ma'am).

Unlike America, where anyone wears anything, clothes here give big hints as to sex. I have seldom seen an African woman in slacks. Although they may have crew cuts or shaved heads, they always seem to wear dresses, or *kangas*—brightly colored prints like tablecloths wrapped around themselves. But sometimes the men wear dresses, too—*kikois,* a length of cloth wrapped around and worn at midi length.

Speaking of clothes, a friend of ours went away for a weekend and his house was broken into and all his clothes, sheets, blankets, dishes, and pots and pans were stolen. Africans won't usually steal jewelry or silver or other valuables because they have no use for them and in trying to get rid of them would be easily spotted, so they take the useful things. Our friend waited until local market day, then went to the African market place about fifteen miles from home and sure enough, spread all over the ground with all the other things for sale, were his household belongings and his clothes. He had to buy them all back.

Somehow that amused me. Possibly because the African's stealing is understandable to me—not right, but so understandable that it seems almost justifiable since many are so very poor and the money is really needed. However, when it comes to being taken by Europeans in one's own income bracket, it is another matter and not so funny.

We were just about to make our first film for our lecture tours, and since I had not filmed anything since the TV documentary on leprosy six years earlier, I felt more comfortable hiring a professional than having all the responsibility myself. So we hired a temperamental French Canadian who told us he was the best cameraman in all of Africa. We paid him a fortune, plus his expenses at the lodges from which we worked. After a tedious week the filming was done, and we took the hour's worth of film to the States with us and gave it to a film lab in Washington to process. Then we invited a few people to come to a little studio room to view the animal and tribal footage at its first screening. Everyone was eager. Even the owner of the lab was there because he was so interested in our African film. When all was ready, the lights went out, and for the next hour we sat in the dark and watched a black screen. Occasionally we could distinguish a vague object on the screen, which might have been a buffalo or an elephant—but whatever they were, they were dark green. We threw all the film away. Shirley Brown could have filmed it as well. Our Canadian had obviously had no previous experience, but he was anxious to get a free safari and some money for himself. We wrote to him, but of course he had left the country and has never returned.

Since we were broke and could not afford another "professional" cameraman, we decided I had to film it myself. One problem was that we did not have a camera, nor could we afford one. Very kindly, Betty Levy, a close friend from Baltimore who was at that time in Nairobi, loaned me hers. She cautioned us to renew the insurance because her policy had just run out that day, and we said of course we would and, naturally, forgot. The next day we set out and drove about seventy-five miles into the bush to a river where we wanted to film. We parked the car, locked it because the camera was in it, and walked down to the river to check to see if we had found the right spot. Returning to the car for our equipment, we found the camera had been stolen. The window had been broken and everything was gone from the car. Now, not only had we no camera with which to film, but we had to dig deeply to find some money to replace my friend's camera. Already it had cost us two thousand dollars, and we didn't have one foot of film. Our sad story, the "Perils of Pauline," got around town and, fortunately, to the ear of Sir Michael Blundell, an old friend, who very kindly saved us by giving us a lot of his excellent film which he had collected over the years.

Like any city, Nairobi has its share of swindlers and con artists.

When Ray Bates was staying with us, he came in one evening with a story about a little African orphan who had approached him on the street. He told Ray that although his parents had died, he had been lucky because a kindly English couple, a Mr. and Mrs. Hale, had agreed to pay the cost of his schooling. Now he had just received the news that the Hales had been killed in a car crash in England. Ray, who is generosity on two legs and who was returning to the States the next day, gave the child his last $10 and his address in Washington, D.C. "Watch it," Jock cautioned.

Ray did watch it. When the child wrote for next term's school fees, Ray promised to send the money upon receipt of a letter from the Headmaster. The reply came, officially rubber-stamped, "St. Xaviers Boys School." The Headmaster's letter said that indeed Mwangi Njuguna was a bright and promising lad and it was not only true but tragic that his sponsors, Mr. and Mrs. H. J. Hale of Kent, England, had been killed. However, if Ray would take their place he, the Headmaster, would personally send a school report three times a year so that he could follow Mwangi's progress.

Ray sent us copies of the correspondence, but kindly refrained from commenting upon Jock's cynicism. I wasn't so kind. I attacked him at once and gave him a lecture on the fundamental goodness of people. Jock shrugged and said, "OK, maybe I'm wrong, but why not call St. Xaviers?" I strode to the telephone and turned to the Nairobi Schools in the book. How much evidence did he need? I looked under the schools run by the Government. I searched through the list of City Council schools, I checked the private schools. I was calming down a bit now, and rang the Ministry of Education. They told me there was no St. Xaviers in Nairobi. Jock reached for the postal address book.

In East Africa each person or company has a P. O. Box number. You can look up the name and find the box number, or you can look up the numbers, which are listed in numerical order for just this purpose, and find out who owns the box. There was no listing under Xavier or St. Xavier in this book either, so he checked the number. The box belonged to one Samuel Ndungu who, for the investment of a $1.00 rubber stamp and the control of a fleet of "orphans" through the city, was doing a roaring business making up fictitious report cards and sending them quarterly all over the world to altruistic tourists. We turned the matter over to the Criminal Investigation Department (so that Jock and I could take over Mr. Ndungu's business, which obviously has real potential).

The con game is not only carried on at street-level. Our Swedish Baron friend told us a story against himself one evening:

Being a businessman, he had long realized the possibility of a profitable business founded on the sale of crocodile and snake skins. One day a retired hunter who had shot many crocodiles approached him with a proposal—the Baron was to put up the money and arrange the marketing, and the hunter's job was to produce the skins.

The first thing they did was to form a company and the Baron paid out six thousand dollars to equip the hunter with basic requirements, of which a large truck was the major item. Soon all was ready and our friend went to say good-by and good luck to the hunter embarking on the first of what he hoped would be many successful expeditions. The brand new truck with "Reptiles, Inc." painted on the sides was glistening in the morning sunlight. Guns, ropes, hooks and supplies were neatly stacked inside. The two shook hands, slapped each other on the back, and the hunter drove off with a confident wave, and to this day our friend has never seen him or the truck again. Years later he learned that the man had driven straight to the Congo, where he had sold the new truck and started another business of his own.

In day-to-day life one must keep awake, too: There is a charming Asian in Malindi who fixes refrigerators. If you take your refrigerator to him to have the handle or some other small thing fixed, he burns holes into the electrical parts or breaks it in some other inconspicuous way and then tells you he has discovered your refrigerator is useless and he will be glad to give you a good trade-in on a new one.

If you are a visitor, beware of con artists: Gambit 1 is the orphan ploy. Gambit 2: Supposing you are on a safari, the driver of your safari vehicle, excellent at his job, cheerful and helpful, could take on a mournful expression a couple of days before the end of the safari. In response to your tender enquiries he finally comes clean. You see, his wife died, leaving him the seven children. His half-sister, who married a drunken no-good bum who has been given ten years in jail for spearing his uncle, has been left to support five children by herself. Since your noble driver is the only surviving male member of the family, he must endeavor to clothe, feed and educate twelve *watoto* (children). Weeping, you dip far more deeply into your pocket than you had intended.

You had wanted to tip him of course, but you had no idea of the weight of responsibility he bore so bravely . . .

Jock knew one bachelor driver with not a care in the world who pulled this one with absolute regularity on each safari. The sad part is that there *are* needy people in dire straits with twelve kids, but how can you, on a three-week trip, tell them from the bad guys? Tip your driver if you think he has earned it, at a rate you find reasonable.

I had an interesting encounter with the Russians here. It was during my interior-decorating period, and I spent many days with the Russian Trade Commissioner and his wife, whom I would describe as pleasant peasants who looked more as if they needed a new plow than a new house. Since they didn't speak a word of English, nor I of Russian, they provided an interpreter. I took samples of curtains, rugs, furniture and lamps, and we discussed things for hours. Sometimes, Mr. and Mrs. Mokshanov would start arguing about the colors or patterns and the interpreter would pause and explain to me, "Mr. and Mrs. Mokshanov are at war," and then he and I would sit in silence and wait for one of them to win. I worked very hard. After four days of giving them all my plans, they thanked me, said they wouldn't need me any more and then used every one of my ideas, doing it all themselves. Perhaps they did this to save themselves money, or perhaps they found out I planned a direct replica of Mt. Vernon decorated with hidden microphones . . .

Speaking of spies and bugging, a Russian who was in Philadelphia on a diplomatic mission was entertained by Colleen Harrity, a very special friend of mine there. She said he knew more about Philadelphia than she did—even that Chubby Checker originated the twist there, as well as all the historical and industrial facts. After their pleasant evening had progressed to friendly banter, she said to the Russian, "If you're so smart, what do you think this is?" and pointed to the elephant-hair bracelet on her arm which she had bought while visiting East Africa. He examined the strands, which looked more like plastic wire than hair from the elephant's tail, and he studied the knots where the hairs were tied together to form the bracelet and pronounced, "It is a micro-phone." (Actually, the only people supposed to wear elephant-hair bracelets are those who have shot an elephant or slept with a hunter. Colleen did neither of those—maybe she slept with an elephant.)

I won't even tell you my experience with the Egyptians, because this is supposed to be a lighthearted book, but I'll give you a hint of how terrible it was by telling you that I did all the work for their trade exhibit, which took me weeks, and they never paid me my fee, nor did they pay me back for the hundreds of dollars of things —chairs, display cases—they asked me to order for them and pay for myself. Then they stood on diplomatic immunity so no lawyer could touch them. But I suppose the Egyptians added color to my life if not charm.

However, most of my decorating stories had happy endings.

Once, the *Time* magazine bureau chief, a bachelor, asked me to decorate his apartment. We went to look at a few things together, but found it was impossible because we both have that terrible affliction—giggling. For no reason at all, except that you are in church and not supposed to giggle or at an earnest meeting and someone sneezes peculiarly, you giggle, and if someone else near you is a giggler, it becomes synergistic and soon you are both un-controllable. The minute he and I went into a store together, if someone said something really funny like, "May I help you?" we would be unable to stop giggling. So finally we had to go into shops separately,—one of us looking at the chair, and the other waiting outside—which is a ridiculous performance for adults. He had to go to Rhodesia for a month and asked me if I would have his apartment finished for him when he got back. I did, and it looked stunning except that it needed a large painting on one wall. I did not want to spend more money without his approval, nor would I want to pick a painting for anyone, so I decided I would make him one myself. Even though I am retarded and unable to paint, draw, sew, or do anything artsy-crafty with my hands, I decided I must make him a giggle. So I covered a large softboard with gray flannel and painted a round orange giggle (giggles are always orange) right in the center. Being sloppy, I spilled some paint, so I covered the various messy splashes with strips of black tar tape, then glued the finished work on the wall. He was delighted with both his apartment and the giggle. One evening several months later Robert and Ethel Kennedy stopped in his apartment and Ethel admired my giggle as serious modern art.

Many of the non-Africans whom one meets in Kenya aren't here just because they were born here, as is the case in so many places in the world. They are here for another reason. They have had enough curiosity or drive or restlessness or trouble or courage or all these things to leave their nests—so what we end up with are individuals. This is not to say you *like* everyone—you may despise quite a few, but you are seldom bored. This is also not to say there are no plain vanilla people here, no forty-watt bulbs, but there don't seem to be as *many*. Or perhaps it just takes longer to recognize a French forty-watt bulb. Or maybe the wrappers on people—for example, the Asian's saris, the black make-up round the eyes, the red dots in the center of the forehead, and other strange Hindu customs—are so exotic that it takes a long time to realize you are still getting plain vanilla underneath. Also, many of the dreary colonial types left screaming, "It is impossible to live here now"—meaning they do not like being ruled by blacks—"so we are going to Australia," and we always think, "Thank God." Because of this I have a strong desire never to go to Australia—it must be filled with kangaroos and everybody else I hate.

But back to interesting people, and I don't mean the obviously interesting personalities—the paleontologists who find man's early origins, those who live with and study the game, the builders of the country—I mean just everyday people who lead sort of kinky lives. We have friends who live in tents with Persian carpets and beautiful antiques, and others who live in an enormous wigwam made from coconut fiber and still another who lives in a box (a waterproof packing crate)—just because they want to.

The first time we went to the house of someone we had just met for drinks, we walked in and the place looked deplorable—

newspapers were thrown everywhere, ash trays were overflowing, even turned over, and empty glasses and beer bottles were strewn around the entire room. He apologized, "I'm sorry about the mess, but"—I was sure he was going to say he had had a party the night before and had not yet cleaned up—"this is how I live."

One night we were at the house of a friend who has eleven dogs and twenty-three cats, and while we were sitting around the living room having drinks, a donkey walked into the room and wandered around. The only thing I could think of to say was, "Get your ass out of the living room," but since my host sort of petted it as he would a dog and didn't say anything about its being there, neither did I.

Another friend, who has an airplane that looks as if he made it from a model kit, lives at the hazardous take-off altitude of ten thousand feet. To get his plane going you have to *push* it. Can you imagine the confidence pushing a plane instills in you before your flight? Whenever he arrives at Nairobi's airport, no one ever says, "Hello," they always look astonished and ask, "You still alive?"

Needless to say, I never accepted his invitation to go for a ride. However, when I haven't had a choice I have flown in some planes I would rather not have been in. Aboard one thirty-year-old plane —a DC 3½ or something—the pilot asked us to stand in the front for take-off because the cargo load was too heavy in the back. And in another, it was so crowded with passengers that they were standing in the aisle, just like a streetcar, and even I know that is contrary to all regulations.

One thing I have been fortunate enough to avoid is the "Bamboo Bomber" which is a 1933 Dragon Rapide—it has double wings like the Wright Brothers' plane and flies around Lake Victoria every day. A few years ago Jock's brother-in-law used to fly it, and I asked why he never brought it to Nairobi; he said, "Oh, it won't fly that high. Its ceiling is lower than Nairobi."

In a small plane on a flight to Lamu, we actually had a pilot with pimples. Can you imagine—pimples? He could not have been more than seventeen years old, we were his first commercial passengers and he looked as frightened as I felt. Pimples; it's just totally unacceptable.

Because of all the different nationalities living here an American visitor, intrigued with the subject, asked an Englishman, who had been born in Kenya but who, like Jock, had given up his British citizenship and taken out a Kenya passport, "You have lived with so many nationalities, you must really *know* them. Do you like the Germans?"

"Hate them," he answered.

"Do you like the Africans?"

"Oh, heavens no."

"How about the Scandinavians? Do you like them?" she asked.

"I despise them."

"The Americans then—do you like the Americans?"

"Not at all," he answered her.

"Do you like the Asians?"

"Worst of all," he said with disgust.

"The British then, you like the British?" she asked hopefully.

"I can't *stand* the British."

"Well, who do you like then?"

"I like my friends."

Time has made friends of my acquaintances. After fourteen years here, I find I can communicate better with Italian, British, Swedish and French friends, who say things like "dis-sip'-lin" and "ter-ree'-ble" and "tru-pli-cate" (for triplicate), than I do with many of my American contemporaries.

I have learned through living here that in this world there are just people and what they do—their actions and attitudes. Nationality or background or color seem to have little to do with whom you really like. You just have to be hooked up on the same circuit with a person somehow, and usually I find it happens through humor—laughing at the same things.

Nairobi is a place with so many races and nationalities and religions that it is a world, not a city—and the fact that all these different peoples get along so well gives hope to the rest of mankind.

VII
Three Little Pygmies

The twentieth century has suddenly been thrust upon an unsuspecting Africa. But there is a price to pay for progress. Jock knows the first African in Kenya ever to get an ulcer. Jock's friend, a member of Parliament, wasn't feeling well, so Jock took him to the doctor who diagnosed it as the first ulcer he knew of in an African. I am sure there are many now. The African must trade some of his laughter and joy for tension and ulcers, which seem to be synonymous with progress. It is a big price to pay.

Once a man came to work for us and said he was saving his salary to buy a bicycle. The day he bought the bicycle a few months later, he came to us and said he was quitting. We asked why and he said, "I *have* my bicycle now." Might it not be good if we in the Western civilized world sometimes quit when we got our bicycle? "Western civilized world." When someone asked Ghandi what he thought of Western civilization he answered, "I think it would be a good idea." I wonder.

While many of the Africans have plunged into the twentieth century, own fancy cars, hold down big jobs, and get television sets and ulcers, visitors are not really interested in these carbon copies of themselves. It is the primitive or backward tribes that are fascinating to the outsider. Africans tend to despise or be embarrassed by their half-naked and more backward brethren, but for the world-weary visitor, primitive societies provide an intriguing glimpse into his own history. When the visitor laughs in the presence of primitive people, it is the laughter of pleasure and rediscovery, not derision.

Some of the tribes in East Africa wandered in from the north centuries ago and others have been here since man himself evolved. Paleontologists keep finding earlier and earlier evidence of the beginnings of the human species in Kenya and Tanzania and Uganda.

Primitive tribes are at their most comic when confronted with modern contrivances. Jock once flew with a game warden in a tiny airplane to a remote region where they touched down on a dry lake bed, becoming the first aircraft to land for miles around. The tribesmen gathered—they had seen planes overhead and were not too frightened—and immediately started to peer with interest underneath the fuselage. Jock couldn't imagine why they were so curious about the belly of the aircraft, until one of them asked him whether it was a bull or a cow plane. Since it moved and flew it must be alive, and if alive it should have genitals or an udder—a perfectly intelligent supposition to people whose very lives depend upon their cattle.

This nature-orientated logic pops up all the time. Years ago, Jock and a friend drove a truck and a jeep across country for several days, eventually arriving at a Turkana village. The villagers had heard about vehicles, but had never seen one. Suddenly there were two in their midst, each with four legs and a mouth and two eyes in the front. Obviously, the little jeep was the child of the truck and would grow to be the same size one day.

Primitive people are usually as friendly as can be toward strangers. They have an unabashed curiosity and will feel your funny straight hair before bursting into peals of laughter. Blond hair seems particularly strange to them, and when I visited the convent on my first trip mine was the first fair hair they had seen, since the nums kept their heads covered at all times and there were no other white people in the area. When the Up With People

musical group from the States played for the Masai last year, the
tribesmen could not get over the fact that one of the American
black girls had a long black wig. She took it off and slipped it onto
the head of a Masai woman who had shaved her head in accord-
ance with tribal custom, and the transformation was thus doubly
spectacular, causing paroxysms of mirth throughout the village.

But it is usually you as the visitor who ends up feeling inferior.
You ask yourself if you would have been so open and friendly if
the tables were reversed and a dozen tribesmen had wandered
onto your carefully manicured suburban lawn and were curious
to examine the inside of your house?

And how confident would you feel if your vehicle, your plastic
water bottles and your canned food were suddenly removed and
you were left standing in the semi-desert, wearing a skin, holding
a spear and gazing at a couple of camels and a few scraggy goats?
I'll bet you would die of thirst before you found out how to milk
that Godamn camel.

No one can ever mention primitive people and leave out the
Pygmies whom we have seen on the edge of the Ituri forest, on
the border between Uganda and the Congo. You smell them long
before you see them—an odd, rather than unclean smell. Along
the road there are fake Pygmies—regular people, but short, bend-
ing over saying, "Me Pygmy, me Pygmy" and asking for money for
posing for photographs. A Pygmy can build his house in ten minutes, and when completed, it looks as if it had taken only five. It
also looks as if his mother made it—which she probably did. The
older women are adorable. Their breasts look like elongated
prunes and some of them have curly hair all over their chests—we
thought of sending a picture of one to *Playboy* for the "Pygmate
of the Month." To get to the Pygmies you stomp through a forest
of marijuana which both men and women Pygmies seem to smoke
all the time, through bamboo water pipes filled with charcoal and
the *bhang*—as cannabis is called here. During the question-and-
answer period at one of our lectures, a lady asked us if that was
why the Pygmies were so small, but as we told her, the Watusi,
who average seven feet in height, smoke *bhang,* too, or perhaps

I should say what's left of the Watusi. For years they held another tribe, the Hutu, in subjugation and near slavery, and in an uprising ten years ago the Hutu butchered thousands of Watusi. Then, in 1972 a further clash took place in which more than 200,000 of both tribes died, so the strange, decadent and unbelievably tall aristocrats have been greatly reduced in numbers. There is a Watusi King who is in exile here in Nairobi, and as you can imagine it is not a bit difficult to pick him out of the crowd.

The Ruwenzori Mountains, which divide Western Uganda from the Congo, are spectacular and romantic. They are sometimes called the Mountains of the Moon, and for centuries it was believed that the source of the Nile was hidden in their thickly forested and misty slopes. The mountains clearly define the western limit of East Africa and are almost as finite as an ocean in terms of what lies beyond. Thus the Pygmies, the Congo River, and the vast Ituri forest are another world, of which we in East Africa are seldom aware.

Their lives are far from being one long safari through the "grass" lands. They have a strict moral code and are a humorous and intelligent people, who are at one to such an extent with their leafy environment that they themselves have become part of the forest life, belonging there as much as the birds and animals. They are incredible and fearless hunters and will stalk an elephant so skillfully that they are able to get close enough, undetected, to plunge a spear into its stomach from below. On their arrows and spears they use a poison—which they brew themselves from bark and berries and roots—that will, literally, knock over an elephant. To test the strength of the poison, they use a technique, common to a number of tribes, of nicking themselves and allowing the blood to trickle down their arm. They then touch the poison to the stream of blood and watch the speed with which it changes the color of the blood and works its way upwards towards the wound. Just before it enters their own bloodstream they wipe it off.

Nobody really knows how many Pygmies are left. Since the Ituri forest lies in the Congo, reliable reports are hard to obtain. They tend to be despised by other tribes for being so small, but in reality they are more intelligent than many of those who look down upon them. Like the Masai, they prefer their own way of life and are reluctant to enter the twentieth century.

We all know by now that the Masai drink blood and milk, live in igloo-shaped houses grouped in *manyattas,* and adorn themselves with red ocre and cow dung. They are crazy about cow dung —not only do they build their houses with it but smear patterns on themselves with it, too. This doesn't make them smell too nice, and when they smile the flies march across their teeth, which turns most people right off. Another thing inclined to appall the fastidious is the children's early morning showers. They stand under a cow that is urinating and enjoy the warm trickle while it lasts.

Aldous Huxley once said, "The entire philosophy of life can be summed up in five words, 'You get used to it,'" and all too soon you have become used to the Masai with their bodies naked except for a cloak thrown over their shoulders, their long spears and their superior attitude—indeed, even the flies. For your interest to be held, you must see them doing something—spearing missionaries or something.

It is the same with animals, as I mentioned before—once you have seen twenty thousand elephant or zebra they cease to fascinate unless they are in action. For example, I have ignored every ostrich I've seen in the last five years, until the other day when I came across two mating—a sight which certainly renewed my interest in ostrich.

But back at the *manyatta* with the Masai. This is the kind of thing that happens. A friend of mine from the States was making some educational films for schools on different ethnic groups, and we had arranged for him to film a group of Masai in the Great Rift Valley. The Masai had agreed and were being paid handsomely. The American cameraman had filmed them in many situations, and they had co-operated beautifully. He then went inside one of the low huts to have a look around and crawled about in there for ten minutes checking the light and whatever else cameramen check. A dozen or so expressionless Masai stood around outside not saying a word. Then he came out and said, "O.K. this one's fine—

let's go in now and film." "No," they said. Amazed, we asked, "Why not?" and they answered, "There's a puff adder in *that* hut." Typical.

A similar experience happened to Jock's brother-in-law who took a short cut through a narrow gorge full of thick bush, while some Masai with him took a longer route. When they caught up, he asked why they had not followed, and they told him that a lone buffalo and a rhino lived in the gorge. The Masai assume that because they know what they are doing, other people should too, and they would not presume to interfere.

The Masai youth, in order to become Morani—young warriors distinguished by a red pigtail down the center of their foreheads—must prove their manhood by killing a lion with a spear. This is a rather final method of separating the men from the boys, and the government, in the interest of wildlife conservation, has tried to put an end to this practice. But in remote areas it still goes on. As warriors who are no longer allowed to fight other tribes or kill lions, the Masai Morani now get their thrills by rustling cattle.

This sport, for that is what it is to them, is enhanced by the fact that they stand the chance of being shot by anti-rustling patrols. This added danger makes the undertaking really fun. The rule of law and establishment of order may have its blessings, but it has removed an element of excitement from lives of young men. Elspeth Huxley has said that if the British have succeeded in doing nothing else in Africa, they have certainly succeeded in boring the Africans to death.

The Masai, however, are by no means an example of what the average African is like. The city African in the 1970s wears elegant Madison Avenue suits and ties, while his rural cousins wear shorts and shirts like Californians. This is fine for them, but no fun to photograph. On the other hand, the Masai are regularly photographed by tourists and the *National Geographic* because they are so picturesque and capture everyone's attention.

The first time I ever ran into the Masai was in 1960 when I visited Henny and Pat Hemingway who were living in Arusha, Tanzania, where there are many Masai. Right away I said, "These

Masai are marvelous! I'm crazy about them!" and Henny answered, "Oh, you and the British—they love them, too, but I hate them." I asked why, and she answered, "The British love them because they are so proud, so superior, so dignified." I said, "That's right. So why do you hate them?" And she replied, "Because they are so proud, so superior, so dignified."

So either you like the Masai or you don't, but it *is* difficult to ignore them.

The incident about the missionary being speared occurred in 1971, when a Dutch missionary asked a Masai if he could photograph him. The Masai said no, the missionary photographed him anyway, and the Masai threw his spear into the missionary's stomach. It didn't kill him, he lives—knowing now that when the Masai say they are God's chosen people, they really believe it. And you had better believe it too—at least in their presence.

I must admit that I am on the Masai's side. If I believed my soul would "go into the little black box" and some foreigner appeared in my back yard while I was hanging up the laundry and asked if he could take my picture, and I said no and he took it anyway, I would certainly *want* to spear him in the stomach. For the visitor there are always other Masai a little further down the road who will willingly be photographed for a few shillings.

A few years ago a Coca-Cola truck overturned way out in the bush, and all the bottles fell to the ground. Some say the driver was dead in the cab and others say he had gone for help, but in any case there was no driver. A Masai wandered onto the scene, saw his chance, and immediately set up a stand and sold all the unbroken bottles of Coke. That's what I mean about doing something.

But I'll confess, I'd like to have the Masai around forever—even if they weren't doing anything. They are among the last primitive peoples alive today, and the world will be a little less picturesque when they become like the rest of us.

How lucky we are to live in the 1970s—a time when the world still has primitive peoples and men are going to the moon. We are so fortunate to live at just this short time when both worlds overlap. In fifteen years I fear all the primitive people will have had the dubious advantage of becoming "civilized." But for these next fifteen years or so, the Masai won't let us down. They won't step on our long-ago dream of far-off Africa and its exotic people. They will continue to fit our romantic image of brave African warriors who spear lion and walk for hundreds of miles among wild animals, alone and unafraid.

VIII
A Leopard in the Cookie Factory

Betty Levy and I once combined to give a dinner party for about sixty-five or seventy people. Her job was to make the chicken à la king, which we decided was a good thing to have because it is a very American dish and most people had not had it before. My job was to do the salad and the dessert. A few days before our dinner party she had rehearsed making a small quantity of chicken à la king and said it was the best she had ever eaten. The morning of the party she arrived early, and with her cook and mine, she prepared the twenty chickens, put in the peppers, mushrooms, pimentos and all the other goodies. By seven o'clock all was ready.

At 7:45 P.M. I wandered into the kitchen and heard a funny noise. The chicken à la king was on the counter making a strange bubbling sound. It was the noisiest chicken à la king I had ever heard. I asked our cook, "Did you just boil this?" "No," he answered, but the concoction kept on gurgling away. Betty and I decided we had better get it into the refrigerator. However, chicken à la king for sixty-five people is a tremendous amount and our refrigerator is very small, so we hauled out all the shelves and everything in there and got the chicken à la king into it.

Ten minutes later we opened the door of the refrigerator to see what was happening and it was like some horror movie—the chicken à la king came pouring out of the refrigerator and all over the floor, still bubbling and making loud funny noises. It was as if chicken à la king were taking over the entire world.

Whenever I get nervous I giggle, so I started to giggle, and Betty burst into tears. In the meantime Jock smelled this terrible smell —did I mention the terrible smell?—and rushed into the kitchen to see what on earth was happening. He saw us up to our ankles in chicken à la king, one of us crying and the other laughing. "What is wrong?" he asked. Of course, we didn't know what was wrong, so he decided the only thing to do was to rush to the little local store before it closed and get something else for dinner. The guests were due to arrive in five minutes. "I'll just get some tinned spaghetti," said Jock, which made my friend cry even more. "We can't give these people canned spaghetti for our fancy dinner party!"

Suddenly I had an idea. "Let's *wash* the chicken à la king and start again!" So we put what was left in a collander and turned on the hot water full blast. All the chicken, mushrooms, peppers and pimentos were saved and the cook made a new sauce. We sprayed air mist all over the house to get rid of the odor and tried to look charming and nonchalant as the guests arrived.

The next horror was that we had run out of water because this was a Saturday night when the man who pumps the water gets drunk instead, as is his usual practice on a Saturday, and we had, in washing the chicken à la king, used up our reserve. Therefore, no one could flush the loos or have water with their drinks, which added another element of charm to the evening.

Dinner was served and needless to say Betty, Jock and I had salad and garlic bread for our meal. We wondered if everyone would be sick and accepted compliments on the chicken à la king with modesty.

About 2:00 A.M. when a few stragglers were still sitting around the living room, our cook appeared and said, "What's left of the chicken à la king is making that same noise again." We went into the kitchen and sure enough it was bubbling and rising and smelling just as it had done before. We buried it alive, and it wasn't until

three days later that we figured out the mystery. In East Africa
we have two kinds of flour, "home baking" and "self-rising," which
contains yeast. My friend had not realized there were two kinds
and merely grabbed a bag which by bad luck happened to be the
self-rising flour. The combination of the yeast and the wine in
the sauce made the chicken à la king ferment and the rising was
due to the yeast.

If you have a sense of humor, Africa can be a very funny place
to live, as long as you don't want to accomplish much of anything
but sitting around laughing all day—but if you have had bad eggs
for breakfast, you may be rendered apoplectic as you attempt to
achieve things as the day goes by. A friend learned to cope with
the petty officialdom, which thwarts almost any undertaking here,
such as paying local government taxes, trying to obtain a visa, or
taking delivery of a parcel from the Post Office, by collecting in-
efficiencies with masochistic glee with a view to publishing a funny
book.

Sometimes I feel as if I am living in one big insane asylum. I
guess my American standards and values have been inculated in
me so deeply that I feel a little peculiar about waking up and thinking, "Well, my zipper is broken in my blue dress so I'll take it to
the Post Office today to have it fixed; and when I buy my cigarettes
I must check the date on them, and then I'll go to the High Class
Fishmongers and get the lady butcher to give me some chicken."
My thoughts are interrupted by the telephone—it is a friend sug-
gesting we meet in the tree for tea, and I agree. That means the
"Thorn Tree," a popular outside cafe in the center of Nairobi,
which everyone calls simply "the tree." The man who does our
mending sits outside the Post Office with his sewing machine
and the "High Class Fishmongers" is the name of our butcher, who
is female. All locally made cigarettes are dated—numbers are embossed on the bottom of the pack so that 118, for example, means
the cigarettes were packaged the 118th day of the year or about
April 28—thus telling you how fresh they are.

One time a cigarette company in Nairobi was sued for using
"inferior tobacco," but the company won the case because they

said they had never claimed to have tobacco in their cigarettes in the first place, and if you do examine the package, you won't find the word "tobacco" anywhere. So I don't know what I smoke in my Kenya cigarettes, but I love them and carry cartons with me whenever I leave the country. They are very mild and pleasant and cost only twenty-seven cents (American) a pack.

So I leave home and I go to the Post Office with my dress, then I drive to town passing a baboon sitting on a post by the road just watching the traffic, and as he looks at me I suppress the instinct to wave. I pass seven giraffe, about twenty impala and one rhino, because the road from our house goes right past the Game Park. I draw up to give a ride to an African who is hitchhiking. As I stop he darts behind a bush and grabs his three live chickens which he holds fluttering in the car. I wish I hadn't stopped. Halfway into town I stop for gas, but the gas station attendant, who is wearing a bathing cap, says, "Sorry, no gas—we've run out," so I get a quart of oil, tip him (it is the custom here to tip gas station attendants) and drive on. I am behind a truck with a long load protruding from the back, and to comply with the law it must have a red flag, but since the driver doesn't have one, he has used red Bougainvillaea instead and it is waving in the breeze. It is prettier than a red flag.

I am coming into Nairobi now—there are only two traffic lights in Nairobi, but many traffic policemen stand on little metal stages in the center of the street and perform hand ballets of traffic signals. The Africans have the most graceful hands in the world. I am distracted by this, and also because my judgment is not as accurate driving on the left, in turning a corner I scrape the policeman's stand, which totters and causes him to fall off. I stop and wait to be lynched, but he laughs, steadies the stand, climbs back on and still laughing waves me on cheerfully. I imagine a New York cop in the same situation.

There are only two small fire stations in Nairobi, a city of almost half a million people. Many of the houses are made of wood and yet there never seem to be any fires. When the fire engines go out it is a big event—perhaps only once or twice a month. In New York there are constant fire engines and sirens. Why are there no fires here? I am reminded that the entire budget of a West African country is less than the New York City Fire Department's. Shaking my head, I drive on to another gas station.

While I am waiting for the car to be filled, I think of the story about a doctor years ago who had a brand new car which had the filler-cap neatly hidden under one of the taillights. He asked the attendant if he knew where the gas tank on this new model was, and the man answered proudly and efficiently, "Oh yes, it is under the taillight." The doctor turned to a case he was reading while his car was being filled, but feeling that it was taking rather a long time, he glanced up and saw that the pump had clocked fifty-six gallons. He leapt out of the car and found that the attendant had the hose under the rear light all right, but under the wrong light which he had levered up with a screwdriver, and the gas was flowing into the trunk so that all his tools and suitcases were floating around in it.

Another time I witnessed a wonderful act in Nairobi that filled me with admiration and made me want to imitate it should a similar opportunity come my way. Ahead of me, some crazy driver cut in front of another car, very nearly causing an accident. Both cars skidded to a halt right across the center of the road. The African driver of the car that had so blatantly disregarded the traffic rules, instead of being chastened or apologetic, immediately started shouting insults and curses at the innocent driver, also an African. The latter listened patiently for a minute, then without saying a word, he backed his car off a few feet to give himself a good run and *charged* the offending car, ramming it with a satisfying crunch.

Just as I am about to leave the gas station, I see a Land-Rover waiting to have a hole through its door fixed. A rhino had obviously charged it successfully. This reminds me to have the dent taken out of our fender, which was damaged when Jock hit a buck which ran out in the road—a common occurrence. So I said, "Could you please take that dent out . . . my husband hit a buck." They said they could, and we agreed I'd return at six-thirty to get the car.

I am afraid to ride the buses here—they are such hideosities. Many are privately owned and to get more business, they race each other to the next bus stop to see who can get the passengers first. They pass each other on curves and turn over and crash and kill people all the time. Once a man leaned out the window as another bus passed so closely in the opposite direction that it cut off his head. No one even noticed until the woman sitting next to him turned to say something, and he was just sitting there without a head.

So I decide to take a taxi. They don't cruise here, so I walk to the nearest taxi stand and discuss the fare with the cab driver. He has a blue net plastic bag on his head—one of those woven ones in which you buy four apples. Since many taxis have no meters, you must always decide on a fare first; we agree to four shillings. I get in and as soon as we start off he asks if I will give him two shillings now so he can get gas. Cab drivers don't have the capital to invest in gas *before* they get a fare, and since this is a standard procedure, we go back to the gas station for twenty-five cents' worth.

On our way to the tree now, we pass a sign that advertises "SABA JUU"—7 UP—literally translated. And now another sign—a neon— "COME RACING SUNDAY." Horse races are run on Sundays only. It is a big social event. The British women look as if they are going to a lawn party. They wear big floppy hats and fancy dresses and sit quietly in the boxes sipping tea and clapping politely if their horse wins, just like in *My Fair Lady*. I am the only one jumping up and down hollering and screaming and embarrassing everyone. There is no starting gate, just a string held across the front of the horses. In addition to the regular betting windows, there are bookies scattered all over the grounds in booths like lemonade stands hollering out better odds for a certain horse than the other bookies. You can bet with them or with the tote. Bookmaking is legal here, on and off the track. In town, the most crowded stores are the "Turf Accountants," or permanent establishments operated by bookies in shop fronts, and every day of the week you see crowds of Africans around them eagerly awaiting the English race results.

Jock's grandmother, who died at ninety-six, never missed a day with her racing forms and bookies. She won all the time but had never been to a race track in her entire life.

Almost to the tree now. We pass an African woman carrying shoes on her head. She will put them on when she has reached her destination, but meanwhile she is walking barefooted in comfort. Some other things they carry on their heads are cartons of milk, gin bottles filled with kerosene, buckets—in fact, anything. As a result they walk with beautiful grace. Moving day means the women carrying their bed and bureau on their heads to the bus stop which could be five or six miles away, waiting for the bus, which could run but once a day, putting the furniture on top of the bus, hauling it off when they have reached their destination, carrying it to their new house and then returning for the other beds and tables and oddments. (Yes, we've come a long way, baby.) No wonder the African woman likes polygamy. When the missionaries suggest she become a Christian, that is fine until they get to the monogamy part and then suddenly it is another matter altogether. "What, *me* do all the work alone?" Can we blame them?

I meet my friend in the tree. A man sitting at the next table has a safety pin in his earlobe. Africans pierce their ears when they are very young and slowly introduce larger and larger plugs until the ear lobes are distended into a loop so large it may even reach their shoulders. In these loops they carry beautiful ornaments like empty Kodak film boxes, empty spools of thread, and sometimes even messages—which Jack Paar christened "Ear Mail." Once we found an old Masai man in Tanzania with a can of peas in his ear (now you know what you can do with your empty tin cans). However, the educated city Africans do not like their loops (the younger ones don't have them done in the first place now)—they want to look like everyone else, so they hook the looped lobe up and around the top part of the ear. Once at a cocktail party in Nairobi, Jane Paton, an American friend of ours, said to an African she knew well and who had his ears wrapped up instead of hanging down, "Oh, come on, John, enjoy yourself—let your ears down," and so he did.

When Jock was about nine years old he went off with his good friend, Nyongo, from their farm to have tribal scars burned on his face, but a servant warned his mother and she stopped him. I wish she hadn't—he would be exquisite with tribal scars. (What is our plastic surgery in the shape of nose jobs, eye jobs and face-lifts but our version of tribal scars—the making of our faces to fit our image of beauty?)

I chat with my friend. I look around as some Americans get out of their Land-Rover with their hunter, returning from a shooting safari. (I remember how I finally met a very famous hunter about whom I had heard so many stories of bravery and skill: there stood a magnificently bronzed specimen with beard and eagle eyes, standing next to a nervous little man who looked like a tubercular chicken. It was the latter who was the legendary hunter and the first a client on his first safari.) The American man has on one of those Australian army hats with a leopard-skin band, his beard is long and he is fashionably seedy and covered with dirt as he thinks John Wayne or Charlton Heston would be. The hunter is hatless, well-shaven and clean. The hunter looks like the client and the client looks like the hunter, but now that I have lived here I can tell the difference.

The view from the tree is in technicolor because of all the brilliantly hued saris flowing by, which is not surprising since there are so many Asians in Kenya. I see African men walking by who are impeccably dressed in gray flannel suits and regimental striped ties. I see others in rags. Some Africans are Oxford or Cambridge graduates, brilliant leaders of today; others live as they did two thousand years ago—not knowing the principle of the wheel. They wear skins and are pagans. The majority are somewhere in between. I watch them and see one who walks by barefoot in a black-and-red checkered bathrobe tied with a corded belt and tassel, and wearing a bowler hat. I watch the British men in their pleated shorts with their pipes sticking out of their knee socks, just as in the funny papers. I see Italians and Germans and Greeks and Scandanavians and Swiss and French, and I think I must be watching the whole world passing by.

I hear the mechanical muezzin, a recording played over a loud-speaker from the mosque summoning the faithful, so I know it is time to pick up my car. My friend gives me a lift to the garage, I thank her, say good-by, and as I walk in the man smiles and says the car is ready, and how it certainly was a big dent for hitting a duck.

Even if I never left my own house in Karen, I'd still know I was living in a crazy place just by reading the morning paper—which is delivered every morning by the dairy and brought to me in bed on a tray along with my coffee about 7 A.M. Before my first gulp of coffee, I may read: "DAR ES SALAAM GOES GAY FOR THE POPE" or "LEOPARD FOUND IN COOKIE FACTORY," followed by a story of how the preceding night a leopard was found stalking through a Nairobi factory that makes cookies. Once there was a headline "OSTRICH COMMITS SUICIDE," with pictures of a male ostrich purposely distracting a lion from the baby ostriches by running right in front of it so the lion would kill him instead of his babies. Then there was a report on the daily passenger train from Nairobi to Mombasa being six hours late because it hit an elephant, and it took six hours to chop up the elephant and remove it from the line and then repair the tracks. Once I read an article on "WOMEN'S LOB" as it was misprinted.

In the Kenya papers even regrettable incidents can sometimes take on a note of unintended humor.

Five or six years ago, a young American missionary girl arrived in Nairobi, filled with evangelical fire and love for all mankind. An immigration or a customs officer at the airport promptly asked for a date and she agreed to visit the Game Park with him. When he picked her up in his car, he had with him a friend and a bottle of scotch. By dusk all three were still in the Park and the scotch was in them—including the non-drinking missionary—because, as she explained later in court, she did not wish to offend the local people by rejecting their hospitality. Finally, the customs man, whom I shall call Odongo, persuaded her to join him behind some

bushes, while the friend lapsed into a drunken stupor in the back of
the car.

At this point the girl realized that things were getting out of
hand and in the attempted rape case that she brought against him,
she testified that she called for help. The drunken friend, according to newspaper reports of the trial, ". . . hearing cries for help,
pulled himself together and went to help Odongo."

The two men were subsequently convicted, but many people,
including ourselves, felt that if silly girls make instant dates (and
you can't get much more instant than the first male you meet upon
arrival at an airport) and then consume alcohol in contradiction
of their beliefs and habits, then something's gotta give. In short,
she got what she asked for—but then to scream rape is a little unfair.

Telephoning in East Africa can also be outrageous.

One day I was trying to telephone home from a telephone booth
in Nairobi. The operator, an African man (telephone operators are
predominantly male in East Africa), told me to put in my one
shilling twenty-five cents (seventeen U. S. cents). I was distressed
because I had thought the call would be only seven cents, and I
didn't think I had any more money with me. "Oh dear, oh damn,"
I grumbled as I looked through my change, "I don't think I have
enough," and was absolutely astonished when a cheerful, "Oh
that's all right—just put in what you do have," came as the reply.

But we have our difficulties too. In one area the giraffe kept
running into the telephone wires, so the poles had to be taken
down and replaced with higher ones so the giraffe, which are eighteen feet tall, couldn't reach the wires. Elephant have been known
to knock down telephone poles by leaning against them to scratch
which might make it impossible to call anywhere for four days.
These things you accept as inevitable. But, when you try to call a
town just a hundred miles away and are told the call can't go
through because the operator has taken his wife to the dispensary
or is out to lunch, or that it is 4 P.M. and he has left for the day and
won't be back until 8 A.M. tomorrow—that can annoy you.

Telephone conversations can go like one Jock had when he called a police station 125 miles away and didn't know if the person who had answered was the operator, the duty constable or the inspector, so he asked,

"Who is this?"

"It's me."

"Who's me?" asked Jock patiently.

"How do I know? You're in Nairobi."

Once I was telephoning various chartered airlines looking for a cheap way to get my son Rick, who was then in Georgetown University, from Washington, D.C., to Kenya for his Easter holidays. Having no success with the first three or four chartered companies because the flight dates were wrong, I dialed the next one on the list and a voice said,

"Hello."

"I'd like some information on your chartered flights—could you tell me the dates your planes are flying and then give me the fares?"

"You want the chartered fares?"

"Yes, but first I want the dates. If they don't fit, I won't need the fares."

"Oh, so you want the chartered *fares?*"

"I WANT the DATES your chartered flights leave and THEN the chartered fares."

"I will try to connect you with chartered fares."

"WHO IS THIS?"

"This Chinese Embassy."

Obviously I had dialed the wrong number, and he thought I had been saying the "chargé d'affaires"—which says a lot for my French. When I told Jock he said he could just imagine the C.I.A. spending the rest of the week trying to decode the secret message between the American lady and the Chinese Embassy, which they must have picked up on their bugging devices.

Another time we planned to meet a friend in town for dinner, but we wanted to change the rendezvous, so I telephoned her, but she wasn't in. Since we were going to the theater first and would be unable to call back later, I decided the only thing to do was to leave the message with her servant.

"Would you tell Mrs. Rocco not to meet us at the New Stanley Grill but to meet us at Lavarini's instead?"

"Uh?"

"We were to meet Mrs. Rocco tonight for dinner at the New Stanley, but now we have to change it to Lavarini's restaurant."

"Oh."

"Do you think you could tell her when she comes in not to go to the New Stanley but to go to Lavarini's instead?"

"Where?"

"Lavarini's."

"Banareves?"

"No, Lavarini's," slowly and precisely.

"Where?"

"Do you have a pencil and paper there?"

"No, *mem-sahib*."

"Would you go and get them please?"

"Yes, just a minute," very cheerfully.

I wait four minutes. Then he says,

"Yes, *mem-sahib?*"

"Now, here we go . . . Lavarini's. L-A-"

"L-I."

"No, A."

"No I?"

"No, A as in Africa."

"A."

"Good! Now—V."

"B?"

"No, V as in Victoria."

"Oh, C."

"No, no, V as Vizuri."

"Ah, V."

"Yes, yes. Now A—Africa again—haha—R."

"What was that?"

"Rrrr"

"R?"

"Yes! Good. Now, next letter—I."

"A?"

"No, I—like India."

"N."

"No, I, like Ishasha."

"Oh, I," very pleased.

"Yes, now N."

"M."

"No, N—like Nairobi."

"Oh, N."

"Now, the last one."

I figured my friend could do without the s on the end, the apostrophe would be impossible, and I had already been on the phone ten minutes.

"I like Ishasha again."

"I."

"Good. Excellent! Now, that's it. Would you please read that back to me?"

And he answered, very apologetically, "Oh, *mem-sahib,* I can't read or write."

As you know, our dog's name is Shirley Brown. Our daughter, Dancy, named her after a school friend. Our Shirley Brown is occasionally very bright (I'd be willing to bet more so than the school friend), and our servants are terribly impressed with her giving them her paw, rolling over, sitting, and all the tricks Africans have never taught their dogs to do. One day Dancy, Jock and I took Shirley Brown into town with us as we sometimes do. While we were gone the telephone rang, and our servant answered. He did not know Dancy had a friend at school called Shirley Brown and a little female voice said, "Is Dancy there?" He said, "No, who is calling?" and she said, "Shirley Brown." "Shirley Blown?" as they always say. "Yes, I'll call later—good-by." He was truly upset when we got home because he didn't *really* think it had been Shirley Brown, and yet he did know that once we had an American staying at our house who actually *had* telephoned his dog in the States, so you never know.

Our Siamese cat's name is Irvink Katz. He's Jewish. When we first got him I telephoned the vet to get an appointment for his required health shots. The vet asked, "What's the kitten's name?" "Irvink Katz," I answered then added rather weakly by way of explanation, "He's Jewish." Puzzled, but quite serious, the vet asked, "How do you know he's Jewish?"

Larry Fellowes, a New York *Times* correspondent, told us that every time he went to Dar-es-Salaam, it was standard procedure for him to call the Chinese Embassy just to ask how many Chinese were in Tanzania, since all Americans are so interested both in statistics and the Chinese. Every one of the four conversations he had had were identical:

"Hello, Chinese Embassy."

"Hello. This is Larry Fellowes from the New York *Times*. I wonder if you could tell me how many Chinese are in Tanzania?"

"Just minute please."

A new voice:

"Hello."

"Hello. This is Larry Fellowes from the New York *Times*—I wonder if you could tell me how many Chinese there are in Tanzania?"

"Just minute please."

Another new voice:

"Hello."

"Hello. This is Larry Fellowes from the New York *Times*—I wonder if you could tell me how many Chinese are in Tanzania?"

"Just minute please."

And the fourth person, always the fourth, came on and said:

"You New York *Times*. You shut up. You go way," and slam went the phone.

Ngorongoro is an extinct volcano in Tanzania where an eruption thousands of years ago formed a crater twelve miles in diameter and 2,800 feet deep. Today this has become a tourist attraction, and visitors stay in lodges on the top, or rim, of the crater and go down into it during the day to look at the game that lives in the bottom—lion, rhino, buffalo, elephant and all kinds of plains game. More frightening than being next to a rhino in the crater is the trip down into it. The dirt road is narrow and twisted, with no guard-rail and room for only one car. We have always worried that if an elephant came around the corner and wanted to pass, which is not unlikely, it would merely push our car over the escarpment and down we would go those 2,800 feet. This has never happened, but we are always sure it will. Since the road is so narrow that two cars are unable to pass, it became necessary to have an "up time" and a "down time." This was a nuisance, for if you were in the bottom of the crater and wanted to go up for lunch, it might still be "down time," and you would have to wait an hour or more before you could go up.

However, progress is with us in East Africa, and not long ago another road was built so that now there is a down road and an up road. The first time we used the new road, there was a sign at the foot of it which read, "UP ROAD. NO DOWN TRAFFIC. ONE WAY ONLY. UP."; then there was a line drawn and printed underneath it was "BEWARE OF DOWN COMING TRAFFIC."

There used to be a store in Mombasa that displayed a sign "Whiskey and Roller Skates," and another that had painted on the side of the building, "Photographic Equipment and Plucked Chickens."

While I am not a golfer I have strolled around on a golf course in Uganda and seen the following sign, "Balls may be Removed from Hippo Footprints." Not much chance of such a hazard at the Greenbriar.

All by itself, standing in the middle of a limitless expanse of African plains through which we pass on our way to Mombasa, there is an official-looking sign offering "Free Parking." (The reason for it is that hidden by the tall grass there is a small motor-racing circuit, used about twice a year, but the passing visitor has no means of knowing this and must be very bewildered.)

Since Independence came to the East African countries there

has been a steady movement to "Africanize" or give jobs to citizens rather than expatriates, so we were not surprised to read in the small ads in a Uganda paper that "Black White-Hunters" were wanted by a shooting safari company.

English is always said to be one of the hardest languages to learn to speak, let alone to write, so mistakes by Africans can be forgiven. Even so, the use of a dictionary might have produced better results for a businessman in Marangu, Tanzania, who had carefully erected a multi-colored wooden sign by the road which read, "African Stile Curvings"—not to promote graciously bent turnstiles, but to advertise his African Style Carvings. But maybe he was right after all, because visitors who passed puzzled over it and stopped to find out.

At the coast there is a taxi called "The Happy Taxi Co." which runs a shuttle between Mombasa and Malindi, and for slightly less money the trip can be made with people, chickens, goats, coconuts and charcoal aboard the "Sweet Bus."

A red L for learners is a tag required in this country for apprentice drivers. The learners sometimes attach homemade signs with a backward L. Which makes one wonder if they will be able to read the traffic signs—especially difficult ones such as "Keep Leet," which is a mis-painted "Keep Left" sign near our house. To get over the difficulties of written signs, purely visual ones have been devised, such as silhouettes of children near a school, of a train at a railroad crossing, or a cow at a cattle crossing.

A bar near Nairobi is called "The Reliable Bar"—can it be relied upon to get one drunk? And in another bar there is a sign that advertises that patrons can have a drink with one foot in the Northern Hemisphere and the other foot in the Southern Hemisphere. This prompted Jack Paar to ask the owner how the exact location of the equator was determined—by regular survey or astronomical means? The reply was, "When one has a bar, one *knows* where the equator lies."

But it was in London that I found my favorite sign. A building had just been painted and propped up against it was the usual torn piece of cardboard upon which was written, "Wet Paint, Darling."

London is a good sign-hunting territory. There is an informal directness about them, typified by one that we saw the last time we were there at a post-Christmas sale in Harrods. Instead of a "Reduced" or "On Sale" sign on the dress rack, there was a simple message, "Grotty Leftovers."

Cheating a little, because telegrams are not really signs, there was a very funny exchange between a locust officer and his headquarters in Nairobi. The locust swarms, which can devastate crops overnight, are a major threat to many countries in Africa. To control them, it is necessary to locate their breeding grounds in remote desert areas of the Sudan and northern Kenya. Once located, the young insects can be sprayed from the air. But the difficulty lies in finding the breeding ground. A young locust officer, dispatched on his first mission, was excited to find his first large swarm breeding and radioed his headquarters, HAVE FOUND LOCUSTS COPULATING. The reply from headquarters read, STOP COPULATING KILL LOCUSTS.

Another telegram concerned the school fees—already extremely expensive—which were raised yet again when Jock was at Eton in England. The mimeographed circular sent to the parents explained the reasons for the increase in fees, but contained a typing error so that it read, "Regretfully, therefore, the fees must be raised from 'x to y' per *anum*." One parent, who had evidently remembered his Latin, cabled the school, UNDERSTAND REASONS FOR INCREASE BUT WOULD APPRECIATE BEING ALLOWED TO CONTINUE PAYING THROUGH THE NOSE AS USUAL.

IX
Hot Dogs in the Rolls

"As I was saying to the Queen, if there's one thing I can't stand it's name droppers."

This is the name dropping chapter. Nairobi is a fun place to live if you like movie stars, and I'm crazy about them. That's why I go to the hairdressers—to read movie magazines. I pretend to be too sophisticated to have this sort of magazine in my own house; but, secretly, I adore them and grasp every sneaky opportunity I can to read them. And to see a real live movie star . . . wow! Nairobi draws many of them, and it is not at all unusual to see them around the city. In the streets we have passed Clark Gable, Ava Gardner, Frank Sinatra, Bing Crosby, Robert Mitchum, John Wayne, Cyd Charisse, Tony Martin, Shirley MacLaine, David Janssen, Elsa Martinelli and many others. We have sat in restaurants only one table away from Capucine, Hayley Mills with her father John Mills, and Hugh O'Brien—the excitement of which made eating almost impossible for me. In Nairobi we have had dinner with Jimmy Stewart and his wife and daughter, Kelly. Jock has had tea with Caroll Baker, whom he said was very quiet and pleasant and not at all the siren of her movies. Jock also knows Sean Connery from the latter's pre-James Bond days when "007" was in Kenya playing a small part as the bad guy in one of the

Tarzan movies. Jock spent about two weeks off and on with him and found him very nice and has since hoped that fame has not changed him.

The location for this and many other movies was a place twenty miles from Nairobi called Thika. This is an industrial center that resembles Pittsburgh more than the jungle. However, in the middle of Thika, where everything from textiles to plastics is manufactured, there is a waterfall and because of this and Thika's nearness to Nairobi, it has often been used as a film location. In one film, as Clark Gable treks through unexplored Africa for weeks in the steaming heat, he at last arrives at the edge of the area sought by him and Ava Gardner. As he parts the bushes and surveys the scene, he puts his hand on her shoulder and says—as only Clark Gable could say—"Here we are—gorilla country." And everyone in the Nairobi theater laughed and laughed, because they knew that what Clark Gable and Ava Gardner were really looking at through those bushes were not gorillas but electrical pylons and The Metal Box factory.

Jock also met Gordon Scott, one of the fifteen Tarzans, and drove him to Thika. At that time Jock had just bought a big new Citroën car of which he was very proud because it was larger than most automobiles in Kenya, but Gordon Scott, a giant muscle man, could hardly get into it. Although you would not know it on the screen, he was not at all at one with the animals and had to steel himself for scenes in which he had to touch or pet them. However, he was as strong, if not as intrepid, as he looked; and one day at a gathering of some Kikuyu villagers, he picked up two large men at the same time and held them aloft—one in each hand —which impressed Jock as well as the villagers.

One day Jock and I were at the Mt. Kenya Safari Club, and a friend of ours from England, who was in Kenya taking temporary jobs as a governess, waved to us, beckoned us to the pool and there she introduced us to a Mrs. Travers, who was very pretty and friendly. Jock, who was certain he had met her before, turned to Mrs. Travers and said, "Don't we know each other?" She smiled and said vaguely that perhaps they had met, but Jock was so certain he kept on trying to determine where. Had she lived in Kenya all her life? Had they met in England? No, she answered, but perhaps they had met in Nairobi before. Her husband joined us, and after a pleasant conversation with them we parted, and then learned from our friend that Mr. and Mrs. Travers were none other than Virginia McKenna and Bill Travers who played the leads in *Born Free*. Virginia McKenna is as well known to English audiences as Natalie Wood is to Americans, and her modesty was charming in not reminding Jock who she was, nor in telling him he only recognized her from the screen, which she must have known all along. Bill Travers, also a famous English actor, became so attached to the lion cubs he worked with in the filming of *Born Free,* that when he went back to England after the film, he raised a lot of money in order to return to Kenya to free the movie cubs himself in just the same way that Elsa was freed in the movie . . . life imitating movies which were imitating life.

An interesting system has subsequently developed governing the use of lions in films shot here. The releasing of lions à la Elsa is very time consuming, very expensive, and only partially successful in the final analysis. There are also very few people capable of even attempting it. The whole object of release is that domesticated lions may lead free lives instead of ending up behind bars.

However, to make films you need tame lions, so instead of capturing wild ones or using captured cubs, why not engage lion actors who are already in captivity? For *Living Free,* the sequel to *Born Free,* the film company has done just that. Twenty lions of different ages were brought to Kenya from "Africa U.S.A." in California. They made the picture, collected their money, and went home. The Kenya Government has insisted that this should be the pattern from now on, so that no more free lions have to be captured. Jock knows Susan Hampshire, the star of *Living Free*—he had dated her a couple of times while she was still in drama school in England.

Lady movie stars, indeed any ladies associated with lions or the larger cats, have to be careful to remember when they are going to have their period. The lions can detect the fact at once and are

inclined to be made restless and edgy by the slightest smell of
blood. Indeed, during the filming of a well-known movie there
was a tragic incident, when a normally placid lion killed a lady
whom it knew and liked, and the only possible explanation
seemed to be that she was in the middle of her period. As a result
of this accident, the producer would not feature a single lion in a
movie that was wholly about the capturing of dangerous animals.

Some of the movies filmed in Africa about Africa and Africans
are outrageous. A few, like *Africa Addio,* are seriously upsetting.
This film presented a series of gory incidents involving the slaughter of men and animals throughout the continent. Things taken
out of context and presented as the commonplace are bad enough
—a film could be made of America for exhibition in Africa, showing nothing but the race riots, senseless crimes and slum areas in
the States and presented as *This Is America.* But *Africa Addio*
went even further than that: The makers of this film presented, as
just one example, footage of the necessary culling of hippo by the
Game Department as a kind of open season for butchers, unre-
strained by the new and irresponsible governments who had no
interest in keeping the animals alive. The accompanying commen-
tary assured viewers that "meat day is every Friday" and that
within a few years there would be no animals left in Africa. This
is quite untrue. The independent African governments have conservation programs and are well aware that a booming tourist
industry depends upon the survival of the wildlife. In other footage
they harmfully misrepresented countries in Africa, highlighting
only one facet of larger incidents in order to shock. Sensational-
ism is appalling enough, but when false and contrived sensational-
ism is presented as documentary truth to a world which is in no
position to judge, then the lack of integrity makes one sick and
frightened of the consequences.

However, harmless and amusing situations in movie making do
arise. For instance, before the movie companies were too careful
about Kiswahili translations, assuming no one in the United States
would understand, one director needed an African messenger to
gasp a Kiswahili sentence to the big chief just as he was collapsing

after running for days with his vital news. The director asked a local Englishman who spoke Kiswahili to write an urgent-sounding sentence in the language. He did, with tongue in cheek, and the African, played by an American black from Hollywood memorized it and played the part beautifully. All was well until the movie was shown in Nairobi (where even the parrots speak Swahili), and everyone present had the drama of that moment reduced to high comedy because what the messenger actually said as he threw himself exhausted before the chief was, "I do not think I am getting paid enough money for this part."

We also laughed at the knowledge that when *Mr. Moses* was filmed in Kenya, the elephant that played a significant role (the best role, as a matter of fact) was an Indian elephant obviously imported for the part. We learned from friends that this elephant was terrified of chickens, and every time a chicken would wander through the African village that was used for the set, the elephant would run away, knocking down huts and fences and causing much expensive time to be wasted in catching it and rebuilding the "set."

Another extraordinary thing to see was an exciting rodeo scene in a popular American television serial about Africa, when the cowboys in Kenya were riding buffalo. It was evidently filmed in California and the "buffalo" were beef steers wearing plastic buffalo horns. One would think that the producers, having gone to the expense and trouble of staging this entire performance—even though we have no cowboys and nobody ever rides a buffalo— would have painted over the white chest and underbelly of the steers, or used Black Angus cattle—buffalo are solid black—because watching two-toned buffalo on television was as startling as seeing striped giraffe.

In addition to itinerant movie stars, there are a number of resident Dukes and Princes, Counts and Barons, Lords and Ladies —most of whom are authentic, but a smattering of whom are self-styled. A few remittance men (those banished to the colonies by their families and paid a fat retainer to keep out of sight) still live in Kenya—including one said to be the illegitimate son of King

Edward VII. As I mentioned before, Winston Churchill's grand-daughter was married here and lived here for a while, and the Aga Khan has a house next door to Jock's mother and makes frequent visits to Kenya. Jock has known his wife since they were teen-agers and used to go to the same parties.

When the Queen Mother visited Kenya before Independence Jock was assigned as her "aide-de-camp," traveling with her and her retinue, helping to organize receptions and generally being on hand during the two-week visit. He says that she is without a doubt one of the truly delightful and warm people in the world, with an incredible ability to concentrate 100 per cent upon whomever she is talking to—most flattering to the person concerned.

Jock said that at a garden party in Nairobi she proceeded down a line of people—dignitaries of one sort and another—chatting with each in turn, and that the men were supposed to bow and the ladies curtsey as they were introduced. At one point in the line there were several ladies in a row each of whom sank gracefully down, back straight, balance steady, after much rehearsing at home. Then it was a man's turn again. In his nervousness, and quite unaware of his action, he unconsciously copied the ladies whom he had been watching intently and made a perfect curtsey. The Queen Mother did not bat an eyelid and made a point of talk-ing to him an extra long time. Afterwards, in the security of Gov-ernment House, she burst out laughing and confessed she could hardly contain herself when it happened—but she made Jock and the others promise never to tell the man what he had done, and to this day he is probably unaware of it.

When she left she gave Jock a beautiful pair of cuff links inscribed with her personal insignia, which we keep having to re-trieve from the bottom of the washing machine in my sister's cel-lar in Baltimore.

I must say I feel more comfortable in a washing machine than I do in a palace. I have been in two. Both times were disasters. When we visited Iran a couple of years ago the Shah's brother, Prince Abdoreza Phalavi, invited just the two of us to his palace for tea, and I immediately spilled mine all over his seventy-five-foot wall-to-wall Persian carpet. I don't normally spill tea but I was so nervous. I got down on all fours to wipe it up and he helped me—I was so embarrassed.

The other time was when I was invited to go on Ethiopian Airlines' Inaugural Flight from New York to Addis along with many travel writers, the press and so forth. We were to have an audience with the Emperor, and not being used to protocol, we were briefed on the way to the Palace that we must address him only as "Your Imperial Majesty," not "Your Royal Highness" or "Your Majesty" or "Sir." The men were to enter first, and on the way to the throne, they were to bow three times. The women were to follow with curtsies. After shaking hands with the Emperor, we were not to turn our backs on him but should reverse, or back away. I remember standing at the back of the long room with Pauline Fredericks and Marion Gough, an editor of *House Beautiful,* and giggling as we watched the men—a real Laurel and Hardy visit with the Emperor. With fears of blurting out "Your Imperial Crab," and remembering tales of former Emperor's cutting out the tongues of people who goofed, they nervously set off in a straight line, one after the other, like parachutists out of a plane. And then came the bowing. Unused to bowing and very awkward at it and afraid they wouldn't get in all three bows, most of the men bent over at a right angle from the waist with the entire top half of their bodies parallel to the floor, and walked this way towards the Emperor—coming up for air three times en route. One seemed to follow the other in imitating this extraordinary approach. Then, as they finished shaking hands with the "Lion of Juda" and backed away, still bent over from the waist, they all began bumping into each other like funny mechanical toys gone haywire.

Spiro Agnew visited Kenya and as I shook hands with the Vice-President I suggested we sing a few choruses of our old school song "To You Forest Park We Are Loyal." He smiled and replied, "I think that would be a good idea," but he sang "The Star-Spangled Banner" instead. I bet because he couldn't remember the words to our school song.

Our friend with the airplane you have to push took Pucci on

safari, and when he asked him what he did, Pucci said, "I am a designer," and for some reason which I cannot imagine our friend assumed he was a bridge designer and spent the next two weeks with him thinking this. When he returned home his wife asked what Pucci's first name was and when she was told "Emilio," she was very angry not to have collected a dress, or at least a personally signed scarf.

We once spent over a week with Mrs. Dan Reeves and three of her daughters on safari. Six months later, when my son Rick was having dinner with one of the daughters in her flat in Paris, he came out of her bathroom and asked, "Why do you have a Los Angeles Ram's bath mat in there?" She said, "We own the Rams." Jock and I had no idea. They never mentioned the football team while on safari with us, much less the fact that they owned them. However, we both know approximately as much about football as my ex-mother-in-law, whose gardener said to her one day in the midst of an exciting World Series, "Some series, ain't it, Mrs. Bruce?" She replied, "Oh, I'm terribly sorry, Mr. Jarvis"—she always called him Mr. Jarvis—"but I don't know a thing about football."

As I mentioned earlier, we have taken Mike Wallace and his wife, Lorraine, on safari, and also Paddy Chayefsky and his wife, and Cy Feuer. They were all kind, alert, interested and interesting people whom we enjoyed being with tremendously, even though their trips were swift. But Jack and Miriam and Randy Paar have become really close friends after many trips through Africa together.

Jack is one of the funniest men we have ever known, and totally spontaneous. We have actually been unable to eat our meals sometimes because he makes us laugh so hard, which is something I cannot say about anyone else we have ever known.

He is also interested in everything and is a born interviewer. He cannot help being genuinely curious. For example, I telephoned him once after Miriam had undergone a serious back operation. He knew she was safely through it, but we, of course, did not.

"Hi, Jack," I said, "how is Miriam?"

"Oh, Betty, good to hear from you—where are you?"

"Baltimore. How's Miriam?"

"When are you coming to New York, when can we see you?"

"Tomorrow. What about Miriam?"

"How are you traveling? Are you going to drive?"

"Yes. Is Miriam O.K.?"

"Gee, you do an awful lot of driving. Do you really like to drive that much? Do you still have that same car?"

And he really does want to know.

But the owner and operator of this quick, inquisitive mind, is above all a man who values his family and his privacy. His wife, Miriam, and daughter, Randy, are both gems—warm and easy going and full of laughter.

As far as Africa goes, Jack has a true love for it, and applies an integrity and sensitivity when making a program which is not always evident in others in his profession. He likes to show Africa as it is, not as the television audience may imagine it is. He will even sacrifice interesting facts for fear of being labeled a sensationalist. Once, we filmed Jack and Miriam petting a rhino that had been raised by a game warden in Tsavo National Park. A few weeks later the rhino turned on and killed a park ranger who was stroking it, but Jack would not include this fact, though he still had plenty of time to insert comments into the program, because he felt it might be interpreted as sensation seeking. I'm glad we live in the same forest with the Paars—they have given us so much laughter and warm friendship and our lives would be a lot less sunny if they weren't in it.

Marchesa Suki Bisletti (a Dutch girl married to an Italian Marquis) raises wild animals as a profession as well as a hobby. One day Jock, the children, and I stopped at Suki's farm to see her, and as we walked into her living room, we gave a shout for her. She didn't appear, but a large lion did, so we waited for her back in the car. While we sat there, Jock told me that Suki had once performed a great trick for a Tarzan movie which he had witnessed being filmed. The script had called for Tarzan to find a scarf, then a shoe and finally the bones of a girl who had been devoured by a lion. Suki suggested to the director that they rewrite the script and film the girl actually being attacked by the lion. She then donned the film-star's clothes and proceeded with her trick. This entailed a game in which one of her pet lions stalks her and finally charges, jumping right on top of her. The two of them fall to the ground, and the lion playfully swats her as a kitten would a toy mouse. Of course the lion was always very gentle and kept his claws retracted. Suitably dubbed with furious roaring and terrified screams, this resulted, Jock said, in probably the most realistic mauling of a human by a lion ever filmed.

Still other friends of ours, Viscount and Lady Mandeville (who will become, through inheritance, the Duke and Duchess of Manchester), specialize as stand-ins in movies when the danger is real and not simulated. This often involves driving Land-Rovers precariously close to rhino or elephant, even allowing them actually to attack the vehicle.

In one movie, I think it was *The Lion,* a hunter friend of ours, Bill Ryan, who is graying and grizzled and looks tough, was a stand-in for the beautiful Capucine in a couple of sequences. He is one of the few who looks the part of the hunter, yet he had to don a long dark wig, make-up and appropriate padding, and drive a Land-Rover and trailer closer and closer to an elephant, teasing it in order to provoke a charge that would result in the trailer being smashed to pieces. It was dangerous work, requiring fine judgment and an intimate knowledge of elephant reaction. On the screen you could not tell that it was Bill behind the wheel instead of Capucine, which I don't think pleased him very much.

But I've been saving my idol, William Holden, till last. For many years I've been a fan of his and have had a schoolgirl's crush on him, from which I have never fully recovered. One day Jock and I were at the Mt. Kenya Safari Club, which is owned by William Holden and another American, Ray Ryan, and although we had been there many times before, we had never seen William Holden. On this occasion we were there with Cy and Jed Feuer. I wanted

1. Our Nairobi house.

2. Dancy, McDonnell and Rick in 1963, on our second trip.

3. Shirley Brown, as a puppy, and Rick, age eighteen.

4. William Holden's former Rolls-Royce, a bargain at $1,200.

5. Irving Katz.

6. Shirley Brown
in her party hat.

7. The Paars on safari with us.

8. Lion escaping from
   tsetse flies in a tree.

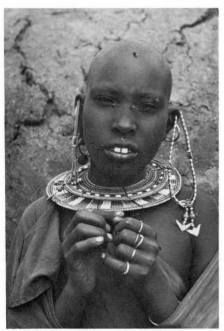

9. A Masai girl.

10. A Masai woman. The beads have two purposes: decoration and a denotation of status.

11. Jock and the Pygmies.

12. Our coast house.

13. Church at Lalibala carved from solid rock.

14. Two visitors at Treetops.

Wife tells of slain husband

By NATION Correspondent

A KAKAMEGA court was told yesterday how a man opened his father's stomach with a spear and took out the intestines.

Before the Kakamega district magistrate, Mr. E. N. Eahirungo, was Khaluchi Nandwa who is facing a charge of murdering his father, Nandwa Omumo, on February 5 at Sianda, Marama Location in Kakamega District.

It was alleged during the preliminary inquiry that the father had heard his son and another man fighting near his hut. When he went out to the scene, the court was told further he was speared by his son who subsequently pulled out his intestines.

The mother, Mrs. Anyangu Nandwa, told the court how she covered her husband with a piece of cloth. She said her husband was bleeding terribly.

The hearing continues.

Millionaire takes his 24th wife

An African millionaire herbalist, Mr. Khotso Sethsuntsa — a spritely 86-year-old — has married his 24th wife.

His latest bride, Nogama Msindo, is a Lesotho teenager and their wedding reception was the biggest he has held.

There were hundreds of distinguished guests, both Black and White, said Mr. Sethsuntsa, who claimed to have slaughtered 10 oxen and 20 sheep for the festivities.

"I still want more children," said the bridegroom, who does not know how many he has by his 23 other wives.

"I don't know how many grandchildren I have either. Twenty of my daughters are married."

He said his teenage wife was not his last. He intended to increase the number of his wives but could not say how many more he would take.

— *Reuter*

There were lions in his luggage

There are certain natural hazards in East Africa to the seemingly simple task of waiting for a bus.

Take the case of the young traveller who was waiting for the midday bus on the main road near the entrance to the Mikumi National Park in Tanzania.

His bus came but, to his horror, so did a pride of young lion. The young man did not hesitate. He left his luggage and ran to the bus which lost no time in moving on.

The lions soon found the abandoned suitcase and playfully batted it around while two others in the pride had a tug-of-war with a towel. The effects were recovered with little damage and were later returned to the owner.

Cholera? Keep your shirt on

KAMPALA, Saturday

SINCE when has there been a connection between cholera and the wearing of clothes?

The answer to the question is the monopoly of 30 Karamojong who have been arrested after mobilising a whole village to attack a county chief who tried to persuade them to wear clothes and thereby, so they believe, causing the present cholera outbreak in Karamoja.

It is the common belief in Karamoja, according to reports reaching here, that cholera broke out in the area because the people had abandoned their traditional custom of going about in their birthday suits.

Witchcraft and love scandal hits church

THE Celestial-Christianist Church in Porto Novo, Dahomey, has been hit by a scandal of unrequited love.

Evangelist Benoit Agabaossi, successor of the founder of the sect the prophet Oshofa, is accused of setting members of his church on to an old woman who tried to seduce the holy man in the early hours of the morning.

In his defence Agabaossi told police he and the rest of the faithful beat up the old woman because she had changed into a dog. "This witch-doctoress changed back into a woman before our very eyes as we beat her," the evangelist said.

Agabaossi, also a healer, explained that at 2 a.m. he and church members sleeping on the premises while under treatment were awakened by the piercing hooting of owls — a sign of bad medicine.

"Next three dogs appeared. For us everything was clear. Someone was trying to cast a spell. We armed ourselves with sticks and stones and beat the dogs."

Two of the animals escaped, but the third, said the evangelist, trapped behind a tree, suddenly assumed the form of the old woman under the blows that rained down on her.

Police are not convinced and have charged the evangelist with assault and battery. The only proof of the truth of the story would be for the woman to change back into a dog, but this, say the Celestial Christians, is impossible since they neutralised her powers by pulling out a tuft of her hair.

When will the kissing start in Indian films?

THE question of allowing kissing on the Indian screen has taken the headlines again. The Central Board of Film Censors has decided that the Indian film has some character at the moment and it should be maintained by keeping off "un-Indian" acts like kissing, since their depiction would not enhance or reflect the true Indian image and the culture of India.

15. Some typical newspaper stories.

16. A Masai youth
preparing to
become a **Morani**.

17. A Masai Morani (warrior).
The hair, prepared with sheep's
fat and sheep's wool, is
worn only by young warriors
who've passed initiation rites.

18. Masai man in ostrich feather headdress.

19. A Masai man with an unusual earring.

20. Jock and I with Masai women in front of hut made of cow dung.

21. Wash day at our Nairobi house.

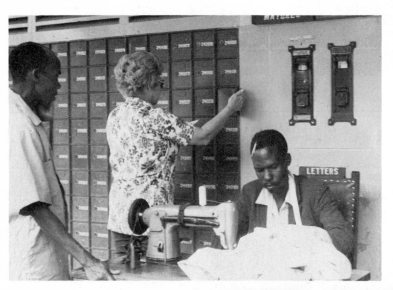

22. A tailor hard at
work in the Post Office.

23. His Imperial Majesty,
Haile Selassie, and friend.

24. Lioness angry at me for photographing her.

25. A decorative means of transportation.

26. Dancy and McDonnell,
sixteen and seventeen years old.

27. Rick, age
twenty-one.

to sun-bathe by the pool, but hadn't remembered to bring my bathing suit. The pool was deserted, so Jock suggested I just put on his bathing trunks and my old sleeveless sweater. I hesitated, but finally thought "so what?" Jock and the Feuers were used to my scruffiness in the bush, so I changed and sat in Jock's baggy trunks and the torn sleeveless sweater with my bra straps showing, trying to get some sun on my white legs (which needed shaving). I looked like a female impersonator—and *that* is when I met William Holden. He came up to greet Cy, for they had known each other in Hollywood, and Cy was too polite to ignore me—the monstrosity with him. I wanted to get up and run, but I knew if I did the bathing trunks would fall off, so I sat there trapped and suffering. William Holden is extremely pleasant and polite and short—about five feet nine inches—which renews my certainty in the theory that great men are little men—like Caesar and Napoleon. (I just said this so that if William Holden reads this he won't be mad at me for telling you he's short.)

Jock and I have since bought a Rolls-Royce that originally belonged to William Holden—a 1948 Silver Wraith limousine which he shipped to Kenya from Switzerland. We paid $1,500 for it and soon after buying it, I saw William Holden in Nairobi walking down the street, so I followed him. (I always follow him.) He went into an electrical store and so did I, pretending I wanted to buy an iron. He was standing next to me buying something very romantic—like a 60-watt light bulb—and I just couldn't get up nerve enough to say anything to him. Finally, to my amazement, he turned around to me and said, "Oh, hello." I was thinking he wouldn't recognize me out of my strange get-up, but I guess I must have still looked pretty funny, so I told him about our acquiring his Rolls and he said that when he first owned it, it had zebra-skin upholstery. We left the shop together and walked down the streets of Nairobi talking and laughing, and do you know that not *one person* I know saw me walking down the street with William Holden?

I adore the Rolls—it is sixteen blocks long, has a glass partition that goes up and down at the touch of a button, a bar, two folding tables and hinged foot rests. We lost the ignition key before even driving it away, so had to leave it parked on the property of the people from whom we purchased it. Every day at noon we would drive in our other little nasty car to the Rolls, then climb into the back of it and eat our picnic lunch in splendor. Sometimes we took friends, and it was becoming the most popular lunch counter in town, but the former owners got tired of the bits of egg shells on their lawn, so we had another key made and departed majestically. All that day Jock and I played Rolls-Royce. Jock would drive and I would sit in the back waving to passers-by and "giving orders to James." Then I would drive and Jock would sit in the back criticizing the way in which I had waved with glee and enthusiasm and showing me how to wave with refined condescension instead. Most of the time in Kenya, both Jock and I would be in front playing chauffeur and maid to Shirley Brown, who would ride in solitary state in the back with one paw on the arm rest, graciously acknowledging the surprised looks of those we passed.

Later we shipped the car to the States to drive it there during the lecture tours we undertake each year. A twenty-year-old Rolls-Royce with a right-hand drive and Kenya tags going 120 kilometers an hour is no longer a usual sight in Idaho. While traveling, I usually type, and we decided we were a hazard on the road because truck drivers would glance into their side-view mirrors as we were passing, and first they would see me sitting there in the "driver's seat," but instead of driving I was typing. The truck would swerve all over the road until the comforting sight of Jock behind the wheel on the right-hand side came into view. We thought of buying a child's toy steering wheel to stick on the dashboard in front of me. We were also a curiosity parked at drive-in restaurants, sitting in the back eating 25-cent hamburgers off the polished walnut tables, or ordering hot dogs in the Rolls.

As a matter of fact, what I was typing was this book. The only place to write a book is while driving in an automobile—for what else is there to do in a car six hours a day? There are no distracting telephones, no bureau drawers to clean, or hair washing, but only mile after mile of solitude allowing us complete concentration. We should have dedicated this book "To our Rolls-Royce, without whose unstinted help this book would never have been written."

X
Hansel and Gretel

Before we built our house at the coast, a friend of ours gave us the use of an empty house on eight hundred acres of his land in a remote area one hundred and thirty miles north of Nairobi, on the edge of what we have been told is the largest cedar forest in the world. Every weekend we hauled some furniture along with us in our Land-Rover, and when we had cut the grass and weeds down from the windows and finally furnished it, it looked just like Hansel and Gretel's house . . . far from tourist-folder Africa.

The forest was filled with buffalo and leopard and colobus monkeys (black and white bathroom rugs) and lots of antelope, but best of all are the Masai who own the land. Frequently, when we walked through the woods following streams, we would find a bright red patch on a rock where the Masai had been mixing their ocre with which they paint themselves. And on an occasional tree would be a dab of red—a signal perhaps for other Masai about some sheep they had stolen and which way to go for the feast.

Every time I walked in the woods I swore I would never do so again. I was too afraid. I'd see recent leopard footprints and hear buffalo crashing about in the bushes. Someone would say, "Aren't the wild flowers lovely?" "Wild flowers? What wild flowers?" I was always too busy looking *up*—for suitable trees to climb to escape from buffalo, or for tails hanging down. I have been told that leopard let their tails hang down when they sleep in trees during the day and that one must not look directly up or the leopard will pounce. You must just turn and walk quietly away. I found walking through this forest was just like riding a roller coaster—I hated it when I was doing it and swore I would never do so again, and yet the minute it was over I wanted to go back.

In our house we had no electricity or refrigeration. Everyone asks how we ever managed without a refrigerator when we were almost on the equator, but the altitude there is ten thousand feet, and it is very cold indeed. We sometimes called it "Withering Heights." Frost often covered our world in the mornings, and in the evenings if it had hailed, we went into the garden and collected the hail-stones for our sundowners (cocktails). A roaring cedar fire kept our stone house warm and made it smell like Christmas all year long, and candles lighted our way inside—it's fun taking a bath by candlelight. Irons were filled with burning charcoal and the clothes pressed beautifully, and the wood stove gobbled cedar, making all the food taste like outdoor cooking. *Everything* was charcoaled—have you ever tried charcoaled jello? Three-minute eggs took six minutes to cook because of the high altitude. There were no telephones, mail, or people, our nearest neighbor was six miles away and our nearest village thirty-two miles—a long walk for a pack of cigarettes. No one was allowed to get sick since getting medical help was far too difficult.

They say, "Getting there is half the fun," and so it was getting to our house in the woods. It was the doughnuts and the Asian dwarf along the way I liked best. We finally hired the cook, David, from the Bell Inn, the only place to eat along the one hundred and thirty miles, because he made the best doughnuts ever—all hot and oozy with jelly. We had jelly doughnuts with martinis and steak and everything; but now, of course, we can't stand the sight of them because we ate far too many. But David Doughnut, as we nicknamed him, stays on with us learning to cook other things. If we could have thought of anything we needed an Asian dwarf for, we would have tried to hire him, too, but instead we contented

ourselves with buying things in his general store, as an excuse to
see his bright face looking up from below the counter to ask what
we wanted.

Then we would continue across the Great Rift Valley—a spectacular geographical wonder and, at five thousand miles long, the
world's largest valley. Driving across it we would see zebra and
baboons and dik-dik and, occasionally, Lord Delamere who lived
there too. Finally, we would begin to climb out of the valley, and
since it usually rained the rest of the time was spent in the mud.
First the children and I would get out to ease the load and push
the car while Jock drove. The spinning wheels left us all mud-
splattered, and we would try to walk on the slippery surface which
wasn't easy, but oh such fun. Our gumboots would sink into the
mud which was almost to our knees and sucked one foot in like
quicksand as we pulled the other foot out. We'd often lose our
balance, plunging in up to our elbows, and there we would be on
all-fours in the mud, laughing so hard we thought we'd never have
the strength to move. If one of us was managing to walk quite
well on the slick road ("road" being a rare British overstatement),
someone else would give him a little shove just so he too could
fall down and join the fun. I have fallen down more between the
ages of thirty-five and forty than I did between the time I was two
and seven.

Jock, who was raised in Kenya at a high altitude, is not only like
a mountain goat, but like Tarzan in the forest as well. When he
married me with my three children, he got a package deal of four
sea-level city people. On one of our first walks through the forest
—I should say one of our first crawls through the forest—we slid
downhill with ease, but found it impossible to walk up an anthill
much less climb at ten thousand feet. Jock waited patiently while
we gasped for breath, pausing every two seconds to rest. Anyone
who has trouble giving up smoking should just go to our house in
the woods—smoking is automatically out—just trying to breathe
keeps you occupied at all times.

We were resting yet again in a glade where the forest bordered
a field when suddenly Jock heard a buffalo crashing through the

bushes and urgently hollered, "Buffalo!" expecting us to react as we had in the "fire drill" of all of this. Being nervous I, of course, giggled. Dancy's reaction in moments of stress is to cry. Both of us ran for a big tree, as we had been instructed previously to do in case of buffalo, but I was unable to climb it because I was laughing too hard, and she was unable to climb it because she was crying too hard. So we both stood at the bottom of the tree in our various states of emotion, presenting a perfect target for the buffalo. McDonnell, then ten years old, had never seen a buffalo before, so he ran to a barbed-wire fence, climbed over it, and stood there in the open, behind a few strands of wire, assuming that he was safe from a charging three-ton animal. Jock was totally appalled by our performance, and the buffalo must have been, too, because it ran off in the opposite direction.

One evening Jock and Rick and I decided to fish for trout. In our secondhand, Second World War Army jackets and high rubber boots, we set out in the cold mist, reminiscent rather of Scotland than equatorial Africa, and walked about six miles into the woods following the river to an eighteen-foot waterfall. Rick had gone ahead and found a promising pool directly above the falls. Pretending to be a good sport, because I was really much more concerned about avoiding buffalo than catching trout, I said, "I'll fish this one," and started to climb down the cliff to a pool in a narrow gorge. I grabbed a branch of a tree in order to lower myself, but it broke and I slid down laughing because I knew I was going right in that cold river—there was no way I could stop myself.

So, howling with apprehension and laughter because it *was* funny, I hit the water and the cold took my breath away. I came up in waist-deep water still clutching my fishing rod, and expecting to climb out, when I was unexpectedly seized by the rapids. Catching my heavy coat, they tumbled me over and over, and though I grabbed at rocks, they were too slippery to grasp. I was being washed closer and closer to the falls. I think of myself as a good swimmer—I got my life-saving badge from the YWCA and all that —but this had nothing to do with swimming. I was totally out of control.

Jock could not reach me—I was being carried downstream faster than he could scramble over the slippery rocks—but Rick, hearing the commotion looked around in time to plunge in and brace himself against a rock so that he could catch me as I was swept towards him. It was a narrow escape, and I had been within feet of going over the falls onto the rocks below, just like Katherine Hepburn in the *African Queen*.

When our children were at our house in the woods they would create things for themselves to do. I fear we Americans invent so many diversions and activities for our children that they have lost the ability to create for themselves. With no bowling alleys, movies, swimming pools, or friends, they became interested in things they had never noticed before—rocks and birds and how ants live. They looked at sunsets instead of TV sets.

One afternoon Dancy and McDonnell announced they were going to go for a walk. We were very glad because we were just about to pretend we wanted to make fudge, hide the sugar, then send them next door to borrow some. This would have taken them about six hours, and we would have enjoyed the peace and silence. Off they went, but within a half hour they returned, wide-eyed with awe. "We just saw the Virgin Mary! She is sitting down there." "Stop being ridiculous," I said, seeing they weren't being ridiculous. "She's sitting on a log on that hill by the stream with her sheep all around her, and she has on that dress of hers with those big long sleeves," insisted McDonnell. "Dear God," I thought, "What do you say to the Virgin Mary?" It might be easier if we were Catholics.

Jock and I felt mildly uncomfortable as we walked with the children to meet the Virgin Mary. The sheep were there, the log was there, and from our side of the stream a shaft of evening sunlight among the shadows cast an uncanny illumination on a bleached split branch attached to the fallen log and resembled a seated figure in white robes. The setting was so perfect that for a moment I caught myself wondering if she really had been there.

XI
Who Painted Them Birds?

I just read somewhere that a man asked a child who had visited East Africa why he liked it so much, and the child answered, "Because people wave back." Children often give good answers. A child visiting here the other day, upon seeing his first leopard said, "Look, Mommy, there's a pocketbook."

On my children's first trip to Africa the ship had docked in Mombasa harbor at night, and in the morning when they had their first glimpse of the continent, Dancy, then seven years old, asked, "Does God live here?" Later, on safari, her six-year-old brother, McDonnell, said, "There's a mouse what has wings," when he saw his first bat, and at Nakuru, where three million bright pink flamingo make a spectacle on the lake, he asked, "Who painted them birds?" Back in Nairobi, after a few weeks in the bush, the waiter at breakfast asked my daughter what kind of eggs she wanted. "Chicken," she replied.

Almost everyone who comes here for two weeks goes home and writes a book. We were no exception. I wrote a book and so did seven-year-old Dancy. Mine was, without a doubt, the worst book I ever read. Here is hers (with her spelling):

DANCY'S BOOK OF AFRICA
TITLE: SAFARAS

Well, we left New Yuork. Then we got on a ship and it's hoter then the sun, and I and my father got seasick every day.

For a month and two days and the first day I met a girl named Jane. I was seven. She was eight. After a half of a month she was nine. I was still seven. My brother was six. After the month and two days were over—we were in Africa. AFRICA—what can I say. Well insted we met a lady named Mrs. Hordon and rented a house. One night we heard a hynena nok over a garbage can. Daddy got out of bed as quik as he could. He ran into the kitchen as fast as he can run but that wasn't verry fast for him. He ran too the back door and called Mommy. Mommy must have thouth the hynena was in the house. Mommy called my brother who was 13 yeas old. It seemed to go by age. My brother aged six did not hear the hynena nok over the garbage can we were fast asleep. It seemed to me that someone could of called us.

One night we went to Mrs. Hordon's house for dinner then Mommy and Daddy and us had after dinner coffee. The next morning Donnell through stones and he broke the window of the guvermints house. Later on Daddy brought a truck for our hole family to go thru the plains. The plains is a place were there is lots of trees and a hole bunch of animuls. Daddy got out of the truck and there was a lion two yards away. Mommy said get in the truck. She didn't like lions. She didn't like buffalos as far as I am concerned she didn't like anything. We came back from Africa by 5 plains and one jet.

The End.

The thing that impressed my daughter most about Africa was the "after dinner coffee" she was served for the first time, and to her what was far more noteworthy about the trip than anything else was the fact that she was still seven after her friend turned nine—age at that time is much more important than lion or elephant. The story to which she referred was when Dan Bruce, to whom I was then married, and the children took our first trip through any game park, which, by sheer coincidence and totally unappreciated by us, happened to be across the Serengeti Plains during the migration. We thought that Africa's game parks must always have 150,000 wildebeest within view. Our Land-Rover (truck) was packed with food and petrol because there was nowhere to buy anything in all Serengeti's five thousand square miles. There wasn't even a road in those days, just a track. We arrived too late at the entrance to the plains, and the game scouts would not let us through until the next morning. No one is allowed out in the game parks after dark, and the scouts calculated we would not have enough time to reach Seronera Lodge—the one point of shelter in the middle of Serengeti—ninety miles away. So we slept in a metal hut at the entrance. Our closest encounter with nature until then had been one trip to the Baltimore zoo; we had never been camping and there wasn't a Boy Scout amongst us, but somehow we managed to light the kerosene lamps (we had seen how it was done in the movies) and eat cold food out of cans. We "slept" on sheetless cots in our clothes and killed a scorpion under the bed; we lay awake listening to the lion roar and once felt the hut shake when a hyena bumped into it. No one had ever been up at 6 A.M. before, but we set out the next morning as soon as the sun came up. McDonnell announced that the only thing that had displeased him the night before had been that "jelly with carrots in it"—the orange marmalade we had for supper. There we were, like Stanley and Livingstone, crossing the Serengeti Plains in an open car, totally ignorant of everything we were doing. Lunacy.

Except for the scorpion, the only animals we had seen thus far in Africa were a cat and a rabbit, but within two miles from the gate, we began to see a greater concentration of animals than I was to see for the rest of my life. Dan announced that the game warden had warned him to be careful because there was a man-eating lion in the area. I was getting furious with him for permitting the safari when we saw our first buffalo—a lone one. Fear joined my anger because a lone buffalo is far more likely to charge than a herd.

"Drive off," I shouted, but Dan had never seen a buffalo before, so he turned to look at it, and as he did so his cigarette went under the seat where the gas tank of a Land-Rover is situated. He had to break the never-get-out-of-your-car rule to search for the lighted cigarette before it ignited the tank. I was waiting for the car to blow up or to be charged, when Dancy said in a happy little girl's voice, "Oh look, there's a lion what has hair!" And so there was— lying in the bushes six yards from my husband. He jumped back into the Land-Rover, and as we drove off we saw that the lion was with a lioness and cubs, three of them. They appeared totally bored, but I assure you we were not. Although the buffalo did not charge and the Land-Rover did not explode, I remained frightened for two days. Even the "herd of birds" McDonnell announced that he saw frightened me. We went up and down gullies, through river-beds and thick bush; branches flew into the car, thorns tore at our arms and faces, and tsetse flies swarmed in and bit us; we flitted the car with spray guns, bounced up and down and arrived covered with dust, nine hours later in Seronera.

The camp was completely deserted when we arrived. My vivid imagination told me that the people had been eaten by a man-eater, but the real reason was that everyone was half a mile away at a poacher's trail. But when the game warden returned, he told us a harrowing story about a woman who the previous week had stood up in her Land-Rover to get a closer picture of a lioness, and the lioness had sprung and mauled her.

I was not comforted by this news, and the next morning when I reluctantly set out again I knew just what the Christian martyrs felt like when they were flung to the lions. Within five minutes af-ter leaving Seronera, we were staring leopard and lion in the face, and I decided I preferred my animals in the zoo where I could imagine I was superior.

The track was much worse than the day before. The road was nothing but deep sand, and we had to pull slowly through it with the four-wheel drive. I thought the only way things could be worse was to have our car break down, and I was soon to find out about that. It was engine trouble. Although Dan fiddled for about two hours, the car would not start. In those days one car a week might cross the Serengeti, and since no one was expecting us at Ngorongoro, the next stop, no search party came to look for us. We had no food or water left, so we considered walking the remaining thirty miles with the children, but we were certain to run into elephant and leopard since we were getting close to their territory. Dan suggested that he walk and leave me with the children. Leave me with the children! He would find me stark raving mad by the time he returned—if he returned. The day before there had been fear; today there was terror. We couldn't go and we couldn't stay. To die is one thing, but to *perish* is another. Hyenas and vultures are worse than lions. I complained that we didn't have our gun with us. Dan asked why I wanted it and told me, "That little pistol wouldn't kill a hyena, much less a lion." I told him at least I could commit suicide.

The children were too young to realize their peril. One motionless giraffe stood and watched us. We saw mirages—thank goodness we all saw them, or I would have been convinced I had already lost my mind. Dancy wondered if the giraffe saw mirages too. I didn't care. After two of the worst hours I have ever spent in my life, the car miraculously started, and we limped along in it for the last twenty-nine miles, passing through a bush fire. A mile before Ngorongoro, our car broke down for good, and we walked that last mile to the lodge, tired but triumphant.

And all my daughter remembered about her African trip was the after-dinner coffee!

XII
Youth in Asia

I often wonder if my children would be the same children they are today if they had stayed in America. I hardly think so, since when Dancy and McDonnell went to the States in the fall of 1971 to go to college, they were not at all like American youth. At sixteen and seventeen they lacked the American teen-ager's so-called "sophistication." They didn't know what the Establishment was, or the SDS, or moratoriums, and neither one had anything but a cursory interest in clothes, smoking, cars, telephones and all the usual American teen-age fascinations. Although they went out with crowds of friends, they had never been out alone with a member of the opposite sex, nor did they or any of their friends particularly wish to, despite the fact that modesty does not prevent me from telling you, they are very attractive.

Two years ago we were in the States for New Year's Eve, and Dancy and McDonnell said to Jock and me, "What are we going to do to see the New Year in?" "We" of course meant the four of us together. It never occurred to them to go out with anyone other than us. And so we went to the theater and had a midnight champagne dinner afterwards which was big treats for all of us. Last New Year's Eve we all spent together, too, in Nairobi's airport seeing off friends. We had champagne which we drank from empty yoghurt cups, we blew up balloons and batted them back and forth with the Africans working there, and rode around in wheel chairs.

Rick, the suave twenty-three-year-old who was in American schools until he was sixteen, then in Kenya for two years of British boarding schools, then back to the States to Georgetown where he got his degree in Foreign Service and Political Science, said to me when he came home his first summer, "Mother, you have got to Do Something with those two—they act retarded." Their naïveté embarrasses him, but it refreshes me.

In Kenya there are no hippies, no skinheads, no heroin, teenage crime, love-ins, or communes, and it has never even occurred to them to hate their parents or leave home. They love home— shame on them. So in this way they may not be as "sophisticated" as their American peers, but in many ways they are far more so. They feel comfortable with adults and can carry on an intelligent conversation with them—they are even articulate. They go to dinner parties with us, are offered drinks, and wine during dinner, liqueurs afterwards, and join right in the discussions of legalizing abortion, homosexuality, pollution, population explosion and so forth. Everyone listens to the other side and either argues or agrees depending upon opinions, not age. In fact, I find the generation gap only with some of my contemporaries, never with the youth here.

We all go to the discussion groups held in Nairobi every other week. An American house guest, a twenty-two-year-old teacher, went with us one evening when the subject was "The Population Explosion." The speaker was saying that now we have death control, we must also have birth control, and someone else went on to discuss euthanasia. When we left, our American guest asked, "Why were they talking about the youth in Asia?" Our sixteen-year-old daughter explained it to her.

Why is it that the youth here is so different from the youth in the States? How did it happen? I think boarding schools are greatly responsible. Since Independence all schools are integrated because the Africans allow the Europeans and Asians to go to their schools. There are a few day schools in Nairobi, but many children

here go to British-style boarding schools where the better education seems to be available. The British send their children to
board when they are six or eight years old, which horrifies me. In
fact, I wasn't pleased about sending mine off at the ages of fifteen,
eleven and ten, but off they went to separate establishments:
clothes-conscious Rick, in short pleated pants and knee socks and
a wide tie when skinny ties were fashionable, to a secondary school
in Nairobi; Dancy to a girl's school just twenty miles from Nairobi;
and McDonnell to an outrageous place eighty miles north of Nairobi
in the middle of nowhere.

His school looked as if it should have had a chain across it with
a plaque reading, "Abraham Lincoln went to school here." Had
it been in America, it would have been condemned by both the
Health and Fire Departments a half century ago, but despite its
abandoned summer-camp-in-the-Maine-woods appearance, aca-
demically it is equal to the best schools in Europe—in fact, many
years before Jock had been accepted at Eton from this same school.
Someone said, "It's a school for boys, not for parents," and so it
was. I thought it was totally unacceptable, but McDonnell adored
it.

Some "swell things" about the school were: The school uniform
was a white (stained) shirt and khaki shorts and bush jacket. No
one ever told them to tuck their shirts into their pants—they just
hung down below their bush jackets. They had to bathe only twice
a week, but three others used the same water, which made it okay.
They slept outside on the verandah. Dogs wandered in and out of
classrooms. They carved their initials into the desks during class—
if they could find any room left to do so. They threw wadded paper at a dog or a friend instead of in a trash basket. The teacher
approved of all of the above and walked around after class with a
gin and tonic or scotch and water while the boys ate flying ants.
(The Africans eat them, too, insisting they are a great delicacy.
You pull the wings off, pop them into your mouth alive, and everyone says they taste just like butter.) So McDonnell ate live ants,
played cricket, rugby and squash; he gardened, and with the
school climbed Kilimanjaro at the age of twelve and threw up when

he got to the top. When the school would go to Nairobi for a swimming meet, they would take homing pigeons with them which they
would release after each event with the results tied to a foot. And
there he stayed, happy as that lark, for five years.

Dancy's school was more presentable, but I would have run
away—if anyone had been able to get me there in the first place. The
girls' uniforms were actually described on the clothing list as "nig-
ger brown" until a few years ago, even after Africans went to the
school. The uniform was a dreary one-piece jumper with a blouse
and a tie—a man's striped tie. And, on their heads they wore men's
straw hats. When she first came home from school with her hat on,
I thought she was in some kind of tap-dancing routine in a school
play, but it really was part of the uniform, and she didn't even seem
to mind. Like her brother McDonnell, she was interested in school
activities—sports, school plays, music, singing in the choir, even
the "Young Farmer's Club." The fact that none of their friends
drove, or dated, or wore fashionable or unfashionable clothes, or
smoked cigarettes much less grass, or wore make-up (because
it is not allowed in schools here until they are eighteen years old),
kept them from being preoccupied with these things.

Holidays happen three times a year here. The schools close for
six weeks at Christmas, four weeks at Easter and seven weeks in
the summer; so instead of one long summer holiday during which
time the children get so bored, not to mention how bored the parents get with them, there are three vacations of roughly six weeks
each year. This seems a much more satisfactory way to me—they
don't forget everything they have learned because the holidays are
not too long, nor do they have to spend weeks reviewing. In the
holidays the children were delighted to come home and get really
decent food—like peanut butter and jelly sandwiches, and they
were delighted to stay up to a really decent hour—like 9 P.M. Parents are wonderful and generous and lenient, and the school is the
bad guy, which I like much better than being the bad guy myself.
And just when they were beginning to suspect we parents weren't
really so marvelous after all, it was time for them to go back to rice
and demerits and lights out at 8:30 P.M.

Home is beautiful and luxurious, and free time is spent with fun-loving understanding parents in the evenings playing Monopoly or card games, or making up plays, or all singing with guitars, or showing old slides, or playing Password. Because we have no TV we'd create our own entertainment or just sit and talk for hours, and in this way they learned the art of conversation and the joy of communication long lost on American youth. They used to get furious when I said "They watch sunsets instead of TV sets," but now I think they are beginning to see the advantages.

They might not know who "That Girl" is, nor do they know they must be blonde to have all the fun, but they do know what it is like to be in a school which once had less than 1 per cent black and three years later had 90 per cent black. They know what being both a minority and a majority feels like. They have friends who are African, Swedish, British, Asian, French, Ethiopian, Greek, to say nothing of Muslim, Hindu, pagan, Catholic, Jewish, Protestant. They have friends who live in mud huts and friends whose parents are Ambassadors, and they know that what is *not* important in life is color or creed. Perhaps they don't know what is important yet, but knowing that those two things aren't, is more than a lot of people ever learn. Perhaps they haven't had as many experiences with drugs and sex and all the other youth syndromes in the rest of the world, but there is time enough for that, and when they do their minds will be familiar with the consequences and ready to cope.

My children learned strange things—what other peoples think and do, and that perhaps there are many rights in this world and not just our American standards and values, which might not necessarily fit everybody.

McDonnell's first encounter with death was in Africa when an old Masai we knew died. McDonnell asked what would happen to Rerema's body now? As he was a Masai, I told him they put it out for the hyenas. "Oh," was his only comment. A little later his grandmother in the States died, and realizing there were no hyenas in America he asked,

"What happens to Granny now?"

I told him they would put her body in a coffin and bury it.

"What's a coffin?" he asked.

"A wooden box."

"You mean they dig a hole in the ground and put it in, then cover it up? Ugh—that's *terrible*."

Interested, I asked, "Why?"

"It will take so long for the worms to get you. Mother, promise me when I die you'll put me out for the hyenas."

"All right," I agreed, "but why the hyenas?"

"Well, it's fast. And at least the hyenas get fed. Something good is done."

One's background certainly is exposed at times. In the States, our burial customs are inculcated in us and we accept them without flinching. But other nationalities don't. The British are appalled by our funeral parlors—Jock didn't even believe me when I told him some Americans are "laid out" for three days and that the coffin is open and everyone goes to see the corpse. He was much more shocked at that than I was about the dead being put out for the hyenas. In Kenya you are buried the day after you die, in an unopened pine box, without being embalmed. You can hold a funeral service at the church or grave side if you want, but to people here funeral parlors are outrageous, barbarian institutions. Recently I noted with satisfaction while reading the obituaries here that, "There will be no funeral, just plant a tree somewhere if you wish." I thought how very nice that was.

My children also learned how to travel halfway around the world alone at ten years old. Once Dancy left school early and came to the States with Jock and me, but McDonnell wouldn't leave his garden, or cricket stick, or whatever it was and insisted on staying at school through the last day. I told one of his masters that I thought he should not travel to the States alone, but should come with us. "A typical American mother—overprotecting her son," was his answer. Jock agreed with the school and assured me he himself was not only flying to England from Africa when it took four days in a "flying-boat" with stops in Khartoum and other exotic places when he was three months old, but that he was also making his own flight reservations. So, finally, I gave in and made all the arrangements for McDonnell's flight from Nairobi to New York with only one change in London. To pray a plane across Africa and then the Atlantic is just too long to pray, and I was very nervous about "mah baby" traveling all that distance alone, so as early as possible I called Pan Am to see if they had a Bruce on the passenger list on flight 662 from London? Yes, they did. I thanked the gods and went to Kennedy International three hours ahead of time in case there were tail winds which blew them in earlier. The plane landed right on time, and I watched every single passenger get out—but McDonnell was not on the plane. Where was he? He definitely was not on board—not even locked in the bathroom. He must have fallen out of the plane over the Atlantic. Pan Am staff dismissed that possibility, but they still looked worried. By this time it had been established that the "Bruce" on the plane was, unfortunately, the wrong Bruce. Where do you start to look for a ten-year-old in the world? Perhaps he had boarded the wrong plane and was going with a group tiger shooting in Nepal. We telephoned Jock's mother in Nairobi, and, yes, she had put him on East African Airways to London. That plane stopped in Athens, Rome, then London—he could have got off at any of those stops and made a wrong connection to almost any remote spot on the globe. The definition of a blotter is something to look for while the ink dries, and we made calls every place we could think of, which gave us something to do until McDonnell arrived in New York—which he did about three hours later. He merely strolled into the customs area with his guitar, whistling. I ran up to him and hugged him and shouted hysterically, "Where have you been?" He looked puzzled, "I've been in school in Africa, Mother," as if I had bumped into him by surprise in New York's airport and wondered where he had been for the last three months or so.

"I KNOW that. Where have you been the last three hours?"

"On a plane flying here," he answered, looking at me as though I were absolutely crazy.

"Which plane?"

"A big one, and the stewardess gave me lots of free Cokes."

"Which airline?"

"Oh, I don't know."

And do you know, that even today no one knows which airline? Everyone tried to find out. We had a letter of apology from Pan Am, but it was certainly not their fault. All McDonnell said was, "I got off the plane in some country and soon I couldn't see any of the people I got off the plane with, so I went up to everybody and no one could speak English. Finally, one man from Ireland said he spoke English, and I asked him if he knew how to get to New York, so he took me to a counter and they wrote on my ticket and told me which way to go."

So from what we could gather and piece together, McDonnell got off his plane in either Athens or Rome and it went on without him. He got his tickets transferred to the next flight to New York and couldn't have cared less. I wish I hadn't cared less.

Finally, they finished school here and went to Switzerland to get a little couth because, as we told them, "You ain't got no couth going to school in Africa." This was also a British school, or "ski resort masquerading as a school" would better describe it. Every day all students must ski between 1 and 4 P.M. (Can you take skiing for American college boards?) In one year they have learned to ski beautifully and speak French, which is more than I learned in all twelve years of public school in the States.

One of the main aims of their school in Switzerland was to teach "leadership." Expeditions were arranged for the boys to go up and down mountains for three days, to build fires and sleep outside, and all those things. Geneva and hitchhiking were strictly forbidden. One boy was the chosen leader of the group and he did all the commanding. After being on six or seven of these expeditions, McDonnell's turn to lead finally came.

Without hesitation he marched his group right off to Geneva to see the latest film on rock music, and after two fun-packed days he led his group in hitchhiking back to school. Unknown to him and his five happy lads, the Headmaster had passed them on the road. When they returned to school he called them in one by one and asked for details of their expedition.

What a marvelous way to find out who has a good imagination. How else can you really tell if a boy has élan or not?

I congratulated McDonnell for learning one of the main aims of the school so quickly and said how proud of him the school must be. They demoted him, which of course was fair, and he had to wash dishes for two months or something like that—but I am sure it was worth it. If you want to dance, you must pay the orchestra, and more often than not it is worth it.

Jock told me that one time at Eton when he was just sitting there conjugating his Latin verbs, the master, with his head still behind a newspaper and without looking up said, "Leslie-Melville, take a hundred lines," meaning copy out a hundred lines of Latin verse as a punishment.

"But, sir, I haven't done anything wrong," objected Jock.

"Take a hundred lines and don't argue."

"But, sir, it's unfair."

"Aha," cried the master, "if I teach you nothing else, but that life is often unfair, I will have succeeded in my task."

However, I must confess I don't take school very seriously. What more does anyone ever really learn—or retain at any rate —than reading and writing? At fifteen no one is ready for geometry —they are all ready for sex. No one actually learns anything until he wants to, and how many children do you think really want to learn the names of the rivers in Uraguay?

I must also confess that I have agreed, or perhaps even suggested on occasion, that instead of going back to school after "half term" (a weekend home in mid-term), the children fake being sick and plan a miraculous recovery in a few days' time, so we could sneak the extra days to go to the coast or somewhere.

Dancy felt the gods were angry with her one time for doing this because an unpleasant incident occurred. We were sitting at the coast enjoying our after-dinner coffee and waiting to go to the movies, when Dancy and McDonnell said they would walk ahead and save Rick and Jock and me good seats. It was chilly and Dancy needed a sweater, but she had only a pink one which didn't go with her dress. My brand-new pale-blue cashmere would have been perfect with her dress and her pink one would have been better with mine, so I told her to go ahead and wear my new one, "But if you spill anything on it, I'll kill you." Off they went down the beach.

In ten minutes we heard a screaming, howling noise which got louder and louder and closer and closer, and then we saw Dancy coming back into the house—totally covered with terrible-looking slime and smelling unbelievably awful. In the dark, she had fallen into a cesspool. It was being repaired and the cover had not been replaced. It was so slippery she couldn't climb out, so she asked McDonnell to give her a hand, which he started to do until she grabbed him, whereupon he let go hollering, "Ugh—DON'T GET IT ON ME!" Somehow she had clambered out by herself without any help from her brother. We threw her into a hot shower, and all the clothes, including the brand-new pale-blue cashmere sweater, we cast into the sea forever.

Speaking of things along these lines, our entire family is crazy about elephant dung. Driving through game parks Rick leans out of the car and puts his finger in elephant droppings along the road to see how long it had been since the elephant passed; if the dung is warm the elephant is close by and if cold, a long way off. This procedure prompted a friend to suggest, "Can't you use a thermometer?"

One day in Tsavo Park, where 22,000 elephant live I got out of our car to see if a famous herd of one thousand was on the horizon. It was not, but walking back to the car I saw some very old elephant dung in the road. Because it is like a ball of dry straw and not at all unpleasant, I picked it up—much to the astonishment of the children, who sat rigid in the back seat of the car with their mouths open—and walked threateningly towards them. She wouldn't pick it up—she wouldn't throw it at us—would she? Yes, she had to. I threw the large elephant dropping at them in the back seat of the car, and it smashed into bits all over them landing on their laps. Instinct told me to run quickly in the opposite direction, which I did, but I was laughing so hard I couldn't run very fast— and anyway there was nowhere to *go*. McDonnell was fast on my trail, and quickly caught me and rubbed the remaining elephant dung in my hair; and we laughed all the way back to Nairobi. You should have smelled the car! It is actually not a bad smell—different —but not bad. I washed my own hair because I didn't know what to tell the hairdresser.

A client of ours once packed a beautiful round elephant dropping in a cardboard box, and with an evil grin, despatched it to a friend in the States—C.O.D.

Our family laughs a lot together, which is the only way I know how to measure happiness. The arrival of report cards is usually an extremely amusing time—we read them aloud and laugh and laugh. McDonnell's usually win because he seems to have very witty teachers. The sacred studies report, "He sews not neither does he reap," which I mentioned before, was a nice one; then came his history report which claimed he seemed to be "having a little difficulty with history—since he cannot tell Napoleon III from Hitler."

His last English report was graded B and the teacher had written, "A very capable boy, but he does not let himself get involved. I am not sure what he considers important, but it is not English." Thank goodness for that—what a relief.

He often plays jokes on me. One day not long ago we had six house guests, four of whom were tiny children whose departure that night was something I was looking forward to with glee, because not only had I been organizing three meals a day for eleven people and doing all the other things required for house guests, but we were packing in preparation for a trip to the States, and it is difficult to move and entertain at the same time. The Rouses, our guests, were on a chartered flight run by a nice little crooked Asian man named Patel. I have talked to Mr. Patel at least twice a week for the last two years arranging cheap flights for us and our friends, so when he called that day I recognized his accent immediately and said,

"Oh, hello, Mr. Patel."

"I am having very bad news for you, Mrs. Melvin"—he never

gets my name right—"the flight tonight with your friends the Louses, is not going, is being canceled."

"Oh my God—you've got to be kidding."

"I am sorry, but what I'm telling you is true."

"Dear God. When does your next flight leave?" I asked, knowing our friends could not afford a commercial flight.

"Not for thirteen days."

Shattered, I started screaming and threatening to sue him, and then I heard him laugh, and I realized it was not Patel at all but McDonnell imitating him.

And because of his humor, when he writes to me, "Mother I love you and miss you, but I don't understand you," I can answer, "I understand you, but I don't love you or miss you," and we both laugh.

Yes, they write every week without fail. To get them to do this, you either frame them or use blackmail. To frame them, you write at the end of your letter, "I hope you can use this little check I've enclosed," and of course you don't enclose the check. They aren't so uncouth as to just write, "Where's the money?" They must write something first and then, "By the way, you forgot to enclose the check in that letter." To blackmail them you only send their weekly allowance when you get their letter—no ticket, no laundry. Both systems work well.

When they were all in primary schools in the States they always worried about my appearance, and before I came to the school play or a P.T.A. meeting or whatever, they wanted me to rent a mother's costume. But as they got older they began to enjoy having their mother the only one without a little hat with cherries and a veil, and the only one not in navy blue and pearls (ladies wear only navy blue and pearls in Baltimore). Instead I wore suede jeans, and I really think they wished I'd ride up on a motorcycle as well.

One time in the States, Dancy was helping me make hors d'oeuvres for a cocktail party. Neither of us was enjoying the tedious work, so I took a break to feed the cat. In doing so I said to her, "You know these people are going to drink so much tonight, they won't know if they are eating those smoked eels or this cat food."

"Let's find out," she said.

And so we put a tin of cat food in a pretty silver bowl with crackers surrounding it on a tray. We added no mayonnaise or seasoning, just a few parsley sprigs, and do you know the guests ate the entire bowl of cat food? When they'd ask me or Dancy,

"My, this is good—what is it?"

"Cat food," we'd answer. They'd laugh and comment on how witty we were, and continued eating the cat food until it was gone.

Another time we were in Florida's Everglades watching an American Indian wrestling an alligator and Dancy asked,

"Is the alligator drugged?"

Rick answered, "No, but the Indian is."

Dancy's finishing school in Switzerland (and I think they just about finished her) gave her an expensive aptitude test and found her ideally equipped to be a "Naval Officer." The fact that she gets violently seasick, can neither give nor take orders, and has no interest whatsoever in any of the armed forces doesn't seem to enter into it.

Why must every teen-ager be expected to know what he wants to do with his life—I still don't know what I'm going to be when I grow up.

I just hope my children know that life is too short to work at anything they do not truly enjoy. I hope they follow that drum beat, whether it is marching along with naval officers or stripping, and that they make sure that whatever they do pleases them and makes them joyous.

XIII
Addis in Wonderland

Just after I returned to Baltimore from my first trip to Ethiopia where I was a guest of the Emperor, His Imperial Majesty Haile Selassie, who had impressed me greatly, I was sitting at the dinner table one night talking about him saying Haile Selassie this, Haile Selassie that, and Haile Selassie the other thing, when the telephone rang for McDonnell, then eight years old. I heard him saying to his friend, "I can't talk to you right now because my mother just got back from Ethiopia—she's been over there with Harry Selaski."

If you ever go to Harry Selaski's country I'd advise you not to eat the food. If you eat your meals in hotels and restaurants, they will be perfectly fine; but I am speaking of undiluted Ethiopian food at an Ethiopian's house. I admit I am a mashed potato and gravy girl and the raw fish in Japan is hard for me to enjoy, and I don't even like going to Chinese restaurants in the States. So it is not surprising that I find Ethiopian food inedible. The second night in Ethiopia I was invited to the Ambassador's house for dinner along with some other Americans.

I had no idea what Ethiopians ate, and when the brass pitcher and bowl were brought into the living room for everyone to wash their hands, I thought it rather a quaint idea and was pleased at the good start. Next came a wicker basket which resembled a birdbath in size and shape, and this was placed in the center of the floor. Around it were placed stools, like milking stools, thus completing the dining table and chairs. It was then explained that Ethiopian men sit on the stools, and the women stand behind them and feed them with their fingers. However, since I was a Western woman, I was allowed to sit with the men.

The first food brought in was *injera*—a sponge-like substance which was placed in the basket just as a pie-crust would be placed in a pie pan. It was gray—it looked just like a gray sponge and it tasted just like gray sponge. Into this was poured a kind of stew called *wat.* I asked, "What's *wat?*" and was told, "Raw chicken and rancid butter!" I wished I hadn't asked. The procedure was to tear a piece of the sponge off with your fingers, and use it as a scoop for the *wat.* A friend there said it was the first time she had ever eaten the tablecloth.

Well, I managed wrapping the sponge around the *wat* but never before had I fed a man with my fingers, so I just shoved it gently into the Ambassador's mouth and it all ran down his chin and onto his tie. The next time I pushed the food so far down his throat he almost gagged. I was a total failure. Another philosophy I always adhere to is, "If at first you don't succeed, give up." So I decided he should feed me instead. I got one mouthful of that raw chicken and rancid butter and knew that swallowing was impossible. This was a terrible position to be in, because as guests in a foreign country, one wants to be polite and to show appreciation for their food.

After a few desperate minutes, I looked around at the editor of an American newspaper who was seated on my other side. His face is normally very lean and angular but at this moment his cheeks were puffed out in great swollen balls. He was storing his *injera* and *wat* like a chipmunk. He whispered, "Isn't this awful? What are we going to do?" I confessed, "I just can't swallow it, if I do, I'll throw up." "Go ahead," he said, "no one will notice the difference." *Tej,* a fermented honey, is drunk along with the *injera* and *wat,* and if you like the taste of sheep dip, you'll enjoy *tej.*

Later, when I returned to Ethiopia to produce a television documentary, I knew the TV crew would be invited to Ethiopian houses, but I didn't tell them about the food. The director of the show had asked what he should take to Ethiopia in the way of clothes, and I had told him only one suit was necessary in case we were invited out to dinner.

Sure enough, the first night there, we were invited to a Government minister's house for dinner, and just before we were ready to leave, the telephone in my room rang. It was the TV director saying in an irritated voice, "Betty, will you please come down to my room for a minute." It was a command rather than a request. When I got there, he was holding his gray flannel suit which he had just got back from the cleaners. "I sent it to the cleaners and they *washed* it." It looked like a suit for a Barbie doll. Thus his mood was not exactly all sunshine and lollipops when he arrived at the minister's for dinner in a suit he had managed to borrow from a giant, with the pants all baggy and the sleeves of the jacket rolled above his wrists.

Then dinner arrived. He sat on the stool, and a lovely Ethiopian lady stood behind him and fed him the first bite with her fingers. He held the *injera* and *wat* in his mouth a minute, paused, swallowed, and said nothing. The second bite came, and he merely held up his hand in protest and said, "No thank you, I'm driving."

However, aside from the *injera* and *wat* and the dry-cleaners, Ethiopia is thirteen months of joy. Don't forget the Julian calendar is still used there, so there are thirteen months in every year and you are seven years younger.

Ethiopia is certainly different from East Africa. The Ethiopians are different too—they don't even call themselves Africans—only Ethiopians. They have two thousand years of roots, culture, Coptic Christianity, and leadership, and can trace their ancestry back to the Queen of Sheba. It is an intriguing country, and Addis Ababa is a wonderfully idiotic city lying exactly half-way between New York and Tokyo. Who wouldn't want to visit magical-sounding places like Addis Ababa which means "Little Flower," and Gondar, Lalibala, Axum and Asmara?

Gondar is near the home of the Falashas—the black Ethiopians who are Jewish, display the star of David and speak recognizable Hebrew.

Way north of Addis is Lalibala, the underground city of thirteen monolithic churches hewn out of solid rock, which still has that rare historic quality that nothing has changed for a thousand years. When Jock and I flew from Lalibala in a converted wartime DC3, we had our suitcases weighed-in at the "airport"—a small thatched open-air hut with a scale outside on the ground. As we waited for the plane to land on the grass field, we saw that some goats were having their legs tied together and were being weighed-in on the same scale as our suitcases, tagged with the same tags and tossed on the baggage cart along with the suitcases. The goats flew with us all the way to Addis—they transport them alive to save refrigeration, slaughtering them after arrival.

Not too many years ago I said to my good friend Hapte Selassie, who is now Minister of Tourism and who was then busily opening Ethiopia for tourists, "Was Addis very primitive when your job started?" "It was prehistoric," he answered.

When I went with the TV director and cameramen to film our documentary on Ethiopia, we went way out into the wilds of the country among very primitive peoples indeed. They had seen few, if any, white men, and they could not speak English, so we really appreciated it when the Emperor gave us everything we needed, especially a little note written in Amharic which told the people not to kill us. We had heard lurid tales about how the Danakils, a primitive tribe in the area for which we were headed, still collect human testicles to take to their intended bride's father as part of the bride price. When the Danakils appeared over a nearby hill armed with their knives and guns, I was shoved forward with the note while the male members of the crew hid, clutching themselves. I tried to smile and managed to hand them the note. They looked at it, then at me, then at the hysterical men, then back at the note—and suddenly we realized they couldn't read. Terror. Just then a plane flew overhead, they looked up at it, said something, and departed in the opposite direction. I memorized their three words, and when we finally got back to Addis, I asked someone to translate what the phrase meant, certain it would be something like, "Big iron bird say white meat bad." But all they had said was, "It must be Thursday," a reference to the one and only flight of the week which passed overhead.

Once, with Hapte, I saw a group of people in sandals and beards way out in the bush.

"Are they the American Peace Corps?" I asked.

"Yes."

"What are they doing—teaching?"

"They are learning," he said, and I thought even if the Peace Corps never does a single thing for peoples of underdeveloped countries, the American volunteers will have learned a lot, which in itself is valuable.

When the Peace Corps first came to East Africa they painted hospitals for free—thus putting twenty-seven Africans out of a job. They quickly changed the approach and now they are teaching almost exclusively, both academic subjects and technical skills, and have, consequently, been of real value.

The Peace Corps volunteers always seem to be involved in some sort of drama, though. One was on trial for murdering his wife—he was acquitted because of insufficient evidence. Another was eaten by a crocodile after he had been warned not to swim in that particular lake. Another ignored the "Don't get out of your car rule" and got lost in the bush and was never found—taken by animals, probably. Yet another drowned—and so it goes. These things seem to happen very often to Peace Corps volunteers.

If a "volunteer" had been invited along on a helicopter trip Jock and I took, I think superstition would have forced me to decline. I was nervous enough about flying in a helicopter and landing places no man—black or white—had ever stood before, and I am incident-prone enough myself without a Jonah on board. Where we were going was totally inaccessible. There were no roads or landing strips nearby—nothing. The only other helicopter in East Africa had just crashed, which meant there was no back-up or rescue for us had the machine decided not to start when we were ready to leave.

At one point on the trip we came down in the middle of about a square mile of sand dunes which lay in the center of a desert of lava rock and stunted bush, miles from water. No African, for the reason that they are absolutely logical about these things, would walk so far from water to see totally inhospitable sand dunes, and even if he did, he would never climb and slide for hour after hour to reach the middle. What would be the point? Since we knew we were the first helicopter in the area, it was fair to deduce that we were the first human beings to stand atop our particular dune.

I could just see us stuck in the desert in northern Kenya with CARE packages being dropped to us as we became international incidents. I went on the trip because I wanted to get film of primitive peoples I had yet to see. As far as the filming went, it was a total failure because the minute the people heard or saw the helicopter they were confused and ran—never to come anywhere near us. They had seen planes flying overhead but never landing, and certainly nothing as strange as a giant spider making dreadful noises and descending. But, in retrospect, anyway, I did enjoy playing Neil Armstrong and standing in places no one has ever stood before.

Speaking of exotic places like Addis Ababa and the Northern Frontier Province of Kenya, last year Jock and I went on a trip to various countries south of Kenya. From Mozambique we rented a car so that we could drive through Swaziland.

The entire country has a smaller population than Nairobi, and this is not hard to believe because we didn't see one animal or person for the first fifty miles. Around every corner we expected to see tribal warfare or a white rhino at least—after all, here we were in Tarzan's Africa, we imagined, like so many of our safari-ers must imagine Kenya. Finally, we did turn that corner and beheld a shocking sight.

In a beautiful and remote African valley there stuck out the ultimate in sore thumbs—a neon sign with a familiar-looking star design on top flashing HOLIDAY INN, and on the marquee was the inscription for that day, "Congratulations, Danny and Ida, on

Thirty Years of Happiness." An identical structure to every Holiday Inn in the States, it had all the details right down to the fake coat of arms in the dining room. There were white plastic palm trees, one-armed bandits, a gambling casino—the entire place was more plastic than Reno. Putting on my plastic smile I said to the manager,

"This is a dreadful place. Can you imagine saving all your life to come to Africa and finding a Holiday Inn identical to the one right around the corner from you in Des Moines?"

He said, "Well, lady, you're only the fourth person out of thousands who hasn't liked it."

Probably the reason that I reacted so violently is that in East Africa they have learned to construct lodges and hotels that blend perfectly with their background—have an African feeling, yet are as modern as tomorrow.

We went on to Durban which was worse—unless you crave Atlantic City's bumper cars, cotton candy and tattooed people wearing hats which say, "Kiss Me Baby." And then I should think it would be easier to get to Atlantic City, and certainly more pleasant, than South Africa, "The Cruel Paradise" as our good friend, Quentin Crewe, describes it—but we won't go into that. That's another book. We are strongly biased that safaris should be done in East Africa and a few other countries such as Ethiopia and Botswana.

XIV
Do You Speak Frangipani?

When Jock and I travel our luggage usually consists of about forty-seven suitcases (with broken zippers and tied together with rope) and a few chic pieces—like A & P paper bags and plastic ones which say "Schrafft's." All of which we purposely abandon in some obvious spot in the first airport we're in. Then we travel around uncluttered for a week or so and have no waiting in baggage areas for luggage to arrive, no sorting of it, no lugging it around, no looking for porters or tipping them, and above all no decisions as to what to wear. At the formal dinner parties we just say, "Sorry about the dried spinach on my blue jeans, but our luggage was lost," and everyone not only forgives our comfortable but slovenly attire, but sympathizes. The luggage always catches up with us at our final destination because we ensure that it is clearly labeled. But meanwhile we've had an unencumbered week's traveling.

However, I hope no one follows this sound advice, because when Jock and I meet our safari-ers at Nairobi's airport we clap if more than half of them still have their luggage. Nobody made us go into the safari business. It is just that human beings do have problems, and when you deal with three thousand people a year you have at least 1,500 problems, just by the law of averages.

Each time we meet a group we wait eagerly to see what abominable problem will be our little challenge for the day.

After a twenty-two hour flight in the prenatal position, our clients arrive looking more like patients who have also been anesthetized with food by the airlines so that they won't notice how long the flight is. (We once made safari arrangements for fifteen *Mad* magazine writers and cartoonists, and when they arrived one of them said the flight was so long he asked the stewardess if the mail had been delivered yet.)

Although we have never lost anyone on safari in East Africa, we did have a group coming to us from the States via the Far East, and a couple of days before they were due to arrive, we received the following cable from the escort, "Lost one member of group drowned in spa bath in Japan."

Another time an entire group was lost, but only temporarily. They had stopped at Luxor on the Nile and were due to leave on Middle Orient Airways, as I shall fictitiously call them so that you can figure out who they are and yet I won't be sued. Their representative went up to our tour leader, whom we call a "courier" or "escort" because it sounds fancier, and said, "You'll have to bump three of your people" (which only means asking them to get off the plane—in case you've never had the pleasure of learning airline dialogue).

Our courier said, "Not me, buddy." He knew the dialogue and continued—"We've had these reservations confirmed for one year. We all have our problems and if you're overbooked, that's yours."

The representative stalked off, only to return again in another hour saying, "I'm sorry, but you'll HAVE to bump three of your people. No one else will get off."

Our courier knew his rights and stuck to them, "Not my group."

Again, the Middle Orient rep stomped off, and ten minutes later they called the flight which by then had been delayed two and a half hours. Do you know who they had bumped? The co-pilot, the navigator, and one stewardess! They overshot the next stop by 150 miles, landed on some desert airstrip, and the passengers had to be bussed back to their correct destination. Moral of Story: next time Middle Orient asks you to get off, get off.

Because lots of our safari-ers are over eighty years old, we have had a few with mild strokes and heart attacks. They go into Nairobi Hospital and our problem is to get them to leave when they are well enough to be discharged. They like the hospital better than the Nairobi hotels—"It's cheaper and the food is better." The same sometimes happens to jobless Africans in jail. They love it and hate to leave. After all, they get a free meal every day and all their friends are there to talk to, and there is time to sit in the sun. No wonder in colonial days jail was sometimes affectionately known as "Hoteli ya Kingi Georgei" (King George's Hotel) and the "guests" were reluctant to leave.

Nairobi Hospital is the only hospital where I have gone to visit patients and found that they were out—not discharged, just out. You can leave your room if you feel well enough and go to town for cocktails or dinner or the movies, or go to the game park or shopping any time you feel like it.

Professional hunters and other men in the safari business have invented a legend that American women, all sex maniacs, crave their bodies. I don't believe it. Just because that single blonde arriving from Chicago finagled Jock to the bar at the first opportunity and, as he poured the soda into her scotch asking, "Say when," and she replied, "Right after this drink," I don't believe it. And just because a seventy-eight-year-old lady lured him into her room on some pretext, hauled off her dress (truly—I swear it) and standing there looking like a turtle in a black boned corset, nudged him and said, "How about a little loving . . ." No, I don't believe it, not a word of it. However, Rick does. After taking quite a few safaris himself, he is thinking of opening his own safari company and calling it "Gigolo Tours and Safaris."

I must say that dealing with so many people has made my estimation of humanity go up. And right now, I'd like to say that Americans are the *best* nationality of travelers East Africa gets. The ugly American is almost non-existent. Out of say five thousand people we have had only two or three swines. Good batting average. You will say I am prejudiced, and I am. Americans are my favorite people.

After living away from them for so long, I see they have many more good qualities than bad, as indeed does America. But Jock, who half expected the ugly Americans he had seen in Europe some years back, is also the first to say that Americans are the best tourists. Although Burroughs, who created Tarzan, never came to Africa, everybody else seems to now. We have taken hundreds of people on safari, mostly Americans, and they include lawyers, doctors, businessmen, retired couples, school teachers, homosexuals, shoe salesmen, widows and Catholic priests—in fact, anyone from five to eighty-five. Most people who come on safari have one thing in common: They may be rich, they may be poor, old, young, educated or illiterate, but they are all travelers—certainly better traveled than we are, and by the time they reach East Africa they have acquired sensitivities that make them tactful and polite in other people's countries.

People on safari do present problems at times. We had one old man who kept taking all his clothes off and appearing nude from elevators in hotel lobbies and again at the bar at Treetops. He wasn't a dirty old indecent exposer, he was merely senile and forgot to put his clothes on. The others in the group liked him and although the escort has the right to return anybody's money and send him home, the group got together and agreed they would take turns watching him, making sure he was dressed before he appeared in public, and they did.

My ex-mother-in-law, on a visit from Baltimore said, "My, there certainly are a lot of colored people around here," and we have had the odd bigot say, in a loud voice in a hotel dining room filled with Africans, many of whom were probably college graduates, "Yur niggers don't seem to be as bad as our niggers." We have also had a few Southerners say they didn't mind "these nigras" as long as they stayed in their place. The huge majority of Americans, however, are kind, generous, interested in learning and anxious to please or help, not to offend.

Perhaps Africa awes people too. Those we meet at the airport are different people when they leave. They have relaxed—they couldn't get a Dow Jones average or even a newspaper if they tried, but the curious thing is they don't mind the lack after a few hours in the bush. No one knows what day it is and no one cares. Your mind is occupied with looking for and finding the game, and perhaps photographing it, so there is no vacuum for a business thought to slip in as there might be if you just lay on a beach where you could always find something to worry about if you delved deeply enough. On safari your greatest concern is whether you are going to find a leopard that day—which is not only important, it is earnest, if you accept the definition of "earnest" as "taking seriously that which has no serious side."

When you do find the animals it *is* absorbing and yet you are free of responsibilities—you don't have to teach them to read or write or keep their city clean, and we Americans have so many responsibilities, or at least think we should, that safari could well be the first time in years you have felt free.

At the zoo, man can still imagine he is important, but in the bush you are the only one in captivity and you begin to realize your insignificance. (One of my favorite cartoons shows a timid little man and his overbearing wife standing at a viewing point surveying a scene of spectacular grandeur, and the wife is saying, "It's not just a feeling George—you *are* inferior.") You begin to sense the triviality of your getting that third TV set for the bathroom in the club cellar, and even if it becomes important again when you return home and re-enter the rat race, it is nice to have had two weeks when you didn't care.

And something might rub off. Perhaps the next time you are trying to understand your long-haired son who doesn't want to run your fire-engine factory because he can't think of a reason why he should work at something he doesn't like for things he doesn't desire in the first place, you'll remember that fleeting moment when tears filled your heart at the beauty and the miracle of the giraffe just standing in a sunset—when you wondered what else could you possibly want in this world and how presumptuous it is to ask for more.

Once we overheard one of our clients trying to question a young Masai tribesman who was standing there in his finery, leaning on his spear. We interpreted for him.

"Do you ever work?"

"No," said the Masai.

"Why don't you get a job?"

"Why?" asked the Masai.

"Because you could make some money and soon you'd be able to retire and do exactly what you want."

"That's what I'm doing now."

The client said, "By God, he's right."

Although we have no such marvelous place as Intercourse, Pennsylvania, from where you can send postcards on which you have written, "We're in the middle of Intercourse," we do have Treetops. Treetops is the famous hotel in a tree in the middle of the Aberdare Forest where all the animals come to drink from the water hole below the tree house. They cannot see you because you are above them, and they cannot smell you either, so you can admire them without their being aware of you. In the bush, the animals are aware of you in your car and therefore beware of you, but at Treetops you can observe them relaxed and undetected. Treetops has many imitations, one of which is Secret Valley, which is said to be so secret even the animals can't find it. However, this is a misleading and unfair label, because Secret Valley offers something which no other place in East Africa will guarantee—leopard. Bait is put in a nearby tree at eye level to the visitor hidden in the tree house, and when the leopard come there is a perfect opportunity to photograph them in the soft floodlight.

Treetops is well known, not only because it is unique, but also because it was here, as the British are so fond of saying, that "Queen Elizabeth went up the tree a Princess, and came down the tree a Queen." Her father died in England the night she spent at Treetops. To go there you must be accompanied by a professional hunter, and when you have reached the tree house, you climb a wooden staircase which is then pulled up behind you and there at your hotel in a tree you spend the night. There are small bedrooms with branches from the huge fig trees coming through your room and upon which you can hang your clothes. There are no private baths, but on each floor there are nice ladies' and mens' rooms with flushing loos. Inside there is a sign "No one can see you except the monkeys," and you do feel silly with the baboons watching. Sometimes they get into the dining room or bar. Very often on the open roof where tea is served, a baboon will grab someone's sunglasses or camera and run off with it. During the afternoon, you see waterbuck, forest pig, bushbuck and other smaller game; and as night falls buffalo, rhino and elephant come to the water hole. If you are lucky, you may see all three together, perhaps ten rhino, an elephant herd of a hundred or more, and buffalo in even greater numbers. Treetops is excellent theater. It used to be open only when there was a full moon, but an artificial moon in the shape of soft floodlighting was tried and the animals didn't notice the difference, so now it is open every night of the year.

Some say Treetops is a "fake," that it is contrived, and that the animals are kept in a corral and let out each hour or so. This simply is not true. I have been there too many times wishing there were a corral because no animals obliged. It is purely a matter of luck. It would be impossible to capture and control the wild animals anyway. They *are* wild. In fact, once, on the way to the tree, an elephant charged the group, and the hunter shot it just a few feet away from an elderly visitor. When Princess Elizabeth visited Treetops, a herd of elephant appeared as she walked up to the tree house, and she had to climb a tree and stay there for hours until the elephant left. They said if she ran her country with the same coolness with which she faced the elephant, she would be a wonderful Queen.

One of the many times Jock and I were going to Treetops the hunter was explaining to his new group of tourists that each tree, on the short walk from the Land-Rover through the forest to the tree house, had a ladder, and that if he blew his whistle once, it meant there was a rhino about and everyone must climb ten feet up one of the ladders. (These have now been replaced by little stockades in which to hide.) If he blew it twice it meant an elephant, and everyone must climb to eighteen feet. One elderly lady said, "My dear sir, I couldn't possibly climb that ladder," and he answered, "Madam, you'll be surprised how fast you learn when you hear the whistle."

Until recently Treetops has been the only place of its kind in the Aberdare forest. Now, a few miles from it on the edge of a glade The Ark has been built—it looks something like Noah's Ark. It is operated on the same principle as Treetops in that you must be installed by mid-afternoon when the drawbridge is pulled up and there you stay until next morning.

Instead of the rustic outdoor charm of Treetops there is a warm glass-fronted viewing room (often welcome in this cold and misty forest), leather armchairs and a crackling fire. Every time we have been there, in addition to all the other animals, we have seen bongo (no, not a small African drum but a beautiful and elusive antelope). Jock, who grew up in the Aberdares, had never seen one in his life before.

One of my favorite things about The Ark is a kind of dungeon into which half a dozen people at a time can quietly descend narrow steps. Peeping out of open stone slits you find yourself on eyeball level with, and only a couple of paces from, whatever animals happen to be at the water hole. You are completely safe, but it is a tense and exhilarating experience to be able to count the eyelashes of an elephant or to smell the hot breath of a buffalo.

A few years ago Dan Bruce took McDonnell on safari. They were sharing a banda (a small hut-type accommodation) and in the middle of the night McDonnell, about ten years old at the time, got up to go into the bathroom, and when he returned only half awake to the dark room, he climbed into the wrong bed—the one where his father was asleep. The mosquito net was down, and as he pulled it aside he felt something in the bed which he took for a baboon that he supposed had climbed in while he had been in the bathroom. Scared to death he started hollering and swinging his fists. Meanwhile, Dan, who was sleeping soundly, felt this lion climbing into his bed, and he started fighting and yelling too. Every one in the nearby bandas was awakened by the commotion and went running to find out who was being eaten alive.

Another night on safari, we arrived with a family at our tent camp to be told that we were one tent short. A twenty-year-old son who was six feet four kindly volunteered to sleep in the same tent with his parents. We asked for a cot to be brought to the tent for him. In a few minutes two servants arrived carrying a baby's crib about three feet long with high sides. What Americans call a crib—a little bed for a baby—is called a "cot" by the British. A camp bed is the word they use exclusively for what Americans refer to as an army cot.

Although you are out in the bush all day long, you rough it in comfort and every night you get back to a hot bath and a cold drink. Most nights you are in a lodge—an oasis in the middle of Africa, maybe two hundred miles in all directions from anything, even a gas station. The lodges generate their own electricity and grow their own food or fly it in. One night out of fifteen you may be in a hotel in Arusha or some such town, and then it is nice to be able to have your hair mucked out in a beauty shop, even if the hotel there has all the charm of Early Airport Transit Lounge and the dining room can double for a gymnasium.

But most people are pleasantly surprised by the comfort in the bush, and they enjoy one night "under canvas" if only in retrospect. The tents, usually in permanent camping sites, stand on concrete platforms and have canvas floors stitched to the sides which keep the awful awfuls out. You have a loo, sort of, and whenever you want, the camp staff will fill a bucket of hot water which is rigged in your private little canvas shower stall outside behind your tent, and by pulling a chain the water sprinkles all over you, like a watering can. As you shower you can gaze at the falling stars. You get into bed, and after zipping yourself in, you listen to the lion roar. You may even feel your tent nudged from the outside as a hyena passes by. This gives a real "African flavor" to your safari and is enjoyed by everyone—except my sister, Evelyn Ireland.

She is the worst advertisement for safaris in the whole world. A gem she is, and a long-suffering one too, to put up so cheerfully with Jock and me, and frequently the children, each year when we all just move in with her in Baltimore. We insisted that she should have a summer of retribution—to repay her for all her generous kindnesses—so two years ago we invited her for her first trip to Africa, to stay with us and go on safari. Evelyn had always said she would love to see our house and stay with us, but she didn't want to go out to see "all those wild animals." However, we knew she would be overcome by the magnificence of it all and dragged her to a game park, reluctant but smiling as is her wont. She was overcome all right. "There's an elephant," Jock shouted with glee, and as we turned to look at her reaction, we saw her crouched down in the back seat with her bush jacket *over* her head and there she stayed, spending what she described as the worst day and night of her entire life. She says she took two safaris that day—her first and her last. If it hadn't been for her son and daughter, Dick and Jeanne, who were also along and who renewed our certainty that this really was fun, Jock and I would have quit the safari business forever right then and there.

Africans in remote places always stare at you, and I like it because sometimes I enjoy staring, too, even though my mother told me not to. Here people sit around and stare at each other forever and no one feels uncomfortable.

We had one safari-er who, in a very remote market place on the way to Mount Kilimanjaro, grew amused with the Africans' staring at him. Without a word, he bought a banana, peeled it carefully, and when he was sure everyone was watching, he put it in his ear, and chewed. Later on that day Jock ran over a guinea fowl by mistake and commented, "I hit us our supper," and our American friend asked, "Couldn't you hit me a hamburger?" I wondered if he knew potatoes would take twenty-three hours to cook when he got near the top of Kilimanjaro? At that altitude, 19,340 feet, you can hold your finger in boiling water and it just feels nice and warm.

Mount Kilimanjaro is the largest lump of land in the world; all other high mountains are part of a range, but Kilimanjaro rises in one majestic sweep from the golden plains and stands alone crowned with snow. Yet this is the only snow the Africans ever see—no wonder they think God lives there. Kilimanjaro used to be in Kenya, but Queen Victoria gave it to Kaiser Wilhelm for a birthday present, and even today it still remains part of Tanzania. If you look at a map you will see a great chunk cut from the Kenya border to include "Kili" in Tanzania.

The youngest person ever to get to the top of Kili was an eleven year old. McDonnell reached the top at twelve, and the only other member of our family who can claim the fame of having reached the summit is Jock. The rest of us would never even consider trying. Eighty per cent of the people who try cannot make it. It has nothing to do with being fit, it has only to do with altitude sickness —which affects some and not others. I have *driven* up to 14,000 feet and I am very proud of that. Jock went up before we were married and he says, "A strange thing happened on the way to Kilimanjaro." He and his party were cheerful and considerate for the first two days and everyone enjoyed not only the climb but each other's company as well. At about 16,000 feet, however, they became extremely truculent and short with one another, would only make enough cocoa for themselves and no one else, and would say things like, "*I* was going to put *my* sleeping bag there." This intolerance lasted until after they reached the top and got down below 16,000 feet again—two and a half days later—when once more they became a companionable and civilized group.

In Addis Ababa, which is over 8,000 feet high, a play ran for years called, "Blame It On the Altitude," and I am always happy to blame my grouchiness on the altitude if I can find no other means of justifying it. Also, at a high altitude you feel your drinks much more than at sea level. On my first trip to Ethiopia with the U. S. press everyone had only one or two drinks at an elegant reception given to us by the Emperor and got falling down drunk.

One well-known TV personality had to be given oxygen, so bad was her condition. No one could make dinner—it was all very embarrassing, so it is also nice to be able to blame getting drunk on the altitude instead of your own overindulgence. (Who was it who said he'd rather be a drunk than an alcoholic because at least he wouldn't have to go to meetings?)

Anyway, our client (who, incidently, owned two dogs—named "Hey You" and "You Too") went on to attempt Kilimanjaro, while Jock and I waited. The client was a boot fetishist. Well, perhaps not to the extent of getting sexually excited about footwear, but he was certainly preoccupied with his mountain-climbing boots. He had sent for them six weeks earlier from Neiman-Marcus, but had returned them and acquired a different kind from Abercrombie & Fitch. Each weekend thereafter he had marched around Philadelphia to break them in. When he arrived in Nairobi, the first thing he did was to take us up to his hotel room to admire the boots. He had by now convinced himself that the mountain could be conquered by fine boots—everything else was secondary. Five days later he returned, dispirited and understandably disappointed, having failed to make the summit. However, it wasn't until he had had a drink or two that the extent of his bitterness emerged. It seems that his African porter-guide had not only strode ahead, though heavily laden, but had made it easily—in bare feet.

We once took twenty-six members of one family on safari. They were all brothers and sisters and cousins and grandmothers and aunts and uncles, and Jock said if twenty-six members of his family went on safari, he'd pay to stay home. They were all athletic types from Milwaukee and used to swimming in very cold water, which no one here would dream of. Where the Atlantic joins the Pacific near the Cape of Good Hope in South Africa, they all decided to swim, to the courier's astonishment. The fact that no one ever swims there at that particular time of year because of the cold and the fact that none of them had bathing-suits didn't matter at all. They dived in in underwear, raincoats, or trousers and shirts. They were on their way to the airport and arrived dripping wet to board the plane. All the other passengers thought they had been shipwrecked.

We also had a Roman Catholic Bishop on safari who traveled incognito—he came as just plain old "Joe Green." I don't blame him; it must be terrible trying to have a vacation, with all the Catholics kissing your ring and wanting to confess and all the Protestants looking at you funny.

When we took three priests on safari we had dinner with some other Roman Catholic priests in Tanzania, who told us a very funny story about the night when they all administered last rites to one another. It seems that one of them had discovered some mushrooms in the forest and they had all eaten them for dinner. Some were left over and they gave them to the dog. Half an hour later the cook came running in to say that the dog had died outside. The priests were miles from any doctor and resigned themselves, after a few moments of panic, to the fact that they were all going to die of toadstool poisoning, so they set about making their peace with the Lord. They sat up all night waiting to die, but other than feeling sleepy nothing happened at all. In the morning they learnt from the cook that the dog had indeed died—but as a result of being run over by a passing truck—not from eating poisonous mushrooms.

Myles Burton, our large, cheerful and very humorous English friend, ran a safari business here for a German company. He not only speaks German and French and Spanish, but is a brilliant mimic and can give perfect imitations of other nationalities speaking English. In fact, Jack Paar once interviewed him on the slopes of Mount Kilimanjaro for one of his television specials, and Myles imitated various clients from different countries he has had on safari.

One of the stories which he once told me, and which I have always remembered, is about the obedience of Germans in groups provided one barks orders and treats the safari as a military exercise. Polite requests to board the vehicles have little effect, according to Myles. He used to line up the group tour members outside the hotel and count them off, "Achtung, you, you and you in bus number one. Schnell! We leave in one and a half minutes. You in the blue coat and you two ladies, bus number two," and so on until they were all packed in. He would then walk down the line of minibuses, poking his head into each one and giving final orders about what to do upon arrival at the next place. Once, as he reached the rear bus, a lady held up her hand and said, "Herr Burton, please may I ask question?" "Of course," said Myles. "Vould it be permitted if I am allowed to ride mit my husband on the return trip? He is in bus number vun."

At the start of one of our first safaris we were sitting in the Thorn Tree with a few of our American safari-ers and some local friends. One of the visitors asked,

"What language is spoken in East Africa?"

A British friend answered, "Swahili."

A few minutes later the visitor inquired,

"What flower is that?"

"Frangipani," we answered.

Then he said to one of the Kenyans,

"I can't wait to see those kangaroos in the jungle. We're going out in the brush today." When all he got in response was a pained expression, he asked, "Do you speak Frangipani, too?"

In the same group were two ladies traveling together; one of whom wore a fake leopard-skin jump suit (I was afraid someone would shoot her) and the other a pith helmet with butterflies and autographs on it. I was embarrassed, and my Kenya friends' eyebrows went up and down as they looked and listened in amazement.

To divert for a moment, I once carelessly left a suitcase upcountry at a friend's house, and just as I told you about leaving luggage, it showed up in Nairobi a few days later. It had been flown down in a small plane and I was to pick it up at the civil airport. The African there had been told an American would collect it, and to make sure he had the right person before handing over the suitcase, he asked me when I arrived, "Are you of the American tribe?" "Yes," I answered and thought how true it was. Perhaps because I *am* of the American tribe, I felt responsible for the mistakes our safari-ers were unknowingly making, so with Jock I sat down and together we wrote the following "Tenthold Hints or Minding Your Manners on Safari." If people want to wear two watches on safari—one with Dallas time and one with local time—fine. If they want to take "Plant Tabs" for warding off Bubonic Plague—fine, that, too, is a personal choice. But so many Americans didn't know what to wear, and what not to say, and how could they? How many Africans know who Martha Washington is and what a BLT on toast is? I've had Kenyans say to me after I've announced, "Today is the Fourth of July"—"Oh, that's the day you Americans eat pumpkin pie isn't it?" When we start taking them on safari in America, I'll write a book of hints for them, too.

XV
Tenthold Hints or Minding Your Manners on Safari

Since Emily Post never wrote a book of etiquette for Africa, we decided we had to because, out of ignorance, visitors frequently take appalling risks with animals or unwittingly cause offense to people. Here, then, are a few tips on manners and behavior.

1. DO NOT FEED THE BEARS—This will not be difficult because there aren't any. However, under no circumstances attempt to offer food or to touch wild animals, no matter how tame they may appear to be. In the bush there is no such thing as a tame animal—some are tolerant, but they are never tame. Dustbin Nelly and her two daughters, a famous elephant trio, are daily visitors to the Lodge at Murchison Falls. A tourist once offered one of them a bun and got away with it, but the danger is that the next tourist may be killed for not offering a bun.

2. DO NOT COMPLAIN BECAUSE YOU HAVEN'T SEEN A TIGER—You won't. There are no tigers in Africa; they are all in India.

3. DO NOT ASK WHERE THE WATER BUFFALO ARE —They are all in India with the tigers. We have Cape Buf-

falo referred to as just plain "buffalo," unless you want to
be very In, and then you say "buff." Other popular animal
vocabulary concerns collective nouns. There is a "pride of
lion," a "troop of baboon," a "pack of hyena or wild dog,"
a "colony of ants," a "herd of elephant" and a "herd of
buffalo, zebra, antelope" and so on. (It is not a "herd" of
birds, but a "flight of duck," a "gaggle of geese," a "flock
of starlings.") If you are uncertain, remember you can always get out of it by saying, "Look at all those giraffe," or
by employing the numerical exactitude dodge, "I saw eight
hundred and thirty-seven wildebeeste."

4. DO NOT GET OUT OF YOUR CAR—Occasionally a
   little notice will tell you that with caution you may proceed
   to an observation point on foot. Otherwise, stay in the car.
   The animals have accepted vehicles as merely other harmless animals in the bush and do not seem to associate them
   with humans, but they instantly become fierce or nervous
   if you alight.

5. DO NOT HOOT—This means do not blow your horn at
   the animals. We once had some Texans on safari and were
   hemmed in front and rear by a herd of elephant on the road
   in Murchison Park. One of the Texans became impatient
   after we had waited quietly for an hour, and he suggested
   we blow the horn to move the elephant off the road. Naturally, we refused to do this, and he thought we were being
   overcautious. The only thing to be done was to sit it out,
   and eventually the elephant did move off the road, allowing
   us to return to the lodge. A few months later we saw a photograph in a newspaper of an elephant with its tusks right
   through the windows of a Volkswagen and out the other
   side, holding the car twelve feet up in the air. The caption
   read, "They blew their horn at this elephant in Murchison
   Park." The photograph had been taken by someone in the
   car behind just before the elephant tossed the Volkswagen

into the bushes. Fortunately no one was hurt. "The Elephant Have the Right of Way" signs mean exactly what
they say.

6. DO NOT WORRY ABOUT SNAKES—We'll be willing to
   bet quite heavily you won't even see one, let alone a scorpion. Indeed, there are very few insects and nasty reptiles
   about.

7. DO NOT WEAR A PITH HELMET—This is about as
   chic as tailfins on an automobile.

8. DO NOT SHAVE IN THE TEA—A dreadful custom in
   East Africa is early morning tea. It is automatically brought
   to you at 6:30 A.M. every morning in the lodges. When
   one of our safari-ers asked on the first day of his trip about
   shaving facilities in tents, we told him hot water would be
   brought to him in the morning, but we forgot to mention
   that morning tea comes first. When he got his tea he shaved
   in it. It never occurred to him to drink it, but this is really
   what you are supposed to do.

9. DO NOT REFER TO AFRICANS AS "NATIVES"—
   Though we may refer to ourselves as natives of America
   or Sweden or whatever, the word in Africa has somehow
   fallen into disrepute and has insulting connotations. Other
   words to avoid are "boy," "colored people," "blacks," "Ne-
   groes," etc. (especially the etc.). The word to use, and the
   ONLY word when referring to the indigenous people is
   "African." This is extremely important. When hailing a
   servant say, "waiter" or "steward" or "porter."

10. DO NOT PHOTOGRAPH AFRICANS WITHOUT
    THEIR CONSENT—Some primitive Africans still believe
    that their soul goes into the "little black box" (camera),
    and the fact that you are trying to capture their image, to

them means you are trying to capture their soul. Therefore, it is important to them not to be photographed. Despite our repeated warnings, one of our safari-ers photographed a Masai moran (warrior) who had already refused to have his picture taken, so the Masai threw his spear at the camera. Fortunately the car was in motion and nobody was injured, but our sympathies were certainly with the Masai, knowing how strongly he felt. However, the sight of money can often have an extraordinary effect in solving the concern they feel about the capture of their souls. It is perfectly in order to bargain with them about money, and if you pay more than four shillings (fifty-six cents) you are being taken. Others, and this includes Asians, have no superstitions about their souls, but just don't like being photographed for the same reason we would not like an unknown African visitor in the United States to photograph us doing our weekly shopping in the Food Fair—even for fifty-six cents. However, many Africans love pictures of themselves and a Polaroid shot produced on the spot as a gift cannot only delight them but can aid you in obtaining many more pictures for yourself. To save film, it is perfectly acceptable to group a few Africans together, and they will not in the least mind carefully tearing the photo to shreds so that each can have a scrap with his own picture on it. Forget the trinkets, beads and mirrors—cash is the thing in Africa in the 1970s.

11. DO NOT BE AFRAID OF AFRICANS—Some may still be primitive but never savage. Someone once referred to the primitive Africans as a "Happy race of children." They are gentle, friendly people who would help you if you broke down or needed assistance. It is much safer to walk through an African village alone at night than down Forty-second Street in New York. Assault, rape and senseless crime are virtually unknown, though a certain amount of burglary and

pilfering goes on in the cities and recently a number of daring armed bank robberies.

12. DO NOT BE EMBARRASSED BY THE SIGHT OF TWO MEN HOLDING HANDS—Both Africans and Asians do this as a gesture of true friendship. There is nothing "funny" about them. (However, do not express your friendship towards your Hunter in this manner.)

13. DO NOT CALL YOUR WHITE HUNTER A WHITE HUNTER—In the old days a white hunter was a white man who arranged everything and took you out to shoot big game. Then Indians started doing the same thing, and in recent years Africans too. All hunters now are "Professional Hunters." This not only takes care of the fact that your hunter may be black or brown, but rightly brings in the all-important word "professional." Only licensed Professional Hunters are permitted to take clients hunting, and to become such a hunter a period of apprenticeship under another hunter is required, as well as completion of a written exam. If a man is a Professional Hunter, it is only because his peers and the Game Department agree that he qualifies. Any malpractice means the withdrawal of his license.

14. DO NOT GO TO A CRICKET MATCH—You'll die of boredom.

15. DO NOT SAY UP FOR UP OR DOWN FOR DOWN—It is "up the Nile" from Cairo down to Uganda, and "down the Nile" from Uganda going up to Cairo. The "brush" and the "prairie" may be correct in Kansas, and the "jungle" in Brazil, but here the only acceptable words are "bush," "plains" or "forest." It is true that Tarzan swung on vines through the jungle, but remember Burroughs had never been to Africa, and he just didn't know that there was no "jungle"

in East Africa. When you get home you tell everyone, "I was out in the bush for two weeks."

16. DO NOT SAY "KEENYA"—Kenya is pronounced KEN- (like the man's name) YA. The British used to call it "Keenya," and most of them still do, but the Africans all say Kenya. Also, the correct pronounciation of Tanzania is TAN-ZAN-KNEE-A, with the emphasis on "knee."

17. DO NOT FORGET TO BRING YOUR CHILDREN OR GRANDCHILDREN—It will be one long picnic at the zoo for them. On safari, you get up early and go to bed early. There are no nightclubs in the bush, so you won't have to find somebody to look after them while you are out on the town. More important from their point of view, there are no dreary art galleries or cathedrals to get bored in—just Africa unfolding fresh every day for all ages to enjoy together. We have taken children from five to eighty-five on safari, and they all love it.

18. DO NOT FORGET TO BRING A TELEPHOTO LENS —If you are a photographer, you will need a telephoto lens to get decent animal exposures, and if you are lucky, some indecent animal exposures too.

19. DO NOT TAKE A TORN OR UGLY BATHROBE—Frequently one is invited "up country" for a weekend. A "weekend" in Kenya consists of a Saturday at noon until Sunday night because banks, government offices and businesses are open on Saturday mornings. Most of the estates, plantations, and farms in Kenya, as well as a few small towns, lie not only north of Nairobi, but at a higher altitude as well. Therefore, anywhere within two hundred miles north and west of Nairobi is generally referred to as "Up country." Many people have elegant houses there, and if you are invited for a weekend, this is what happens.

If you arrive early enough you may be asked if you would like to go for a ride. This means on a horse, not in a car. Or perhaps you would like to shoot? This means birds or maybe an antelope. At sunset, which is at 7 P.M. all year round because Kenya lies on the equator, you return to the house for "sundowners"—this means cocktails. You will then note that each time your glass is empty your host or hostess will ask, "Would you like the other half?" or "Will you have a drink?" but NEVER "Have *another* drink?" It is bad form to draw attention to the fact that "you drink," even though it may be obvious to you and your host and everyone else. After two or six sundowners, do not be alarmed when your host or hostess says, "Would you like a bath now?" This is not a reflection upon the inadequacy of your deodorant and there is nothing wrong with you—it is merely what people up country *do*. After cocktails everyone goes into his room, takes a bath, dons his pyjamas and dressing-gown (bathrobe), and returns to the drawing room (living room) where everyone foregathers before trooping into the dining room for dinner in night clothes. Fairly soon after dinner, which is usually served about 9 P.M., everyone goes to bed, and I must say it is nice to be all ready. This custom came about for a sensible reason. People living up country on estates get up early and work hard all day. When they return home in the evening, they are dusty and dirty and in need of a relaxing drink before they tidy up. It seems silly to change twice if you know there is no possibility of going out, so the logical answer is to bathe and prepare for bed. As a visitor on safari it is unlikely that you will encounter this, since it applies to private houses rather than hotels and lodges.

Jack Paar was so taken with the idea that he filmed Miriam, Randy and himself at a bathrobe dinner at our house for one of his "African Special" programs.

Many visitors worry about their health in Africa and visions of the plague, malaria, blackwater fever, cholera, leeches, snake bites and tsetse flies dance in their heads. Americans are very sterile, and hesitate to eat salads here. But Kenya is a very healthy country and human fertilizer is not used as I am told it is in Asia and India.

When on safari it is wise to drink the boiled and filtered water that is put in carafes in your bedroom; in the cities, the carafes are filled directly from the bathroom taps because the water is perfectly pure, but the gesture is made to comfort the tourists.

If you *want* to worry about something, "Bilharzia" is the best thing to be concerned about. For ease, many people refer to it as "Bill Harris." Once a young Peace Corps girl had a telephone call on her birthday from her father in the States.

"Happy birthday, darling, how are you?"

"Oh, Daddy, all right thank you, but right now I'm in bed with Bill Harris."

"Who the hell is he?"

Bill Harris is a liver disease contracted when going into lakes or streams or rivers where there are reeds. Tiny snails live in the reeds, and as you bathe the invisible organisms somehow get into your system. The disease does not necessarily kill you, but I understand you wish it would, you feel so depressed and lethargic. The cure takes months and is said to be worse than the disease. Almost all Africans who live near lakes and rivers have Bilharzia, and this is why many are so lethargic. It is not, as some people say, because they are lazy—they are sick.

I have actually seen an African fall asleep while riding a bike and tumbling off by the roadside. In addition to Bilharzia, he probably had malaria and a degree of malnutrition as well. Few Africans enjoy positive good health as we understand it, and it is incredible how they keep going when we would have quit as a result of only one of their complaints.

If you, as a visitor, stay out of water where reeds grow and take an anti-malaria pill each week, you can forget about any health worries.

The only thing I ever got after fourteen years of living here is green toenails. I went to the doctor and his suggestion was that I kept them painted with dark polish so no one could see them because they are so ugly. I have also developed an allergy to tsetse flies, which I have thoroughly enjoyed because it is such fun when completing medical forms in the States that ask, "Are you allergic to anything?" to be able to say, "Yes, tsetse flies." The allergy is probably cumulative from being bitten so many times. Now when it happens my ears turn all purple and swell and just hang from my head like eggplants and my feet swell so that I look as if I have elephantiasis, which is another spectacular disease. But all of these things are easily controlled now, so don't worry. Jock is allergic to bee-stings, so we carry antihistamine with us when we can remember and ignore our various allergies. I just hope that if ever I have an accident in New York City and am taken to the hospital, I am not with my good friend who lives there and is allergic only to camels—they'd never believe us.

Generally speaking, the food on safari is a pleasant surprise—unless you are like our friend Quentin Crewe, a British gourmet critic from London, whom we have taken on safari two or three times, and who claims that we are just too insensitive to notice how bad the food is. One day at lunch we were served beautifully fluffy pale-green and pink puddings. We were very enthusiastic about them, but he declined adamantly. After the first few bites we remarked,

"You know, this pudding doesn't have much taste."

"Well, you can be grateful for that," he replied.

We once took Jock's mother on safari with us, and after the first breakfast we all had together, she took me aside and asked if I had noticed how Harvey, an American with us, had eaten? I said no, thinking he must have eaten his eggs with his fingers and wondering how I could have missed it, but she went on to say, "I have never seen anything like it in my life—why, he ate his toast and marmalade with his eggs!" I waited for her to finish the sentence seeing nothing peculiar in this, but that was all there was to it. The British eat toast and marmalade *after* their eggs.

There is no restaurant in Nairobi that serves African cuisine—no buffalo stroganoff or hippo under glass.

In Tanzania you may from time to time see zebra or wildebeest steaks offered on the menu because the sale of game meat is legal there under certain conditions, but it is illegal in Kenya. The meat of both zebra and wildebeest is hard to tell from beef.

The whole question of game skins, elephant hair bracelets, ivory chessmen and curios made out of wild animals is a difficult one. Part of the trouble is that there are too many "experts" with conflicting views, and the ordinary visitor does not know who to believe. Even the Game Departments are not sufficiently adamant either way. This is the problem.

Man's expansion, both in population and agricultural endeavor has forced the animals into ever-reducing areas. To protect them Game Parks and Game Reserves have been defined. (A Park has a network of roads and usually a lodge or two where people can stay, and no shooting is ever permitted. A Reserve is not developed for ordinary tourists, but hunting or photographic parties with special licenses can camp in them.) No agriculture is allowed in either Parks or Reserves, but the nomadic tribes, like the Masai who have lived in these areas for hundreds of years with their cattle and goats, continue to do so. The Masai do not eat game meat and live peacefully alongside the animals. Around the Parks and Reserves industrious and hungry man is busily developing intensive agriculture. Man has his area, the animals have theirs, and one might be excused for thinking that all is well. But it is a cruel illusion.

Nature is supposed to keep the animal population balanced, yet we expect this to happen in a situation which is no longer natural, for the animals have been artificially confined. The numbers of elephant or hippo, for example, may multiply to the extent that they are eating the available vegetation in their reduced area faster than it can regenerate, and the resulting shortage of food affects not only them but all the other animals that graze and browse there. The antelope population diminishes and the predators who feed on them then start to suffer. The repercussions mount. "Leave it to nature" is no longer the answer.

Parallel with this there exists also the problem of poaching—for protein and for profit. The Africans adjacent to the game are as short of meat and cash as all other Africans, but they are in a position to do something about it.

By nipping over the boundary, the hungry poacher can trap or hunt down a delicious and sustaining supper. From his point of view, he is doing himself a doubly good turn because the tiresome animals are constant pests that raid his crops which he struggles so hard to grow. Meanwhile, the mercenary poacher strikes deeper and with more daring into the heart of the Reserve in search of rhino, elephant, leopard and cheetah. The horns and ivory and skins can fetch a nice profit on an illegal market, and there are plenty of outlets. It is not an exaggeration to say that most of East Africa's curio dealers sell poached goods, and it is not difficult for them to get away with it since there exists a legal umbrella under which they can purchase skins and ivory shot under license, and the system of controls is not tightly enough enforced. A skin is a skin and it is impossible to tell in the shop whether it was shot legally or poached illegally. Crooked dealers are, therefore, the truly bad guys. They pay a pittance to the primitive and hard-working poacher, who risks his life hunting dangerous wild animals, they make a huge profit themselves, and they are the means of popularizing that which an aware, conservation-minded, ecologically oriented tourist should not be buying anyway. After all, if people don't buy the things, the market will dry up and mercenary poaching will cease. Alleluiah!

But wait. Back in the Reserve an elephant has just dropped dead from hunger and three emaciated lion cubs have died because after their famished parents had finally killed an impala and satisfied their own hunger there was nothing left over for the cubs. Too bad.

Simultaneously, a magistrate in Mombasa has just sentenced four poachers to three years imprisonment each for shooting elephant with poisoned arrows. He used the occasion to inveigh against the wickedness of such men whose greed endangers the country's heritage of priceless wildlife. . . . The poachers shrugged. A few days before they were caught they had counted twenty-two elephant in Tsavo Park that had died of hunger during the preceding month, and they had been told that four or five thousand had perished in other areas of the eight-thousand-square-mile park. It seemed to them a bit like their goats—in the dry weather some of the weaker ones die for lack of grass and leaves. Or they can slaughter them before they die—what is the difference?

So what is the answer? Maybe an entirely new approach is needed, devoid of sentimentality, running counter to long-held beliefs and based upon a new and practical premise.

Why not regard all game areas as vast ranches in need of careful and deliberate continuing management? Scientific studies underway at present will soon reveal how many animals of which species can be supported to the square mile in a given area. Man has thrown out the balance, and man must now adjust by encouraging one species or culling another. The culling presupposes animal products, meat, skin, horn and ivory, all of which are highly marketable. Instead of taxing poor overtaxed man or collecting from charitable and concerned individuals, why not let the animals pay for themselves? They could do it handsomely.

Ultimately, why not give potential African poachers a piece of the action? If an African "game rancher" had five hundred zebra in his concession area, he could probably shoot 150 a year without reducing the population and from the skins would derive a good income from a source that was self-regenerating; and heaven help anybody who tried to poach zebra from his area! Similarly, he could enjoy for himself and also sell quantities of delicious protein—and look forward to a never-ending supply of it.

If this line of thinking is carried through, then the sale of wild-animal products should eventually be encouraged, not decried. The proceeds from the plentiful species that had to be culled could be poured back to protect the scarce and endangered species like the spotted cats and the white rhino.

It may be sad, it may upset those who write and emote about the "freedom of the wilds." It may also be the last chance for the animals to survive in our world. But until the authorities will grasp this nettle and establish controlled marketing of scientifically culled animal products, the purchase of skins and horns will only encourage indiscriminate mercenary poaching which could spell the end of the game.

I got quite heavy for a moment there, didn't I? (Don't you just hate it when someone makes you feel guilty about something you hadn't even thought about before? And you really wanted that zebra-skin rug too.)

To be more cheerful again, you don't have to worry about hunting safaris—not at their present level, anyway. Hunters pay very heavy license fees and the money is ploughed back into conservation projects. Licenses are issued only for areas where there are plenty of whichever species are to be shot, and in any case, the numbers of animals killed by bona fide hunters are minute alongside the estimates of those which are poached.

Several times we have come across a "giant speckled flower," as Isak Dinesen once described giraffe, lying dead from a poisoned arrow, with only its tail missing, and its child standing by looking at its dead mother, as bewildered as we—even more so.

Jock has no desire to hunt, and I have a revulsion against it. I have tried. On hunting safaris with friends I think, "I'll shoot myself a skirt," but as I raise the gun to fire at the impala I see only the eyelashes like awnings over those trusting eyes, and I couldn't begin to pull the trigger. But then I put flies and spiders out of windows instead of swatting them.

But evidently, there is something in hunting that escapes me entirely. Isak Dinesen claimed there were aesthetic reasons and values involved and wrote, "A man who hears a beautiful tune and doesn't want to whistle it, a man who sees a beautiful woman and doesn't want to make love to her, a man who sees a wild animal and doesn't want to shoot it: this man has no heart."

I can't even understand that. I've heard our hunting friends say that killing an animal makes it immortal, and although I don't agree that that is a good enough reason for wanting to kill an animal, at least I understand what they are talking about. So I will stay with camera safaris. I find them just as exciting because no guns are allowed, and when the animals charge, which they do frequently, you can only run—and we've done a lot of running. Also you have to get closer to the animals to photograph them than you do to shoot, so there is as much exciting adventure shooting with cameras as with guns, and it is a lot less final for the animals as well. When Dancy just saw a collection of heads about to be shipped to someone we know she said, "Ugh! What are they going to do with all those faces?"

To each his own, but not everyone wants faces hanging on the wall. If heads appeal to you, why don't you stuff your own dog or cat when it dies and hang that up over the fireplace? No, hunting is not for us, but that is purely a question of personal choice.

If you think I am being stuffy about leopard-skin pocketbooks, elephant-hair bracelets and so forth, you should meet Michaela Dennis. She is a household word in Europe because of her and her late husband, Armand's, TV series on animals. At her house for lunch one day she served duck. I started to eat and then noticed she didn't have any duck on her plate, and said,

"Oh, I'm sorry, I thought you were served."

She answered, "I don't eat meat. You go right ahead."

I asked if it were because of religious beliefs and she said, "Oh, no, it is because I love animals so much. I don't eat meat, use any make-up or soap unless it is especially made without animal fats, and I don't wear any leather—only plastic or fabric."

I glanced at myself and I had on an elephant-hair bracelet (that was in the days before I knew) and a zebra belt and leather shoes and lipstick—I felt like a murderer.

She continued, "I do eat eggs—because they have no personality."

I disagree with her very much there—eggs have a tremendous personality. They are so friendly and cozy.

However, when we were leaving she said, "Do watch out for the snakes, I saw a few puff-adders in the driveway this morning."

I forgot to ask her if she swatted mosquitos, but I bet she doesn't. And so, as always, you can carry everything to extremes, and I, personally, feel it is all right to eat the meat and wear the skins of domestic animals, but I do draw the line at the wild animals. I am sure a giraffe gives much more joy to others loping across the plains for them to see than being killed only for the hair of its tail to be worn as a bracelet. As our good friend and conservationist Jack Block said, "The leopard skin looks better on the leopard," and as I said in the beginning of this book, "It would be terrible if our grandchildren had to ask, 'What was a lion?'"

One of the greatest problems for most travelers is language. I, personally, am never concerned about language difficulties. Everyone smiles in the same language and someone always speaks enough English for all the tedious things like, "What time does the flight leave?" For the rest, I find it a relief not to be able to understand what people are saying. I remember once sitting by a swimming pool in Addis Ababa and noting some people next to me were speaking Amharic, others Italian, and still others Greek, and I was unable to understand one word of what I overheard. It was beautifully private—I didn't have to get angry at what they were saying, curious as to what they meant or worry about the outcome of the stories. Best of all, I didn't have to get bored with their chatter.

The director of the TV show I was co-producing then was an Italian called Franco who spoke little English. The producer, an American, was trying to teach him, and they had become good friends.

Soon Franco and I became good enough friends for me to do the same, too. My children always said "pubby" for pudding when they were babies, so when Franco asked me how to enquire from the waiters about dessert I said, "Say 'what is for pubby?'" The waiters thought he was retarded.

Most Americans traveling here assume, because they have been told they are going to a country where English is spoken, that they will be able to understand English. What they actually understand is American, not English. There is a 20 per cent difference between English and American, and you don't realize it until someone says to you:

"A fortnight ago, a lorry driver's hooter got stuck on a dual carriageway near a roundabout, so he stopped and opened the bonnet. While at a petrol station seeking help, he heard on the wireless that a lady with a pram was stuck in a lift between the ground floor and the first floor over a chemist shop where she had been buying nappies and flannels. Realizing it was his wife . . ."

We all know that petrol is gas and that a fortnight is two weeks. However, there are some words that I would understand no better if the British spoke in Chinese. Flannel is one. Did you know a flannel is a washcloth? I didn't know that. How about this—"re-valley"? Yes, valley like *Valley of the Dolls* with a soft "re" in front. Re-valley. That is how they say it, but what they mean is "reveille"—the bugle call sounded at daybreak. They spell it correctly but pronounce it re-valley. Can you imagine?

It is obvious from such words as "flannel," "trailers," "sweets" and so forth that there is a need for a translation between English and American. East Africans, of course, have adopted British words and intonations. We list here a few of the English words that baffle Americans most:

lorry	truck
bonnet	hood
boot	trunk
hooter	horn
petrol	gas
roundabout	traffic circle
dual carriageway	divided highway
wireless	radio
lift	elevator
ground floor	1st floor
first floor	2nd floor
second floor	3rd floor, etc.
fortnight	two weeks
biscuits	cookies
scones	biscuits
sweets	candy
pudding	dessert
chemist	drug store

trailer	coming attractions
cot	crib
flannel	washcloth
loo	toilet
cloakroom	another word for toilet
torch	flashlight
gaol	jail
blinds	shades
tap	spigot
cupboard	closet
basin	sink

Jock and I have overcome our semantic problems the hard way. After we had been married a few years and thought we knew all of each other's language peculiarities, I said to Jock about Shirley Brown's chewing the rug after having been told repeatedly not to,

"Shirley Brown doesn't mind very well, does she?"

"Shirley Brown doesn't mind very MUCH," he corrected.

Confused, I repeated, "Shirley Brown doesn't mind very WELL."

Jock grew impatient, "I know what you said, and it is not grammatical."

"What are you talking about?"

And so our argument went until we discovered that the British do not know the use of the word "mind" in place of "obey."

When we were first married and bought our house, we had the following conversation:

"Where are the screens for the windows?" I asked Jock.

"The what?" he asked.

"The screens."

"The WHAT?"

"THE SCREENS."

The British in East Africa, or even in Britain, don't use screens because there are so few insects that screens are unnecessary. "Screens" to them are not the wire mesh contraptions on windows, but a folding screen that stands on the floor, such as those used in hospitals, to block a view. And speaking of hospitals, you might read in an African paper that somebody "went to hospital." It is not a misprint, the word "the" has not been left out by mistake; the British say, "He went to hospital," as we say, "He went to church."

"Loos" are bathrooms and you may well be confronted with the need for a sudden decision. In the rest rooms in the airport, and elsewhere too, you may see signs "European toilet" or "Asian toilet." The European toilet needs no description, but the Asian toilet is the same piece of porcelain ware, without the seat, sunk in the floor. If you've done your knee-bend exercises regularly, you'll have no problem in addressing yourself to this fixture. A black American visiting Kenya for the first time was incensed that the "Europeans" and the "Asians" were catered for, but that the Africans were overlooked in this necessary field. However, he was quickly comforted when he learned that the description merely referred to the style of the installation, and that all races could make their choice. Recently a number of public toilets have been relabelled "Western style" and "Eastern style."

We had a friend who was extremely shy and uncertain of himself but was drafted into the Kenya Police force during the Mau Mau emergency. Left in charge of a police station in Nairobi on his first night, he was appalled at his new responsibility and filled with apprehension over the magnitude of the crises with which he might have to contend. The emergency call came in, and he rushed with his constables to a nearby Asian house where disaster had struck. A very fat and elderly Asian lady had missed her footing while using the "Asian toilet," and her pudgy ankle was firmly trapped in the S-bend. Eighteen hysterical relations had failed to pull her free, and he had to smash the fixture with an axe to release her . . . the things one had to go through in the Mau Mau.

But to go back to the vocabulary problem, all nationalities have difficulties. A Dutch bachelor friend of ours in Nairobi, flirting with one of our young American safari-ers said to her, "The moment I saw you last night, I flopped over you," and was crushed when she just laughed. And no one ever told him the word is "flipped."

An English friend of ours here, a judge, was in the States and a New York cab driver, after a short conversation, asked him where he was from.

"East Africa," the judge answered.

"REALLY? Gee, you speak English real good."

He was totally confused by our friend's hostile answer, "That is the ONLY thing I speak."

Never tell an Englishman you like his accent. He will say, "But I have no accent. I speak English as an Englishman—it is you who speak my language with an accent," and you will feel silly.

Jock learned Swahili at the same time as English, when he was a small child, so he is fluent. In a way it might have been easier for me to learn Swahili if I hadn't had him to lean on, because it was all too easy to say, "Jock, will you tell him not to mix the chocolate pudding with the mashed potatoes?" But finally I went to school to learn Swahili, for three months, from 8 A.M. to 4 P.M. every day. I don't know if I learned much Swahili, but it kept me off the streets. I quote Steinbeck now when people ask me if I speak Swahili, "I can ask questions but I can't understand the answers." The school was a missionary school, and I was the only one not a missionary and also the dumbest in the class. I am extremely bad at languages—I got fourteen (out of a possible one hundred) in my Spanish exams in high school, and after two years of it, it is still impossible for me to count to ten. Unless you are going on safari or have an unusual fascination for Swahili or details, you won't miss much if you skip the rest of this chapter.

However, with Steinbeck's quote in mind, we decided to list a few Swahili phrases which don't need answers, such as greetings and thank-you's, or ones to which answers can be indicated by gestures.

shillingi ngapi   How many shillings? Answered by holding up
                    three or four fingers.

wapi choo?	Where is the bathroom? Answered by a point in the right direction.
naweza kupiga picha yako?	May I take your picture? Answered by a nod or a shake of the head accompanied by the words "ndio" or "la."

ndio	yes
la or	
hapana	no
jambo	hello
kwaheri	good-by
asante	thank you
asante	
sana	thank you very much
tafadhali	please
Bwana	Mr. or Sir, etc.
Mem-sahib	Mrs. or Miss

Men will be addressed *Bwana* and women *Mem-sahib* or *Bibi*. *Bwana* is a term of respect, and it is nice for you to use Bwana when you are speaking to an African. They use it when addressing each other all the time. *Mama* is the equivalent word to *Bwana* when you speak to an African lady.

English will be spoken by most Africans with whom you come into contact, but in case you run into a waiter in one of the lodges who does not speak English, here are a few useful phrases:

	chakula	food
	maji	water
Tafadhali	kahawa	coffee
lete	chai	tea
(Please	mziwa	milk
bring)	barafu	ice
	tembo	booze, or elephant (be careful not to confuse the two)

If you buy a Swahili phrase book in Nairobi it may contain such handy sentences as, "How many men in this camp have syphilis?" (An even handier one that appears in a Spanish phrase book is, "My grandfather's postillion was struck to death by lightening.")

Don't bother to look up Tarzan's *ngawa*—it doesn't mean anything.

A fun Swahili sentence is, "Wally, wally, wally, wally, wally"—at least that is what it sounds like. The correct spelling is, *Wale wa Liwali wale wale* and it means, "The people of the Arab chieftain eat cooked rice." The correct pronunciation is "Wally" five times, and I'm sure you'll find this almost as useful as the postillion sentence.

Swahili has an identifying sound with life. For example, "sleep" is *lala*. There are some Tarzan-sounding words too, such as *ua*—pronounced "oo-ah"—which is the word for "to kill," and *au*—pronounced "ah-oo," which is the word for "or."

A lot of Swahili words are taken from English, such as *motokaa* —the phonetic spelling for motor car. Others are:

sinema	cinema—pronounced see-nay'-ma
chizi	cheese—pronounced cheesy
toasti	toast—pronounced toasty
sheeti	sheet—pronounced sheety
shirti	shirt—pronounced shirty
hoteli	hotel—pronounced hotely
shillingi	shilling—pronounced shillingy
bekoni	bacon—pronounced bacony

The word for bird is *ndege* and the same word is used for aeroplane.

My Kiswahili teacher was Edward G. Robinson's understudy in *A Boy Ten Feet Tall.* I don't know about Edward G. Robinson, but my teacher was a tremendous ham. He didn't teach his Kiswahili classes in an orthodox manner but rather performed them and used limericks to impress grammatical points and vocabulary upon his students. For instance: the Kiswahili word for "gourd" is *mbuyu,* and the word for "this man" is *huyu,* so Mr. Wood recited:

> There was a young girl from Kikuyu,
> Whose belly swelled like an *mbuyu.*
> When her father inquired
> How this had transpired,
> She said *"huyu"* and *"huyu"* and *"huyu."*

The interesting thing about Swahili, or Kiswahili as it is more correctly called, is that it is used by very few people indeed as their natural language. There are 220 tribes, therefore 220 dialects in East Africa. Swahili is basically a Bantu language, but its name comes from an Arabic word meaning "coast"—there are many Arabic words in the language. It was carried inland by Arab slave traders and by missionaries, and it is the only means by which the different African groups can converse with one another. Thus, Swahili is a second language to the vast majority of those who speak it, and it is the lingua franca of East Africa. In really remote areas, you will find Africans who speak only their tribal language and cannot understand Swahili. The rising generation of Africans will be tri-lingual, having learned their tribal language from their mother and Swahili and English in school.

Efforts have been made to make Swahili the compulsory national language because, it is argued, unity among the tribes will be achieved more easily by the use of an African rather than alien tongue. However, this would seem to be a retrogressive step if only for the reason that so many Africans already speak English. Also, it has the advantage of a technical vocabulary which Swahili lacks and which would have to be invented. Parliamentary proceedings are conducted in English, as are administrative matters, and the medium of instruction at the University of East Africa is English. Nevertheless, Swahili is spoken by the ordinary man. We, ourselves, find it quite useful in conversing not only with Africans but also with Asians, Italians or Greeks living here, who do not speak English. It is a very easy language with no difficulties in spelling or pronunciation and the missionaries taught the Africans to read and write it phonetically. Every word ends in a vowel, the next to last syllable is always accented, and it is written in either our alphabet or in Arabic characters.

Many Swahili words have been incorporated into English as spoken in East Africa. You already know one—"safari," a pure Swahili word. (Literally translated *safari* means "journey," and in East Africa everyone takes a *safari* to church or the drug store as well as in the American connotation of the word—a trip into the bush.) Other common Swahili words used in everyday English conversation are:

kali	sharp, fierce, grouchy, peppery, etc. A knife can be *kali* as can a person or a dog.
duka	a store, usually a small general store.
shenzi	definitely derogatory, meaning cheap, common in the nasty sense, of a low order, tatty, etc.
maradadi	beautiful, fancy, elegant, etc.

Now you will be able to understand when someone living in East Africa says, "I was very *kali* when I got home from the *duka* and found they had sold me the *shenzi* writing paper instead of the *maradadi* brand I had asked for."

FOOD

On safari the day starts with early morning tea (you can request coffee) which is brought to you at 6:30 A.M. in the safari lodges. When the sun rises about 7 A.M. you go for a "game run" —a drive around the reserve looking for and photographing animals—and return about 9 A.M. for a breakfast of fruit, cereal, eggs and bacon or sausage, fried tomatoes, toast and marmalade —always marmalade—and coffee, tea or milk. In towns, mid-morning coffee and a "biscuit" is quite usual. Lunch will be a five-course meal and will start with soup. Fish comes next, then meat, potatoes, vegetable and salad, followed by dessert, then cheese. Each course on the menu is numbered, and if you only wish to select certain things, you indicate this to the waiter by quoting the number. Thus, when he takes your order, you say to him, "I'll have numbers one, three and five, and I'll let you know about six later." Do not be shy about ordering everything on the menu—many people do. The only time you'll be served sandwiches, except on a picnic, is at tea time (about 4:30), and then you'll get tiny little cucumber or egg-salad sandwiches, little cakes and tea. I miss hot dogs, bacon, tomato and lettuce on toast, and cheeseburgers so much that every time we return to the States we gorge ourselves on them. (Last time we counted seventy-two cheeseburgers in one month.) Dinner, about 8 P.M. is rather similar to lunch but a "savoury" may be added. A savoury is a hot prune wrapped in bacon called "devil on horseback." (An "angel on horseback" is something even worse.) A Welsh rarebit savoury is a small open grilled cheese sandwich. In other words, savouries are what we may serve as hors d'oeuvres, which the British call "toasties," insisting that hors d'oeuvres are little bits of smoked herring, caviar, olives, etc. that are eaten at the table as a first course before soup. In any case, savouries are served after dessert, or "pudding" as it will be called. Pudding may be cake or pie or ice cream. However, you may select things on the menu in any order, and if you wish to start with the savoury first, no one will mind—very much. As I have tried to explain, having savouries, cheeses and celery served to you after your butterscotch sundae, is comparable to having mashed potatoes and gravy served after your apple pie. The British are just as rude about serving fruit salads with meat, maple syrup on pancakes, marshmallows on sweet potatoes, or candied sweet potatoes with ham, etc. because on the whole they do not mix sweet things with the main course, and think it is quite barbaric to do so. Pancakes are rolled up, filled with jelly or jam, sprinkled with sugar and served as dessert. A friend of McDonnell's remarked that we "ate backwards" when we gave him pancakes for breakfast. The outrageous pronunciation of the word "ate" was one of the first things I noticed about Jock; even the children, soon after meeting him, nudged me and whispered with a frown, "He says 'et'!" After I knew him well enough to question his grammar (and most of the time you never know anyone well enough to question his grammar) he answered, affecting a pompous and superior air, "The Queen and I say 'et,'" and seriously insisted that all civilized English pronounce the past tense of ate "et" (but spell it "ate"). Our fears were allayed.

MAIL

Letters take no more than five days from the States, and three to five days to the States. As mentioned earlier, there is no delivery service—everyone has his own box at his local post office and his own key, and at any time of the day or night he can check his box. Mail is even sorted and put into your box on Sundays. Since there is no mail delivery (nor telegram delivery nor special delivery) all mailing addresses are Post Office Box numbers. None of the houses have street numbers—your name is put on a board outside your house, and it is up to your friends to be able to find it as best they can. One of our friends from the States, with whom we had been corresponding for some time, claimed he was relieved to find when he arrived to stay with us that the people lived in houses and not in boxes.

As far as letters go, we'd guess that nine out of every ten get through . . . that is if no one flushes them down the loo. The entire plumbing system at Mwanza, a small town in Tanzania, was once stopped up because the post office clerks cut the stamps off the letters that had just been mailed, threw the letters down the loo and resold the stamps. This is what could happen to your letter to Mother. Hers to you could end up in the loo, too, because the post office clerks sometimes grow tired of sorting the mail, so they flush the letters away—which *is* easier than sorting—and faster as well. However, be optimistic and have your mail sent to you care of your hotel in Nairobi and have your friends and relatives write, "Please hold for arrival," on the envelope. If there is an emergency while you are out on safari, even in the most remote lodges, there is a two-way radio by which you could be reached from any major city. International telephone calls are very efficient and cost only ten dollars to the States. Remember, telegrams (or cables as they are called in East Africa) are received only as letters—there is no delivery.

CLOTHES

Many people use up precious air allowance poundage or pay exorbitant overweight by filling their suitcases with film and medicines and make-up and other things that could be bought in Africa for the same price and sometimes cheaper. For example—a bush jacket can be tailor-made for you in Nairobi in twenty-four hours for about nineteen dollars. Tennis shoes can be bought for one dollar and desert boots for seven dollars—then you can throw them away after you've finished your safari (that's how we get all our shoes). If you want to have shoes handmade out of leather or suede, they will cost a little more, but it will be worth it. The shoemaker, usually an Asian, makes you stand in your stockinged feet on a piece of paper or on a page of a special book he has, and while he sits on the floor and traces the outline of your foot with a pencil, you stand there, trying to stop giggling because it tickles so much. He measures both feet carefully to take into account the fact that most people have a slightly larger right foot, and three or four days later when you pick up your shoes, they will not only be beautiful but the most comfortable you'll ever have. Everything from Revlon lipsticks to false eyelashes and hair rinses are available. Speaking of hair, hairdressers do rather elegant work in Nairobi—there are French and Italian and Greek hairdressers as well as African and British; but in the bush there is nowhere to get your hair done at any of the lodges, so buy a scarf and forget it until you get back to the city. Comfort is primary, there is no best-dressed list for safari. If you feel comfortable in slacks, then wear slacks; if you don't, wear a dress.

Bring a few sweaters for early mornings and evenings, one nice dress for cocktails and dinner in the cities—and for the rest, comfortable, cotton traveling clothes. Men should bring two or three pairs of washable pants, comfortable shirts for safari, one or two sweaters—or a sweater and a lightweight jacket—and one suit and tie. Most people bring far too many things. As they alight from the plane, we can divide people into "tourists"—four to ten pieces of luggage—or "travelers"—one to two cases—and "seasoned travelers"—a toothbrush stuck in a book.

TIME

There is an eight-hour difference between New York and Nairobi time. Nairobi is already relaxing with a sundowner as you are gulping your coffee and rushing to the office. Usually on your safari when you wonder what old so and so is doing back home "now," he will be asleep, for days and nights are nearly reversed.

If you ask an African for dinner at 6 P.M. do not be surprised when he arrives at noon. This is because the Africans use the old Roman method of time where the first hour of the day is the first hour of daylight (7 A.M. to you, one o'clock to them) and the first hour of darkness is the first hour in the evening. As an easy way to cheat and avoid calculating all of this, merely look at the little hand on your watch and figure directly opposite on the far side of the dial is African time. Thus nine o'clock in your time becomes three o'clock in theirs, 6 P.M. becomes 12 noon and so forth. Actually, African-cum-Roman time makes very good sense, and the best thing for you to do is to forget the whole thing because, unless you speak Swahili fluently, it will never arise.

MONEY

East African Shillings are used, and there are roughly seven of them to a dollar, so if you know your seven-times tables, you will have no problems. (One shilling is written as shs.1/–.)

Shs.14/– is $2; shs.70/– is $10; shs.7,000/– is $1,000; etc.

One shilling is fourteen American cents, two shillings is twenty-eight cents and seven shillings ninety-eight cents. The shilling is divided into one hundred East African cents, but the ten-cent piece—worth less than one U. S. cent—is the smallest unit you will encounter. You will use one ten-cent piece to unlock the door of the ladies' room, four for a local telephone call, and two for matches, which are sold in rectangular wooden boxes and not given away in book form. The fifty-cent piece is another coin, and it is half a shilling and equal to seven American cents. The next size up is the shilling, and the largest coin, in both size and value, is a two-shilling piece. In addition there are shs.5/–, shs.10/–, shs.20/–, shs.50/– and shs.100/– notes, each of a different color and size to avoid confusion and mistakes.

Tipping

One tips people for services in the same way one does in the States—and in East Africa about 10 per cent of the bill for a waiter and about a shilling a bag to a porter, is the going rate.

There are a half a dozen banks, each with multiple branches, in Nairobi that will take care of any financial problem you may have.

CUSTOMS

A word about customs:

I had shipped a lot of things by sea—oddments we had bought for our house and Christmas presents we had received that were too heavy to bring by air—and when the crate arrived about eight customs officials opened it and started going through everything to decide what the duty should be. It was a very frustrating experience for me and the customs men. I had never before realized what a lot of junk we had bought or acquired and how difficult it is to explain these things to people who are not accustomed to frivolous luxuries like our "sex meters" for example.

"What is this?" asked the customs official opening the first box which contained two of those glass bubbles—one on top of the other—with colored fluid inside that goes from the bottom bubble to the top one when you clasp the lower one.

Should I tell the truth and say a "sex meter"—how could I explain that?

"A toy!" I exclaimed brilliantly.

"A toy? How does it work?" As he picked it up he saw the label which read, "Caution: Poison."

"You have toys with poison in America?"

"Oh yes; this is what you do . . ."

We finally got through that and he picked up a stuffed partridge I had bought to put on top of our pear tree at Christmas.

"A dead bird?" he asked. "What do you do with this?"

"Put it on top of my tree."

"Your tree? Which tree?"

"The one inside my house at Christmas—the holiday for Christians."

"INSIDE your house? It grows there?"

"No, we cut it down or buy one cut down and bring it inside and put things, like this bird, on it." The whole Christmas tree routine was beginning to sound ridiculous to me now.

The next item he picked up was a jar of douche powder. "Oh my God," I thought, "toothpaste. Toothpaste," I said quickly and shoved something else into his hand.

Someone had given us a glass which said "On The Rocks" and in the bottom of it were glued two stones. His first reaction, naturally, was to throw the stones away, so he instinctively tried to pick them out. Of course they wouldn't move. He looked at me and I stammered, "Ummmm . . . let see . . . you see, in America we have a custom which is drinking beverages with ice."

"Yes, I know that."

"Well, sometimes we call the ice 'rocks.' "

"I see."

"We say, give me a drink 'on the rocks,'" pointing hopefully to the glass.

"But it is ice you *really* want?"

"Yes," I answered enthusiastically.

"Then why do you have rocks in this glass?"

The next item was a bottle of . . .

"Toilet Water?"

"Well it isn't really toilet water," I said.

"But it says right here 'toilet water.'"

"Yes I know, but it *is* perfume—or 'scent' as the British call it."

"Then why would you ever call it 'toilet water'?"

"Oh, I don't know." I answered wondering why we would ever call it toilet water.

As we neared the bottom of the pile he picked up a small brown paper bag containing a hard object which he could feel through the paper. As he opened it to peer in, I remembered what it was. One of McDonnell's awful friends had given him a joke dog mess made of plastic and looking 100 per cent realistic. The customs official looked at me. I looked at him. Neither of us said a word.

ET CETERA

Excellent animal and bird books and maps are obtainable in East Africa. They are difficult to find in the United States, as well as being expensive. As they are published in both Britain and East Africa, why not wait until you get there to buy them, and save on your overweight too? If you accumulate quantities of books, curios, gifts and so on, you can send them back to the United States by parcel post. If you buy something large, like a drum or a real stuffed elephant, the *duka* where you buy it will ship it to you and you will receive it in two or three months' time.

PLANNING

Having given you all the tips about what to do on safari, I should warn you that to organize a safari yourself is at best hazardous. Unless, for instance, you know the difference between Namanga and Oltukai—both serve Amboseli Park—you can be in big trouble because one is good and situated in the optimum area of the park, while the other is unacceptable and fifty miles away from where you really want to be.

Unless you recognize and understand the behavior of game, you might not drive away fast enough when an elephant comes at you with his trunk up, or you might panic and run away too soon missing all the fun when he comes at you with his trunk down and is only bluffing. If you know to stop quickly when a rhino charges and not to move at all with other animals; if you know how to speak enough Swahili to ask a Masai if he will walk sixty miles for help when you have broken down (this happened to a visitor a few years ago and he only survived by drinking water from his radiator); if you don't mind missing most of the game, because without trained eyes you just won't see it though it may be right in front of you—then go alone. In short, you need *to know,* and you can be sadly led astray by folders because a number of tour operators include some pretty terrible places just because they are cheap. Good itineraries will always include expensive places such as Treetops or "The Ark" (about thirty dollars a night), Mount Kenya Safari Club (thirty dollars per person or fifty-four dollars for a double), Amboseli, Manyara, Ngorongoro, Serengeti or Keekerok, because the good places are not the cheap ones.

A guide can tell you where the animals are, how to interpret their behavior, and can speak Swahili in emergencies. Without a suitable driver or guide you will miss a lot of the history, anecdotes, politics and just sheer gossip about the country and its inhabitants.

There is really no best time of year for a safari in East Africa.

May and June can be wet, with sudden rainstorms, but there are long sunny intervals in between. Many ardent photographers deliberately come then because the air is incredibly clear and there is no heat haze or dust in the atmosphere. At this time of year you can see Mt. Kenya from Mt. Kilimanjaro, a distance of about 250 miles—the equivalent of seeing New York from Washington, D.C. (Maybe that is where they got the title for the musical *On a Clear Day You Can See Forever*.)

The busiest months from a tourism standpoint are January and February and July and August, but this is dictated not so much by conditions here as by people escaping the winter and by the traditional holiday months. Actually, July and August tend to be damp and gray in Nairobi, but since most of the game parks covered on a safari are at lower altitudes in arid areas where it doesn't rain much even during the rainy season you needn't worry. Because the game is always here and the weather doesn't vary that much anyway it seems to me that these busy months are the times not to come so as to avoid crowds in hotels and lodges.

Plan your safari with a reputable operator and agree on price before you set out. (You might as well come on safari with our company because Jock and I are planning to wear rented gorilla costumes from the States, and in the night, beating our chests, we will stomp into the tents of all those traveling with rival safari companies and scare them to death.)

XVI
Safari Anyone?

So here you are out in the bush on a dirt road driving to a game park with your safari leader and three other visitors. You think you notice that in every car you pass the passenger in the front seat leans forward and presses his hand against the center of the windshield, but this is ridiculous. You can't mention it until you are sure. Yes, again it happens, and again, and you *are* sure. "Why do they press the windshield?" you ask, but before you get an answer there is a loud explosion and you think someone has shot you—for asking that question? But you aren't shot—it was the windshield shattering into millions of pieces of broken glass, which surprisingly don't fly around but stay there making the whole windshield into an enormous opaque jigsaw puzzle. This must now be knocked out, and you help to brush away all the broken pieces of granulated glass. Your safari leader, who says his name is Stretch Sox, explains with his flashing Rock Hudson smile, "If you hold the windscreen this doesn't happen. Stops the stones thrown up by passing cars from breaking it." Then you drive on, and although you need all the light you can get for looking for game, you wear sunglasses because the bugs are flying in right through the front and popping you in the eyes and you hope no birds come flying in and that it doesn't rain.

As you turn into the park Stretch says, "Let's all make a bet as to how many elephant we will see before we get to the lodge. We'll each put up ten shillings and the closest number wins." Everyone agrees enthusiastically and you bet seventeen (because that is your favorite number), someone else says six and another twenty-five. There is a hopeful bid for forty-two. Your safari leader says 647 and you all laugh, and for the next hour you are busy searching and counting and not bothering your guide, which of course was the purpose of the game in the first place—just a decoy to give him some peace.

You are on a lonely twisted dirt track which goes on and on, but finally you see a little signpost with an arrow saying, 13 MILES TO VOI LODGE. In ten minutes or so you see another little signpost with the comforting arrow still pointing in the correct direction saying, 16 MILES TO VOI LODGE. Your safari leader doesn't seem to mind. You do, but you are afraid to mention it. Eleven elephant now. You might win.

You see a herd of oryx, the crossword-puzzle animals (gnus are another) and Stretch tells you that for every animal you see, fifty see you. You look harder. Suddenly you spot the lodge on a nearby hill and as you turn a corner, walking down the road right toward you is an elephant and behind it a buffalo and behind that a rhino, and bringing up the rear some ostriches—WOW—Africa. Then right behind them you see an African with a little stick who is tapping the rhino on the rump as they do in circuses, and your heart sinks and you think, "The whole thing is faked." But Stretch is saying, "Are we lucky! The orphans."

He goes on to tell you that the orphans of Tsavo are a collection of animals that were rescued when they were babies and raised at the park headquarters. Originally they may have been separated from their parents or their parents could have been killed by other animals, and the park rangers found them and raised them. Now, the ill-assorted family have come to regard park headquarters as home and the staff as their parents and though they are quite free to wander wherever they like in the eight-thousand-square-mile park, or to mix with herds of wild animals all around, they are afraid of them and feel more secure on territory and among friends they know. The orphans appear tame, and indeed act that way most of the time, but a short while ago one of the rhinos, Rufus, which was then three-quarters grown, turned on one of the park rangers and killed him. Wild animals are just that—wild—even though they may acquire a veneer of tameness. Dogs and cats and horses and cows, after thousands of years of close association with man, are probably the only animals that fit the description of "tame" with accuracy. They transported Rufus to a distant corner of the park and turned him loose, but because he was not really used to the ways of the wild he was attacked and eaten by a pride of lion.

You arrive at the lodge, and after you have had the most glorious bath you have ever had because never before have you been this dusty, you hear the dinner drum. Stretch tells you that this just means the beginning of dinner—you can eat any time within the next two hours, so yes, you will all have a drink or nine with him first. Everyone pays him the ten shillings because just when you were sure you were going to win—fifteen elephant was the count—Stretch, who had ignored the game until then, called out in excitement—"Look at that," and in the distance was a huge herd of what everyone agreed must be five hundred elephant. You are determined to say 555 tomorrow and win.

Buffalo and elephant come to the water hole in front of the lodge to drink, and Stretch tells you about two elderly but enthusiastic American lady school teachers who, after completing their safari, decided to hire a car and to drive themselves the three hundred miles between Nairobi and Mombasa. Earlier, in a shop in Nairobi, they had seen and admired some earrings made of lion claws mounted in gold, but decided they could not afford them. The Mombasa road passes through the Tsavo Game Park and to their surprise they saw a large dead lion lying a few yards from the edge of the road. Poor thing, maybe it had been hit by a car. Anyhow, there seemed no point in passing up a good opportunity, so one of the teachers took her penknife—she was the kind who always has one—and prepared to get her own lion claws—free. As she approached, the lion awoke and was so astonished by the sight of a lady with a small knife about to attack it, that it fled in disbelief. Moral—let sleeping lion lie.

When Stretch tells a story he doesn't want to be bothered with the facts, but this doesn't matter.

After dinner you have coffee and brandy overlooking the water hole and Stretch tells more stories and you hate to see the favorite day of your life coming to an end, but you must now get some sleep to be fresh for whatever tomorrow may hold. How the games and stories have added to the enchantment of it all.

So, just in case you ever want to become a safari leader, I will now list some stories for you to tell your clients, and games to play with them to distract them when you can't find one Godamn animal.

GAMES TO PLAY

In addition to betting games about the number of animals you may see, here is a question and answer game:

1. What do camel and giraffe do that no other animal does? They walk by moving both legs forward on the same side simultaneously. All other animals walk in a diametrically opposed fashion.
2. Why do the lion in certain areas climb trees? To get away from the tsetse flies, which stay close to the ground and don't fly that high.
3. Which animal is so prone to heart attacks it can't be used for work? Zebra.
4. Which animal is susceptible to pneumonia? Wart hog.
5. What has four toes in front and three in back? An elephant.
6. What has five toes in front and four in back? A lion.
7. What is the tallest animal in the world? A giraffe—18 feet.
8. What is the egret to the crocodile? A toothbrush. The crocodile sleeps with his mouth open, and the birds come

along and pick food from between the croc's teeth, thus acting as a toothbrush.

9. What is the tick bird to the rhino? Its eyes and a de-ticker. (The rhino is very short-sighted and the birds act as an early warning system.)

10. What is the fastest animal in the world? A cheetah—clocked at seventy-five miles per hour.

11. How many kinds of elephant are there? Two—Indian and African. The African is much larger and much more dangerous. Its only enemy is man who has exploited the species for so long for its ivory that it has come to hate man and instructs its young in hatred of man too.

12. How many kinds of giraffe are there? Three—Reticulated, which means the patterns are clearly defined and look like a jigsaw puzzle; the Masai giraffe, which is sort of spotted; and Rothchild's giraffe, which is darker patterned and has a long protrusion on its head, like a third horn.

13. How many kinds of zebra are there? Two—the Burchell's, which is the most common and the one usually seen; and the Grevy, which is found in Northern Kenya where it is very hot and where the narrower stripes blend with the heat shimmers for camouflage. The Burchell's zebra makes a barking sound and the Grevy cries.

14. Do you see that alligator in the water? No, you don't, there are no alligators in Africa, just crocodiles.

15. Which animal is an excellent road engineer? An elephant. Human engineers planning roads in difficult places measure and survey and do all those things engineers do, and in the end follow elephant tracks, because their gradients and curves are about right for cars.

16. Which animals are the best water diviners? Elephant. Other animals will follow them in arid country because elephant know where to stop and dig for water with their tusks.

17. What is ambergris? Whale throw-up. (They may think you indelicate here. But when you go on to tell them that it is an export commodity from Kenya because it is used in per-

fumes, they will be impressed with your store of knowledge and will never feel the same about perfume again.)

18. What is the paleontologist's favorite animal other than man? The black rhino because it hasn't changed at all in two million years.

19. What is a paleontologist? One who studies fossils.

20. What color is a white rhino? Unlike George Washington's white horse, a white rhino is brown. ("White" is a corruption of the Afrikaans word meaning "wide," referring to its wide lips.)

21. Which is larger, the white or black rhino? The white rhino is a third again larger than the black.

22. What does Hippopotamus mean? It is the Greek word for "river horse."

23. Why does a hippo stay in the water all day? To keep from getting sunburned. They come up every four minutes for air.

24. When does a hippo eat? It grazes all night long, eating up to three hundred pounds of food.

25. When does a hippo sleep? No one can figure it out.

26. How many feet can an impala leap? Thirty-five in length and ten feet high.

27. What has the body of a cat and the feet of a dog? A cheetah.

28. Which is the only cat in Africa with a tuft on its tail? A lion.

29. What color is the tuft? Black.

30. Do you see that deer over there? No, you don't, because there are no deer in Africa—just antelope.

31. What is the difference between deer and antelope? Antelope have single spikes for horns, whereas deer have branching antlers. Antelope means "brightness of eyes" in Greek, and gazelle means "bright eyes" in Arabic.

32. Who are the garbage collectors of Africa? The vultures, which is why they are protected and not allowed to be shot.

33. At what time are those buffalo over there? Those who have been in the military will know that twelve o'clock is straight

ahead, three o'clock directly right etc., but the women won't know what you are talking about.

34. What do wine and animals have in common? Neither travels well. Flying is extremely painful to animals' ears, and the only creatures that fly happily in airplanes are birds.

35. Why do we eat antelope and elephant trunk, but not lion or hyena? We don't eat the flesh of animals that eat flesh.

36. In what way is the tiger's tail different from the lion's tail? Lions have a black tuft on the end of their tails and tigers have a white tip to the tail. Both cats flick their tails from time to time while stalking their prey. Researchers are wondering whether, in fact, they are passing signals to other lions behind them who may be helping. The black tail shows up particularly well against the light-colored grass of the African plain, and the white tip on the tiger's tail is readily visible in the dark forests where they hunt.

Game II

Ask each person if he were an animal which one would he choose to be. It is very interesting to hear the surprising things people choose: a vulture—protected from man, beautiful in flight, no enemies; a leopard—so beautiful and mean; a chimpanzee—to make people laugh; a Grade-A bull—for obvious reasons. I'm sure a psychiatrist would see all kinds of things in the choices.

Here is a list of questions I promise you the safari-ers will ask you. Here are some correct answers—and also some lies to tell:

1. Are there any snakes? No. (Lie) Bet them ten dollars they won't see one on the entire safari, to instill false confidence in them, and mainly to give yourself some peace otherwise you will be harassed every few minutes to, "walk into my room with me to see if there are any snakes," and "we can't get out here for a picnic—what about those snakes?" As one slithers across the road in front of the car, point out the back window and holler, "Look at those colobus monkeys

in the trees, 'over yonder,'" (as they will say) and keep them busy looking through binoculars until the snake gets lost in the grass.

2. Are there any bugs? No. (Lie) Otherwise, they'll bring sordid things like flypaper from Neiman-Marcus and hang it up in the car, and it will swing and hit you in the back of of the neck and get caught in your hair.

3. What is the most dangerous animal in Africa? The mosquito, because of malaria. (True)

4. What is the second most dangerous animal? Crocodile. Mainly because African women go to the streams and rivers to wash their clothes and are taken by crocs. (True)

5. What is the third most dangerous animal? Since we shoot with cameras instead of guns, the most dangerous animal for us is the elephant because of its size. If a rhino or buffalo were to charge the car, the worst thing that could happen would be that they might turn us over. But, by its very size, the elephant could trample us to pieces even in the car. (True)

6. Is this trip dangerous for us in any way? Yes. (Lie) Do not deprive them of their feeling of having an exciting, harrowing adventure. Make sure they have some noteworthy experiences. Instead of using that new bridge across the river—it is far too civilized—take the old route and ford the river. Be sure to get stuck, or at least pretend to, so they can all get out in the water with their shoes on and push. Splatter them with mud so they can take some "dirty pictures" of themselves to show back home to the folks, and so they can thoroughly enjoy their bath when they get to the lodge. When you get stuck in the river, they will ask,

7. "Is there anything in this water which could harm us?" No. (Lie) If they know about the crocodiles, they won't push you out.

8. What on earth is that television set doing in that tree way out here in the bush? Africans have a thirst for education, and because of the lack of schools and teachers, the gov-

ernment cleverly televises educational programs in Uganda.
(True)

9. What are the four different ethnic groups of Africans in East Africa? Hamitic, Nilo-hamitic, Bantu and Nilotic. (True) They don't want to know, but they want to see if you do.

10. What do the average Africans think of Americans? They don't think of Americans. (True)

11. What about Mau Mau? Robert Ruark and other sensationalists gave the subject exaggerated world prominence in the mid-1950s. The facts are that primarily one tribe, the Kikuyu, were involved and nine tenths of the African population in Kenya did not participate actively. That only thirty-two European (white) civilians were killed by the Mau Mau. (More Europeans died in traffic accidents within the precincts of Nairobi during the period of the Emergency than were killed by Mau Mau.) That the aims and objects of the movement, namely the end of white-colonialist domination and a redistribution of land owned by white settlers among Africans, were obscured by the violent trend the movement took which divided the Kikuyu tribe itself, all of whom probably supported the objectives (as indeed did the other tribes), but not all of whom agreed with the method. (True)

12. What of Kenyatta's role in Mau Mau? Jomo Kenyatta started a political movement but was arrested together with the main leaders who were his lieutenants. They were tried, convicted, many say unfairly, and detained in a desert miles from possible communication with the people. His now leaderless movement was taken over by others and became the Mau Mau which the world saw. Nobody, probably not even Kenyatta, could tell what would have been the course of events had he remained free. One thing is certain however; in the years since becoming President of his country Jomo Kenyatta has shown himself to be a fair and merciful man, without bitterness, without thoughts of retribution or re-

venge. More than this though, he has become an outstanding statesman in Africa, often mediating in disputes between other independent countries, and always anxious to de-fuse situations that might lead to violence. (True)

13. Does anyone ever have wild animals for pets? Yes, lion and cheetah and zebra make excellent pets and the latter are supposedly more intelligent than a dog. Hyenas make good pets too. (True)

14. What is that funny-looking tree over there? Baobab.

15. And what is that elephant doing rubbing against it? Brushing its teeth. (True)

Baobab trees are in a class by themselves. They are enormously fat, not very high, and have branches that are without leaves for most of the year, making them look as if the tree has been pulled out of the ground by a giant and stuck in upside down, so that the roots are waving in the air.

Growing in hot and arid areas, baobabs have a property that may spell their downfall. The trees store considerable quantities of water in the soft pithy centers of their massive trunks. It is said you can predict the weather from the amount of water the baobab stores—a lot in preparation for a drought, and not so much if there is going to be good rainfall during the following season. Elephants know this, and in the very dry weather when no other water is available, they will work away at the baobab trees with their tusks until they can chew on the watery fiber for the moisture. Not infrequently, over the period of a month or so, elephant will totally demolish a baobab tree in this way and since they take hundreds of years to grow, in areas like the Tsavo National Park where there is an increasingly dense elephant population, the trees are seriously threatened.

There is another thing about the baobab tree. Cream of tartar is obtained from it—an ingredient used in many toothpastes. It is nice to suppose that the elephant know this,

since they frequently appear to be polishing their tusks as
they work at the demolition of the trees.

16. Where is the elephant graveyard? Sorry to spoil it for you,
but there is no elephant graveyard anywhere. (True) Elephant do not go to a secret spot to die, they just die in the
bush like everybody else, spread out all over the place,
wherever they happen to fall. The legend started, most
likely, because hunters would come across a number of
tusks together and assumed the graveyard theory, when in
fact they were finding poachers' caches of ivory that had
been abandoned or never collected for some reason.

One question *you* must ask *them* because they will be embarrassed to ask it themselves for the first few days is, "Does anyone
want to stop for rest rooms?" On second thought, don't ask, just
stop—this prevents anyone from even having to admit he goes to
the bathroom. Just stop and tell them there's a rest room behind
every bush, boys on this side of the road, girls on that. You will
notice one lady will never get out of the car. Just like a camel, you
think, but the truth of the matter is she has on a jump suit which
is much too complicated in the bush, so she'll just get kidney
trouble.

The worst thing is when you are starving because you had to
give your picnic lunch to Sarah Sue because she dropped hers in
the elephant dung, (you probably would have brushed it off and
eaten it anyway if they hadn't been looking), and you finally get
your group to the dinner table and you are just getting your fork
up to your mouth when somebody says, "Oh, I've just been dying
to ask you this and at last I have the opportunity! Would you tell
me the story of your life?" (Or the history of Africa.) So you smile
your plastic smile and condense your life-story enough to pretend
you aren't being rude, or not earning your money, and finally, just
as you dip into your food again, that dirty old man asks, "How do
crocodiles breed?" To avoid these constant questions while you
are eating—or trying to—plot your tables so that you have someone
who just loves to talk at *your* table, and as you sit down—don't let
anybody else say anything first—you say, "Oh, Mrs. Patterson, I've

just been dying to ask you this and at last I have the opportunity! Would you tell me the story of your life?" Then you can eat away and nod occasionally so she won't know you're not listening.

As it nears bedtime you may find yourself still sitting up with those of the group who slept late and don't realize, or care, that you had to get up with the 6 A.M. enthusiasts who have long since gone to bed. They are still asking questions, and your voice is beginning to go, but don't worry about that because Americans love statistics, and if you can memorize a vast quantity of numbers, everyone will think you are highly intelligent. If you had eleven million fingers, you wouldn't have to speak even once—you could just hold up the right amount of fingers. For example:

1. What is the population of Kenya?   11,000,000.
2. What is the population of Nairobi?   478,000.
3. How many game parks and reserves in East Africa?   70.
4. How many species of game in Tsavo?   70.
5. How many square miles is Tsavo Park?   8,000.
6. How many elephant in Tsavo Park?   22,000.
7. How many tons does a full-grown elephant weigh?   8.
8. How many pounds does an elephant weigh at birth?   300.
9. How many hours does an elephant eat each day?   16.
10. How many gallons of water does it drink per day?   40.
11. How many pounds of food does an elephant eat each day?   500.
12. How many miles will an elephant travel overnight eating?   40.
13. How many species of birds at Lake Nakuru?   400.
14. How many species of antelope in East Africa?   63.

As you drive into the first lodge you can tell them this little story to prepare them for the food they are about to get:

At the lodges in the middle of the game parks, all the food has to be delivered by truck or flown in. There are no stores for hundreds of miles. Some of the lodge managers bravely try to grow a few fresh vegetables to supplement supplies. One night at Ngorongoro, the guests were served roast beef, mashed potatoes and gravy, and canned baked beans. The manager came in looking harassed, and apologizing for the beans cried, "The elephants ate the brussel sprouts! The elephants ate the brussel sprouts!"

As you approach Olduvai Gorge to look at the site of Dr. Leakey's excavations of early man, you can tell about the group of paleontologists who were in the northern part of Kenya, referred to as the NFD, on a camel expedition because the terrain was too rough for cars. Each night they camped, and each night they heard terrible noises, and the following morning one of their camels would be gone—taken by lion. Finally, since all their transportation was being eaten, and they risked being marooned in the desert, they had to post one of the members of the expedition near the camels each night until the lion was finally shot.

Another expedition story: Zoological groups from all over the world come to Africa to collect specimens—sometimes alive, sometimes dead. One such group from the States on an expedition in West Africa included a bat expert who was overjoyed to capture a dozen or so large, rare bats. The day before he was due to return home he made one final sortie into the forest but found no more and returned empty-handed. He wasn't too upset, since he had been so lucky earlier, but when he returned to camp he found that the porters had *eaten* his entire collection.

As you get to Arusha you will no doubt stop in at Count von Nagy's, a wildlife enthusiast who has an excellent private zoo. This gives you the opportunity to tell the following:

One of the inmates of his zoo is a fine male lion who used to belong to a traveling magician and would appear with him on stage, and, between engagements, would ride in the passenger seat of the magician's car.

The magician's final disappearing act was from Dar-es-Salaam in a sailing boat, and he couldn't take his sophisticated lion with him—magic notwithstanding.

Dr. von Nagy agreed to adopt him and sent one of his African keepers the three hundred miles to bring the lion from Dar-es-Salaam. Chatting about the journey, someone asked whether the lion wasn't very hot in a crate in the luggage hold for all that distance. "Oh no," said the keeper, shocked, "he would never agree to ride in a crate—I bought two tickets and he sat in a seat next to me all the way." You can bet the bus lost a good number of regular passengers that day.

Another story concerning lion happened during the war at a remote Air Force base in Ethiopia. One of the men had a pet lion which he had raised from a cub and which soon became the mascot and was a favorite of the airmen. One afternoon, just as an aircraft was on its final landing approach, the lion was spotted standing in the middle of the runway. One of the groundcrew grabbed a stick and ran to chase it off just in time before the plane hit it. Returning to the hangar, the man was horrified to see the mascot lion fast asleep in a corner—where it had been all along. He had just chased off a real wild lion with nothing more than a stick!

It is only during the last two or three years that a scientific study has been made of lion. One of the first problems to be solved was finding a means of positive identification for different animals. People who knew individual lions, in the sense that they had watched them in the wild since they were cubs and were able to recognize them, were of no real help. They probably could tell the lion they knew from others, but how could they convince anyone else or explain to anyone else which was which? The answer, based upon nothing but acute observation, turned out to be extremely simple. Lions' whiskers, or even a domestic cat's for that matter, grow in parallel lines on the upper lip and each individual whisker springs from a tiny black dot, visible from, say, ten paces. This turned out to be the lion's finger print, as it were. The arrangement of black whisker dots in relation to each other is different for every single lion and can be entered on a chart or detected from a photograph which could easily be taken from a vehicle. Since this is a brand-new discovery the vast majority of zoologists, zoo directors, and the like, do not yet know this fact, so if you have any friends who fall into one of these categories, you can now display your knowledge and astound them.

There still is no way of identifying an ostrich.

This next is a great piece of information to just toss out casually. Look diligently for a German stork. If you can't find one, point to any old stork and tell your companions that the instincts that control the behavior of certain animals are often unbelievably strong and sometimes produce the most dramatic results. East Africa has a large population of migratory birds from Europe each winter, among them large black and white storks from Germany and Holland. These birds have two peculiarities. They are strictly monogamous, and some are East Africa "orientated," while others migrate always to West Africa.

Upon arrival in North Africa, having crossed the Mediterranean on the southward journey, the storks in their thousands rest, and then proceed to the East or West African countries, as their instinct compels them. They are creatures of such habit that individual birds not only return to the same country and district year after year, but even to the same actual tree. Inevitably some die on the trip each year, but those bereaved are allowed to remarry. On the return to Europe from East Africa, they meet up with the West African contingent and all mix freely. Marriages may take place between East Africans and West Africans and children are subsequently hatched. All is well until the next migration when the families arrive in North Africa. At this point, for those who are unfortunate enough to have unwittingly married unwisely, the instinct to go East or West is more powerful than the instinct to stay with their new partners. The young of such unions now discover a shocking fact—they find themselves to be schizophrenic. Which parent should they follow? They zigzag back and forth, first after their father, then after their mother, finally collapsing in the deserts, exhausted. Thousands of young birds who are unfortunate enough to be the offspring of such marriages are found dead each year along the North African coast.

However, stories with the personal touch are always more dramatic. Have some harrowing adventures yourself and collect them to tell. In the next chapter are some true stories Jock and I have collected over the years.

XVII
Harrowing Adventures

Many readers will probably remember seeing Jack Paar's television special on lion. In it he featured an adorable little cub that he raised at his home in Bronxville. He was given the cub by Lion Country Safari in Florida, following a chain of events for which we were originally responsible and which led to Jack's interest in lion.

Our friends, Francesco and Suki Bisletti at Naivasha, have a small private zoo and among their animals were three young fully grown lionesses who were the cubs of the stars of *Born Free*. (I think seven different lionesses played the part of Elsa.) Now large and in their prime they were expensive to feed—thirty-five pounds of food per day per lion. The proper cages at the Bislettis' were already occupied with other animals, and they had nowhere to put them except in a rather unsatisfactory wire-netting enclosure from which they escaped into a neighboring pen where they killed a pet leopard. Francesco and Suki feared they might escape all together—possibly kill somebody—and having tried without success to find a home for them in a zoo, they were arriving at the point where they felt they might have to shoot them. We heard of the plight of the lion, and cabled Jack Paar. In less than twelve hours there was a reply that he would save them and would fly them to the States.

How do you get three fully grown lion onto an airliner? We all have our problems, and this was ours. Recognizing that this was stretching our talents somewhat, we enlisted the aid of an animal trapper, and Jack flew an expert from the States to travel with them. Crates were hastily built and we all assembled at the Bislettis. Suki, who was able to walk among the lion and to pet them, was nevertheless quite unable to persuade them to enter the crates. The lion lay lazily in the sun on some high rocks at the back of their enclosure and could not be tempted down. Some small children were brought to the edge of the enclosure. Lion hate baboons and eat them whenever they can, and they mistake small children for baboons, so the theory was that they would come down to crate level to investigate or to eat the kids. It didn't work. Finally, after hours of cajoling to no effect, it was decided to tranquilize them. The drugs had a sad and undignified, but at the same time comic effect, because the lion staggered around as if drunk, before finally becoming so sleepy that they could be manhandled into the crates. They were loaded aboard the airliner, and we all relaxed and got loaded on the ground.

In the meantime, unbeknown to us, Jack Paar was very far from relaxed. Having cabled us with such alacrity to send the lion, he was, in fact, having a very hard time finding a home for them. Lion breed well in captivity, and the problem in most zoos is not that of acquiring specimens but of unloading a surplus population. Now here were three fully grown lionesses winging their way towards him in Bronxville, but what was he to do with them?

At the eleventh hour Lion Country Safari, a five-hundred-acre open park in Florida agreed to accept them. Alert to the prospect of dramatic television, Jack flew down to Florida having made arrangements to have the cameras rolling for the uncrating ceremony. One of his most endearing features is his ability to see the humor in situations, even when the laugh is on him. As he told us later, he could envision himself opening the crates, and to the strains of *Born Free* the lion would bound into the Florida sunset, safe and as good as free.

All was ready, the doors were sprung, and none of the lion would leave its crate. Food was offered. People shouted and banged on the crates. Nothing happened. A jeep was driven gently at a crate with the idea of jolting or tipping one of them out, and this worked. A startled lion emerged, took one look at Florida, and bolted back into the crate again. Finally, when it was too dark to film very much, and in their own good time, the three emerged and within a few days had settled happily into their new surroundings.

The rescue cost Jack more than seven thousand dollars before he was through—three times as much as he originally anticipated. None of us had any idea how expensive it is to fly large animals around the world. Jack, being a very kind person, as well as an animal lover, didn't mind about the money for a second.

A sequel to the story, which Jack included in one of his television specials, was a reunion with Suki and her lion a year later. Remember, no human being had touched them or approached them during this period, and they were living as if wild, with the exception that they could only roam over a few hundred acres and their meals of raw meat were provided. Suki swore that they would remember her and walked gently towards them, calling them by name. Once more the cameras rolled, but this time there were no disappointments. The lion ate her on the spot. (I'm kidding.) She caressed her "babies," they rubbed against her, and Jack Paar, the NBC television crew, and the hunter who had been standing by with a gun, all relaxed.

Some funny things happen in the States too. We once lunched at the Bronx Zoo with the Director, Bill Conway, and afterwards he asked the curator of mammals to show us around. In the primate house we saw two gorilla sitting cross-legged with their heads resting on their fists in their cage, totally absorbed in a television show! We were intrigued by the television set which had been placed in front of the cage for them to view and were told that in the summer when the gorilla could be outside they were fine, but in the winter, cooped up inside, the male would become so bored that he would beat up his wife, just for something to do. But now they sit there all winter glued to their television set. From time to time the male does get up, shambles over to his wife and gives her a little slug, which we all agreed we liked to think was during the commercials.

When I lived in Baltimore I frequently visited my good friend Robert, the gorilla in the zoo there. A splendid personality, he would wait for a large crowd of onlookers and then he would vomit generously. A few would turn their heads and leave. Then Robert would recline propped up on one elbow and would eat his vomit like a Roman emperor enjoying grapes. Almost everyone would leave then but me, and I would catch Robert's eye, and I swear I have seen him wink.

Soon after Jock and I were married in Kenya we went on our first trip together to Baltimore to visit friends and family. One evening at a dinner party Arthur Watson, Director of the Baltimore Zoo, was present. Jock, of course, knew nothing of Arthur Watson nor of Robert, who had recently died. After a while somebody asked Arthur,

"How did Robert die?"

"Of lung cancer," replied Mr. Watson.

Everyone looked appropriately sad.

"How old was he?" asked another.

"Eleven."

Jock, who supposed the conversation was about somebody known to the rest of us, looked startled.

"At the time of his death he weighed five hundred and twelve pounds," added Mr. Watson. Everyone continued to look downcast, and there were murmurs of sympathy. Jock could hardly wait to get me alone so he could ask about this deformed relative of Mr. Watson's—perhaps a nephew or even his brother?— who ate himself to five hundred and twelve pounds in eleven years and who must have smoked four cartons of cigarettes a day as well. He seemed faintly disappointed to learn that Robert was merely a gorilla.

But, back to Africa.

The safari, or marching ants, give a certain amount of trouble from time to time. They will form themselves into a column about half an inch wide and maybe half a mile long, and as you drive along a road you may easily mistake this black line for a snake. These blind ants come in two sizes. The larger ones are warriors, about half an inch long, and on their heads they have powerful pincers. The ants attack and eat any living creature that gets in their way—from little beetles to an elephant. "Siafu," as the Africans call them, are supposed to be the elephant's only fear because once they get the ants in their trunks there is nothing they can do about it. Imagine having a whole bunch of ants biting the inside of your nose.

They are not dangerous to humans, or to most animals that can just walk away. Tiny children or dogs chained up can be in a lot of trouble though. The three-month-old baby of a friend of ours was attacked in its carriage in the garden, and the mother saved it by plunging the screaming child into a tub full of water to get the ants off. Their bite is not poisonous but is powerful enough to draw little drops of blood, and while half a dozen would just make you jump around a bit until you had pulled them off, several hundred or a thousand could be quite another story. I have had them bite me a number of times just walking around in the garden. You don't feel them crawl onto you but suddenly about ten will nip you all at once, as if by a prearranged signal. Every ounce of modesty departs. Right then and there, no matter who is around, anyone will whip off a pair of pants in record time and start picking the ants off. So long as you are not the one being attacked it can be very funny. The expression "ants in your pants" now has real meaning for me.

The ants live in large underground nests and are controlled by half a dozen or so queen ants, who are nothing more than helpless white slugs about an inch long. To disperse the ants from a nest—to utterly demoralize the colony beyond hope of recovery—all you have to do is to remove the queens. Sounds easy. We had a nest at the bottom of our garden and we hired an expert, an intrepid African steeped in ant knowledge, and it took him a whole day to dig them out. He was bitten and attacked for every second that he worked, but other than swearing for the duration of the job he seemed unaffected by them. I filmed some of the proceedings and show the footage in one of our lecture films. In the middle of everything a small harmless snake, disturbed by the commotion, fell into the hole and within minutes was eaten up by the ants. More than a year has elapsed since the great ant excavation and the removal of the queens, and we haven't seen *siafu* in our garden since.

The intelligence evident among colonies of ants is both remarkable and mystifying. For instance, among white ants—they are wood-eating termites and we have them in the garden too— there is an inexplicable method of instant communication. If you disturb them yards away from the nest, the news gets back to the main nest and the queen instantly. Ants in her vicinity are alerted to a possible emergency, and the news has traveled from the disaster area at a speed that rules out a messenger. In all their behavior there is concerted action, method and precision.

Though I have never seen it done, I am told that the Africans use *siafu* to stitch a wound. If they cut themselves they will pinch the wound closed and allow a warrior ant to bite them in such a way that its pincers grip either side of the cut. When the ant has a good grip they tweak off the body, leaving the head and pincers as a perfect suture.

THIS PAGE IS FOR THE BIRDS

Ornithologists will hate me, but I find birds very pretty and somewhat dull. In fact, the truth is, I don't even find them very pretty—their little beady eyes are too harsh. The spectacle of three million bright pink flamingos on Lake Nakuru does grab me, I admit, but I think it is the color more than the birds. Generally speaking, I don't like anything that flies—birds or airplanes—and I prefer snakes to bats. If only birds would do something interesting—just once. At least with a kongoni, which is the most boring animal in all of Africa—plain vanilla—there is a chance you might find it being grabbed by a crocodile or copulating or something noteworthy. (I know, I know, I am told birds do all kinds of miraculous things, but you can't *see* them.)

The honey birds are exceptions. They have a working relationship with man. These birds love the grubs from the honeycomb but cannot extract it from the bee's nest in trees, so they find a man and deliberately lead him with their call to the tree. The Africans love honey but have no way of finding it in the forest without the help of the bird. The men always leave plenty of comb and grubs as a reward for the bird.

Jock's mother had a parrot that I thought was more interesting than most. He was an African Grey from the Congo, a species that speaks far more clearly than any other kind of parrot. A good African Grey can sound exactly like a human being and does not have that scratchy squawk of most parrots. Jock's father had originally obtained him from a zoo in Nairobi which folded, and he came to the family with a spectacular vocabulary of swear words in Swahili, Kikuyu, Hindustani and English.

He was allowed to wander freely, but his wings were clipped so that he would not fly away and get lost in the forest. Unfortunately, there are many birds of prey in the African skies and one day an evil buzzard spotted the parrot strutting on the lawn below. The buzzard swooped down, grabbed the parrot in his talons and carried him aloft. The parrot, however, knew who to call upon in an emergency and shrieked, "Kamau!"—the name of the cook. Kamau dashed out of the kitchen and sized up the situation in a trice. He yelled at the buzzard, by now a hundred feet up in the air, and hurled a stone. The buzzard was so surprised—after all nothing like this had ever happened to him before—that he dropped the parrot and flew away. Because the long feathers of his wings and had been clipped only the week before, he made an extremely heavy vertical landing and was very sick for some days afterwards as a result.

Parrots sometimes live to be more than a hundred years old.

The male and female birds of the African Grey look alike and for twenty years Jock's mother had assumed that hers was a male —he had that kind of personality. One morning however, to everyone's astonishment, there was a single and absolutely spherical egg—exactly the shape and size of a ping-pong ball lying in the bottom of the cage where "he" slept. The effort had evidently been too much. The bird became listless and sickly, and a few weeks later they found the poor thing dead in the cage.

As I mentioned earlier, neither Jock nor I are interested in sports, neither is he concerned with breaking records as a means of proving something. He does, however, enjoy a certain inverted delight from holding a record he acquired not only without trying but, if the truth be known, by mistake.

The coast of most of East Africa is bordered by a coral reef about a mile offshore. Between the beach and the reef the water is relatively shallow, but beyond the reef the ocean is very deep and it is here that large fish are found.

One day Jock was cruising around with some children and a dog in a small borrowed boat propelled by a little engine, and he was keeping well within the reef. He knows as much about fishing as I know about gardening—almost nothing.

Lying in the boat was a large fish hook, a length of light rope and some bait. Just for something to do he baited the hook and threw it over the stern to trail behind, and having secured the rope to the boat he sat back to enjoy the sun. Almost at once there was a violent jerk and he found himself being dragged out to sea in the little boat. Whatever it was had more power than the engine, and Jock looked desperately for a knife to cut it free, but there was none. Nor was it possible to untie the knot because of the tension. After a few minutes the fish tired and he and the children gradually hauled it up. The moment they saw what it was they let the rope out again. An enormous sting-ray had taken the bait and they say that these fish will leap out of the water and lash people with the dreadful sting in their whiplike tails.

Now that the enemy was known one of the children started to

have hysterics, the dog began barking at the general commotion, and Jock stalled the engine. The ray, having had a brief rest, started off again and with no engine to fight made good time in the direction of India.

Eventually it tired, Jock managed to restart the engine and they struggled back to shore. Upon being beached, the ray gave birth to a sixteen-pound baby—a fully functioning exact replica of itself —sting and all.

The ray weighed 317 pounds (less baby) and was thought to be easily the biggest fish ever taken inside the reef in East Africa— and, as Jock readily admits, the whole episode was an awful mistake.

A sequel to the adventure was that despite giving the details and a picture to the newspaper, no story ever appeared. Jock maintains that because it happened right in front of some hotels it was thought that the publicity given to fearsome fish would scare away people who liked to come to swim.

Swimming. This brings me to an elephant story. In fact, many elephant stories. Since elephant are probably the most intelligent of all the animals, with perhaps the exception of the chimpanzee and porpoise, elephantologists—I just made up that word—are trying to find out now just how smart they are.

One morning during the heavy floods of 1953, visitors sunning themselves at Malindi were astonished to see an elephant swimming to the shore from the ocean. It waded in through the surf, took a look up and down the beach and disappeared inland without delay. Evidently, it had been swept out to sea by the flooded Sabaki river and was making its way home again. Elephant swim with great ease and have the perfect ready-made snorkel in the shape of their trunk. Unable to believe their eyes, a number of the carefree holidaymakers swore off booze then and there.

At Paraa the famous elephant christened Dustbin Nelly is frequently seen around the lodge with her two daughters. The family help themselves out of the garbage bins put out at the back of the kitchen. Finally, for the amusement of visitors, the kitchen staff took to disposing of potato peelings and lettuce leaves right in front of the open verandah of the lodge so that they could watch the elephant family feeding. Not content with potato peelings Dustbin Nelly has acquired a taste for alcohol. She has learnt that if she approaches the verandah, the tourists will back away in alarm, leaving their drinks on the little tables so that she can syphon out the contents of the glasses with her trunk. The lodge in fact has a wonderful photograph of Dustbin Nelly with her trunk in a glass of beer, and standing on a table is an empty bottle of Tusker Beer, a brand name that has a picture of an elephant's head on the label.

Jack Paar woke up one morning when we were with him at Paraa Lodge and looked out of his window in time to witness what could have been a tragic accident. Three little Dutch boys were teasing Dustbin Nelly, who despite her habits is a completely wild elephant and has learned to tolerate humans only so long as the humans do not bother her. The little boys were running around and throwing stones at her and Dustbin Nelly suddenly reached on to the verandah, picked up a steel chair with her trunk and hurled it at the children, fortunately missing them but causing them to run screaming into the safety of the lodge.

Dustbin Nelly is not the only elephant who has acquired a taste for alcohol. At Mweya Park years ago we met George. George was an elephant that came to the lodge every Wednesday and Saturday when the barrel containing the customers' leftover drinks and beer was put outside to be dumped. Old George liked his booze. How he knew Wednesdays and Saturdays no one will ever be able to tell, but those were the only days when he came. Once, by mistake, the barrel was not put outside, so George merely lifted the thatched roof off the building and reached over to drink from the barrel inside.

The power of a sleepy-looking elephant can easily be underestimated. On the Nairobi-Mombasa road a large truck and trailer ran into an elephant at night, injuring it but not killing it. The truck went off the road and turned over on its side. The driver who was unhurt clambered out and very wisely made for a tree.

The elephant's friend which had not been injured, then set about the truck and such was its rage that it succeeded in tearing the axle and wheels out of the chassis.

At Aruba Lodge in the Tsavo Park elephant used to come extremely close to the little *bandas*—separate houses where the guests stayed. Since this made visitors nervous, and could also have been dangerous, the owners dug an enormous ditch around the lodge. Jock and I peeped out of our window early one morning to see an elephant approach the ditch, sit down on his rear end, as on a sliding board, swoosh to the bottom and clamber out, all of which was done quite effortlessly. We were happy that the tourists felt secure but were amused to know that the elephant did not regard the barrier as a barrier at all. In hilly country, elephant usually choose an easy incline down which to walk, but if they come to a particularly steep bit they will sit and slide down on their backsides—one of the funniest things you could ever wish to see.

A renowned figure among game buffs was the late Major Lynn Temple-Boreham who for years was the warden of the Masai-Mara area of Kenya, an animal paradise that visitors can now enjoy by staying at Keekorok Lodge.

One of the great conservationists, T.B., as most people knew him, worked closely with the Masai people and successfully sowed the seeds in many of their minds that the animals around them were a great natural asset. Instead of spearing lion for sport why not save them for spectacle?

Though the stories about T.B. are endless, one that has always impressed me is primarily his about his wife, Joan, who is stone deaf. Before they were married she had a dress shop in Nairobi and was not particularly oriented to animals and the bush. Perhaps as compensation of a sort for being deaf, she quickly developed the most fantastic eyesight and could amaze even her husband with her keen game spotting.

One day T.B. was called to shoot some marauding elephant that were devastating crops and threatening people living on the edge of the game reserve. He and Joan drove to the area in a small truck in the back of which they often slept on a mattress to save the trouble of having to pitch a tent. At dusk they located the elephant which disappeared over a small hill. T.B. decided to follow them early next morning and at first light accompanied by a game scout, he set out leaving Joan slumbering soundly.

He found the elephant just where he expected over the hill and he and the scout started to shoot. Several crashed down as the two men fired and within a few minutes the job was done.

It was still early and he decided to return to the truck for breakfast. Retracing his steps he was horrified to see that where a few minutes before the scout had shot two dead elephant, now there was only one. (It sometimes happens that a heavy bullet can stun an elephant without killing it.) The tracks of the wounded animal led directly back over the hill towards the truck. Appalled, T.B. instantly envisioned what was, actually, at that moment taking place.

Reaching the crest of the hill the wounded elephant spotted the little truck and started its charge—seven tons of enraged and lethal pachyderm on a downward slope, aimed at a deaf and sleeping lady.

The unsuspecting Joan sat up in bed, stretched, and reached over to part the canvas cover of the truck to see what kind of a day it was going to be. Eventful. Directly in her line of vision there appeared a large and furious-looking elephant, coming towards her down the slope at full tilt.

Beside her, between the mattress and the edge of the truck, lay T.B.'s second rifle with a loaded magazine. Though not an experienced shot, she slammed a bullet into the breach, jumped out of the truck and fired. A perfect hit. The elephant's front legs folded under and it came to a sliding halt, stone dead, a few paces from the truck.

Jock had two adventures with T.B., one resulting in a scar which he received from a lion while in the Mara. He was reading one afternoon, sitting in a canvas camp chair totally absorbed in his book, when a three-quarters grown pet lion which T.B. had brought on the safari decided to stalk him from behind. Jock said everybody in the camp held his breath and watched as the lion crept up and positioned himself for the final spring—but nobody warned him because that would have spoiled a good laugh. Launching himself at Jock the lion reached the chair in a single bound and with a playful underhand swat caught him on the rear end through the stretched canvas of the chair. To this day he has a neat scar about an inch long and though from time to time he mentions, *en passant,* that he was clawed by a lion in the Mara, I will not let him exhibit the scar too often.

The second experience had all the potential for a fatal disaster. T.B. led Jock and several others on foot through a belt of forest about a mile wide. The vehicles and drivers were to follow along a rough track half an hour later, giving the walking party a chance to move quietly through the forest, observing birds and animals that would have been frightened away by the cars.

As they walked out of the forest they disturbed a herd of elephant and there was much crashing and excitement. For safety, the party moved to a large anthill fifty yards from the forest edge affording a 360-degree view, and T.B. perched on top with his gun. They waited for the cars to pick them up. After forty minutes or so, it was evident that something was holding up the vehicles, and because it would soon be dark Jock suggested that he go back to look for them. T.B. said that with the elephant activity he himself had better remain with the main group but that he would walk a little way with Jock, and the two set off, Jock about twenty paces in front. The track led through some thick tall grass and Jock was suddenly aware that T.B. was no longer following. Glancing over his shoulder he could see him standing on the path, smiling at him, and he gave a little wave, signifying that all was well and that that was as far as he was coming. Jock continued alone for half a mile, found that the Land-Rovers had been held up by a dead tree having fallen across the disused track, cleared a way round it, and drove to pick up the others. He found them in a great state of excitement about his narrow escape. Unknown to Jock, as he and T.B. had walked through the long grass, a lioness with four tiny cubs had suddenly appeared on the

path between them, only feet behind Jock, switching her tail and
ready to defend her cubs. It is really only with young that lions
are aggressive towards man unless they are cornered or wounded.
She lowered herself onto her belly at the edge of the path, seemingly about to spring on Jock from behind when she heard T.B.
behind her. They saw one another simultaneously and both froze.
At this moment Jock glanced back, fortunately seeing only T.B.
He undoubtedly owes his life to T.B.'s quick reaction, or rather
the masterful lack of it. Instead of shouting or shooting—Jock was
in line of fire so that would have been dangerous—he merely stood
still, smiled, and gave his little wave allowing Jock to walk un-
hurriedly away from the danger. Had Jock been alarmed and
started to run the lioness would have certainly pursued him. T.B.
quietly retreated and the lioness slunk back into the grass.

Jock has always been mad that while he was having the closest
call of his life, he was totally unaware of it. It makes one wonder
how often one has been incredibly close to death but completely
oblivious of any danger.

As I have already told you, one very rarely encounters snakes
or even sees them in Africa. They are there, of course, but they
are in no way a part of daily life. I have seen more snakes in Baltimore than I have here and from all accounts there seem to be more
in Texas or Florida or Arizona than in Africa. However, one does
hear stories of encounters with snakes from time to time, and Jock's
brother-in-law, Martin, had an unnerving experience with a python.
First, I must explain, there persists a belief among certain African
tribes that a python does not in fact suffocate you by coiling about
you and squeezing so hard that you can't breathe. Instead, they
say, it inserts the tip of its tail up your nostril and in some way
not clearly defined, this results in your demise.

Martin, who was running a large ranch at the time, was walking with two or three African herdsmen through some long grass
when he stepped on a sleeping python. Like a steel spring it coiled
all around him and gripped him, but he managed to stay on his
feet.

The herdsmen fled in panic and Martin was left to struggle

alone. In the end, ashamed of themselves for running, they came to his rescue and managed to free him. He said the weirdest thing about the whole frightening encounter was that the tip of the snake's tail kept flickering around his face and trying to enter his nostrils . . .

Of course the most harrowing of all adventures is crossing the street in Nairobi. I still look the wrong way, and this is how I shall die. No exotic African death for me—like getting mauled by a lion or something marvelous like that. I'm going to get run over by a truck—that's all. Very embarrassing it will be.

And now I'll close this chapter with two of my favorite stories, both poignant; one about leprosy and the other about Sally.

When I was still living in Baltimore, I traveled to Tanzania, which was then Tanganyika, and did that TV documentary on leprosy I mentioned before. Since this isn't an everyday occurrence, I'll tell you how it came about: Two friends of mine at Westinghouse TV in Baltimore were interested in doing an hour show on leprosy and wanted a half hour of it to be filmed in Tanganyika. Since I had been in the country, they asked me if I would show some of my slides to them and their cameraman, just so they could get an idea of what the country was like. I did. The next morning they telephoned me and told me they weren't going to send the cameraman after all, they were going to train me to use a camera and send me instead.

"But I don't know anything about photography," I objected. "You saw my slides and they are terrible."

"They are dreadful," they answered, "but you said all the right things, and you have an eye. All you have to do is to learn the mechanics."

And so I went to Westinghouse TV and learned how to use a 16-mm movie camera, and set off for the leprosarium in Tanganyika. After disembarking at Nairobi airport it took four days and four nights traveling overland to get there.

Seven Lutheran missionaries ran the leprosarium which was situated on about five hundred acres of land, and there were five hundred patients. When I got to the mission a missionary told

me that church would be in the morning at eight o'clock. Having
arrived in the evening I had not seen any of the patients and I
welcomed the opportunity to go to church because, frankly, I
was very nervous about confronting them and I knew nothing
about leprosy. I didn't know how I would react upon seeing
them, and I thought it would be awful if I fainted or did something
terrible to embarrass myself or them, so I welcomed the opportunity to see these people before I had to stick a camera in their
faces. I have never had such an experience in my life as the service next morning. The church was stark; they had built it themselves. There was nothing in it, and I mean nothing. There were
no pews; there was no altar. Where the cross should have been,
they had cut a cross-shaped aperture in the wall and the sun was
shining through. The simplicity was beautiful. Of the five hundred
leprosy patients, about a hundred were Christians. About twenty
more came because they liked to sing hymns. The congregation
sat on the floor. I had been told that the man giving the sermon
was the most positive case of leprosy in the entire leprosarium.
He was reading from the Bible, and when he got to the part that
says, "And Christ came upon a group of men who were lepers.
And they called unto Him, 'Have mercy unto us,'" he stopped and
said, "And look at the mercy that Christ has had on us. Look at
what He has given us." Well, I looked around at those people
and the only thing I could see that they had was leprosy. They had
nothing else. There were thirty-two children patients there. They
didn't have one doll, one crayon, one piece of paper, one pencil.
They had nothing. But they were so thankful for that which they
did have—medicine and somebody taking care of them—that one
by one they shuffled or crawled to the altar where they placed a
potato or an ear of corn in thanks for what they had. I had never
felt so ashamed in my life, just thinking of all I had, for which I
was really not very thankful at all. Yet these were the happiest
people. I stayed there for four days and four nights filming, and
I had never seen such joy. They laughed, they sang, they danced.
We had no communication with the outside world at all except
at seven o'clock in the evening when the news came over the

wireless. The last night that I was there it came over the air that Marilyn Monroe had committed suicide. I thought of the girl with beauty, fame, money—everything, and she had committed suicide. And here were people who had nothing but leprosy, and who were filled with joy. It was the first time that I began to wonder about standards and values.

The other story is of a completely different nature. Jock's friend T.B. is, as far as I know, the only man ever to have made a friend of a fully grown wild lion.

Driving through the reserve one day he found a badly wounded lioness lying under a tree. She had been mauled terribly in a fight, fairly common among lions, and was unable to fend for herself. T.B. drove his Land-Rover very close and inspected her carefully. He decided against getting out of the car, but by leaning from the window he managed to place a large camp basin full of water within reach and he also left some meat—but he held out no great hope for her.

Returning next day he was heartened to see that she had drunk and eaten. This time he had brought some antibiotic powder and he was able to flick and sprinkle some of it into the wounds. He christened her Sally and spoke to her as one would speak to a dog, but he stayed safely in the car.

For two weeks he returned every day with meat and water and spent hours just talking to her. One morning she was gone, and T.B. knew that she must have returned to the pride. He was glad he had saved her, and the episode, in his mind, was over.

A couple of months later he was camping in the area and had left the flap of his tent unzipped to get more air. At first light a violent thunderstorm broke and the rain drummed loudly on the taut canvas. Half awake, T.B. was suddenly aware of something standing in the canvas porch of the tent.

Peeping out he saw it was a fully grown lioness. He lay absolutely still and stealing another cautious glance he could see from the scar marks that it was Sally. Full of apprehension he stayed unmoving and silent, and the lioness lay down and started to lick the rain off her coat. In a few minutes the storm was over and

without even looking at T.B. she stalked off. He thought he had
had a very lucky escape and congratulated himself upon having
kept calm and still.

A few days later he suddenly saw the long grass near the tents
part, and Sally sauntered into the camp. She padded silently up to
within a few paces and flopped down. After a minute or two,
T.B. spoke to her very softly, calling her Sally, and using the same
special tone of voice as when he had looked after her. She looked
at him contentedly. It was the beginning of a friendship that was
to last nearly ten years.

Every time T.B. camped in Sally's territory they would seek out
one another and she would come to the tents. Soon the relationship became very comfortable, and T.B. would go about his business while Sally slept nearby or followed him around like a dog.
There was one strict rule that he made at the outset and never
broke. In all the years of their association he never once touched
Sally. Jock asked him about this, and he said he never forgot that
Sally was a wild lion and quite different, therefore, from those
raised from cubs by humans. He said that he sensed the friendship
was entirely upon her terms and he had no thought of abusing it.

Jock saw Sally once, though she never came to the camp when
he stayed with T.B. However, he went out with him one day and
when they reached Sally's area T.B. stood on the roof of the car
and called her name several times, then got back in the car and
waited. In about ten minutes she appeared over a rise followed
by thirteen other lions and cubs. By now she was the queen of
the pride. The others stopped about twenty yards from the car
but Sally came right up and rubbed against the wheels of the Land-
Rover as a cat will rub itself on your legs. Then, Jock said, T.B.
opened the door, but still sitting in the car he put a large basin
on the ground and poured some water into it from a can. Sally
had a long drink and then returned to her family.

XVIII
The Magic That Is Africa

Once, an African guide we had throughout an entire safari would say whenever we saw a lot of giraffe or zebra, "Too much giraffe. Too much zebra." Or if we saw a large pride of lion, "Too much lion." He obviously had the words "too much" confused with "many."

So now I would like to say "too much thanks" to you for joining me on this book safari. I hope you come and walk here one day yourself because as many books as you may read or pictures you may see, you still won't be able to hear it or smell it . . . the wood fires, and the drums. For those of you who have already been here, I know you have been captured. It has been said, "Africa captures you and won't let go." As early as the eighteenth century an explorer wrote, "He who drinks of African waters shall return." Africa is a disease, and there is certainly a magic that keeps pulling you toward it and is impossible to explain.

Why do I like living in Africa? What's so good about Kenya— a country that has no escalators, no bowling alleys, no Hershey bars with or without almonds, no sour cream or funny papers; where people still twist to last year's music, and the radio goes off altogether in the middle of the day, and where there is no mail delivery or street lighting in the suburbs?

But where else in the world would you read in the morning paper a story about a leopard getting into the cookie factory, an advertisement for "Black White Hunters," and an obituary notice ". . . he is survived by 438 grandchildren"? Where else is the race track open on Sundays only and women play polo? The horses run backwards too. (I've been told they don't, that it is "clockwise," but it still looks backwards to me.) Where else can you sit in the bathtub and watch monkeys swinging around in trees, and share the drive-in movies with giraffe looking over the wall? And I know of no other place in the world where fences grow, do you? Perhaps it's because fence posts are chemically treated in other places, but here they sometimes take root and sprout leaves. Do you know of any other place where they blow up avocados— because they fall off trees by the thousands and you get so tired of eating them, you let little boys put firecrackers inside and turn them into hand grenades?

You hardly ever see elephant on the New Jersey Turnpike any more, yet we have many on our main roads here. And at night we have the Southern Cross and lots and lots of stars. Does New York have stars any more?

I like it here because blacks are married to whites and no one even notices, and people wear "truck skin" shoes made from old discarded tires. And how long has it been since you went to a glass blower for a new butter dish? And on your birthday has anyone ever sung "Happy Birthday for You?" I like it too because they call surgeons and dentists "Mr."—only general practitioners are called "Doctor." In the States everyone seems to have a dentist called "Dr. Schwartz," but here you'd have to call him "Mr. Schwartz."

In Kenya no one ever knows the temperature, but it is never very hot and never very cold. And the country is pretty too. I like our mountains topped with marshmallow snow all year round. I like our green agricultural lands and Tarzan-type forest areas and wide open spaces and plains like America's West. I like the deserts with camels, and on the Indian Ocean the dhows still sail as they did in Biblical times . . . all this in a country smaller than Texas.

But best of all are the people. They are varied too. Where else could you go to a dinner party and find eight out of the eight guests of different nationalities and religions? Kenya is the world in microcosm.

And when I am away from it for any length of time, I begin to miss the variety. In the States when I see an occasional sari flowing past, worn by a lovely Indian girl, the beautiful waving colors make me smile, and then I long to see a tall, half-naked warrior with a red cloak tossed over one shoulder going into Woolworth's. And in the bank on Fifth Avenue I never see a woman with a Pepsi bottle on her head standing in the teller's line nursing her baby. Nor do I see her barefooted friend who wears a pretty cotton dress and carries her high-heeled shoes on her head. Where is the man in the gas station who wears a bathing-cap with his regular clothes—just because he wants to? And no one in Chicago carries messages in his ears. In Kenya lots of people do. And regular earrings never make me laugh.

But most of all when I'm in the States I miss feeling safe. While problems of Vietnam, ghetto burning or student unrest need not affect everyone's daily personal life, it *is* terrible to feel afraid to walk to the corner mailbox after dark. In Africa I may have sugar stolen from my shelves by servants and clothes may be taken by thieves, but I do not live in fear that I would be harmed. If I were a poor African, I would steal too. Relatively, people like us have so much, and they have so little of material things that a simple man couldn't possibly imagine that we would miss one of twenty-six shirts, or a cup from our ten-pound bag of sugar which we buy without a thought. (My mother-in-law uses cube sugar so she can count every cube.) But what is this pilfering compared to rape and senseless murders and other hideosities? I would walk through any African village alone and unafraid at night. If I broke down out in the bush, I would be helped by Africans—I might be uncomfortable in their mud hut, I might hate sleeping on the floor, but fear for my safety would be the farthest thing from my mind. Some Africans may still be primitive, but by nature they are not as savage as the civilized.

However, at times I do miss the States. I love the noise and the rat race and all those neon signs. To me; the only thing prettier than a river is a river with a bridge across it—especially if that bridge has lights.

And where else do mice wear clothes and talk?

One time I took a plane from New York to London on Thanksgiving Eve, and as it was coming into London I said to an American stranger sitting next to me, "Just think, today is Thanksgiving —and we will have no turkey, no cranberry sauce, no pumpkin pie, no family dinner." And he replied, "I know, isn't it wonderful?" But sometimes I would like to have Thanksgiving and the Fourth of July.

The States is very "now," and living in Kenya has little to do with living in the 1970s. Vital issues pass us by. When the astronauts first landed on the moon, we had no visual reception—only crackly radio which we could hardly hear—and at such times I feel very left out of things and that life here is rather irrelevant. With Vietnam and assassinations and drug addiction, I begin to feel almost guilty—the world around me crumbles, and here I sit in my ivory tower wondering if the gardenias will bloom. Then I wonder what I'd be doing about it anyway were I living in the States. Wouldn't living in the midst of the turmoil just cloud the view of the good things about America? You can never see the ground you are standing on, and from this distance America still looks good to me.

People ask, "Where would you rather live, in Africa or in the States?" Must I make a choice? Can't I have both? How can I say if I like steaks better than fudge sundaes? I like them both for different reasons. I love the complexities and sophistication of the States and the way it makes me work on all twelve cylinders. I feel so alive. I love the merry-go-round of the theater and the business and fashion worlds. I like the vertical view of skyscrapers. I like both worlds, and I like living in both worlds. In Africa, I like the horizontal view and the other joys of nature, I like the simplicity of life—and besides, in the African sky, the Big Dipper is upside down.